W9-CDB-482

Low Pay and Earnings Mobility in Europe

Concern for man himself and his fate must always form the chief interest for all technical endeavours... Never forget this in the midst of your diagrams and equations.

Albert Einstein
Speech given at the California Institute of Technology, 1937

Low Pay and Earnings Mobility in Europe

edited by

Rita Asplund

Research Supervisor, The Research Institute of the Finnish Economy (ETLA), Finland

Peter J. Sloane

Jaffrey Professor of Political Economy, Vice Principal and Dean, Faculty of Social Sciences and Law, University of Aberdeen, UK

Ioannis Theodossiou

Senior Lecturer in Economics, University of Aberdeen, UK

EUROPEAN LOW-WAGE EMPLOYMENT RESEARCH NETWORK (LoWER)

Edward Elgar

Cheltenham, UK • Northampton, MA, USA

Published by
Edward Elgar Publishing Limited
8 Lansdown Place
Cheltenham
Glos GL50 2HU
UK

Edward Elgar Publishing, Inc.
6 Market Street
Northampton
Massachusetts 01060
USA

A catalogue record for this book
is available from the British Library

3 2280 00609 6838

Library of Congress Cataloguing in Publication Data

Low pay and earnings mobility in Europe / edited by Rita Asplund,
    Peter J. Sloane, Ioannis Theodossiou
        Includes contributions of the European Low-Wage Employment
    Research Network (LoWER) members and invited speakers at the first
    LoWER Conference on the Problems of Low-Wage Employment held in
    Bordeaux on 31 January – 1 February 1997.
        Includes bibliographical references.
        1. Wages – Europe – Congresses. 2. Labor Mobility – Europe –
    Congresses. I. Asplund, Rita. II. Sloane, Peter J.
    III. Theodossiou, I. (Ioannis), 1954– . IV. LoWER Conference on
    the Problems of Low-Wage Employment (1st : 1997 : Bordeaux, France)
    HD5014.L69   1998
    331.2'1'094 – dc21   98–17708
                                                                               CIP

ISBN 1 85898 854 3

Printed and bound in Great Britain by
MPG Books Ltd, Bodmin, Cornwall

Contents

v

PART TWO
LOW-PAID EMPLOYMENT: THE SHORT-RUN HORIZON

PART THREE
LOW-PAID EMPLOYMENT: SOME FURTHER PERSPECTIVES

PART FOUR
LOW-PAID EMPLOYMENT IN THE OECD COUNTRIES: AN INTERNATIONAL COMPARISON

List of Figures

List of Tables

List of Contributors

Mahmood Arai is Acting Professor of Economics, Department of Economics, University of Stockholm. His research interests include labour economics, internal labour markets, wage determination and applied microeconomics.

Rita Asplund is Research Supervisor at the Research Institute of the Finnish Economy (ETLA). Her main research interests centre on labour markets, educational and technology issues and especially the interaction of the functioning of the labour market, technical progress and education and training in the success and failure of individuals and enterprises.

Erling Barth is Senior Researcher at the Institute of Social Research in Oslo. He is also a Professor in Microeconomics at the University of Tromsø and Managing Editor of the Norwegian Journal of Political Economy. His main research fields are wage structure, bargaining institutions, job and worker flows and labour market performance. Among his current research themes are the returns to education in Norway, the relationship between wage structure and mobility, and wage-setting institutions in the public and private sectors.

Paul Bingley is a Research Fellow at the Centre for Labour Market and Social Research (CLS) in Aarhus. His research interests include labour supply, programme participation and wage determination.

Bruno Contini is Professor of Economics at the University of Turin and Research Director of R&P Richerche e Progetti, Turin. He has written extensively on various aspects of labour economics and industrial organization. Current interests include applied economics, firm demography, labour market dynamics, job re-allocation, wage inequality and earnings mobility.

Tor Eriksson is Professor in the Department of Economics, Aarhus School of Business and the Centre for Labour Market and Social Research (CLS). His research interests centre on labour economics and industrial organization.

Michelangelo Filippi has been a researcher in R&P Richerche e Progetti, Turin, since 1993. His main activities include the development of statistical procedures for ensuring quality control of institutional data and the formation of longitudinal data on workers' careers. His projects include wage dynamics, labour mobility and job and worker turnover.

Mary Gregory is Lecturer in Economics at the University of Oxford, Fellow and Tutor at St. Hilda's College and a founder member of the European Low Wage Employment Network (LoWER). Her research interests cover both macroeconomics and labour economics, particularly employment and earnings, on which she has published widely. She has worked as a consultant on these issues for the European Commission, the OECD, the Confederation of British Industry and the Trades Union Congress.

Robert Jukes has recently been employed as statistician at the Office for National Statistics, London. Prior to that he was employed in the UK Department of Trade and Industry and the Department for Education and Employment. His current work centres on the econometrics of unemployment. He also maintains an interest in the analysis of European bond markets.

Mark Keese is an economist in the Directorate for Education, Employment, Labour and Social Affairs, OECD, Paris. His current research interests include low pay, earnings mobility and the impact of statutory minimum wages on employment and poverty.

Claudio Lucifora teaches Labour Economics at the Cattolica University of Milan. He has also taught at the University of Paris II and the London School of Economics. His research activity has mainly involved labour market issues, particularly wage determination and collective bargaining.

Abigail McKnight is a Research Fellow in the Institute for Employment Research at the University of Warwick. Her main research interest is in the distribution of personal income generated by the labour market. Her research has mainly concentrated on the effects of education and employer provided training, labour mobility, unemployment benefits and income transfers to the lower-paid members of the workforce.

Agnès Puymoyen is an economist at the Directorate for Education, Employment, Labour and Social Affairs, OECD, Paris. Her current research interests include earnings mobility and the transition of youths from school to work.

Peter Sloane is Jaffrey Professor of Political Economy in the Department of Economics, University of Aberdeen and Vice-Principal and Dean of the Faculty of Social Sciences and Law. A founder member of the European Low Wage Employment Network (LoWER), his current research interests include the economics of discrimination, labour market segmentation, the economics of job satisfaction, over-education and the economics of sport.

Mark Stewart is Professor of Economics in the Department of Economics, University of Warwick. His research interests include labour economics, income and earnings distributions, low pay, unemployment and applied econometrics.

Joanna Swaffield is Research Officer in the Institute of Economics and Statistics, University of Oxford. Her research interests include labour economics, wage differentials and low-wage employment.

Paul Swaim is an economist in the Directorate for Education, Employment, Labour and Social Affairs, OECD, Paris. His current research interests include earnings mobility and population ageing.

Ioannis Theodossiou is senior Lecturer, Department of Economics, University of Aberdeen. A founder member of the European Low Wage Employment Network (LoWER), his current research interests include labour market segmentation, low pay and earnings distribution, unemployment, employment status and psychological well-being and job satisfaction.

Rocus van Opstal is an economist and Head of the Incomes and Prices Division, CPB Netherlands Bureau of Policy Analysis. His interests include the policy analysis of the labour market and income distribution, and the econometric analysis of micro data.

Claudia Villosio has been a researcher in R&P Richerchi e Progetti, Turin, since 1995. Her main activities include the development of statistical procedures to ensure the quality control of institutional data and the construction of data on earnings mobility and inequality in Italy for the OECD. Current research interests include wage dynamics, labour mobility and job and worker turnover in Italy.

Rob Waaijers is an economist in the Incomes and Prices Division, CPB Netherlands Bureau of Policy Analysis. His research interests centre on labour economics and the econometric analysis of micro data.

Niels Westergård-Nielsen is Professor of Economics at Aarhus School of Business and Director of the Centre for Labour Market and Social Research (CLS). He has conducted research on a large number of labour market issues using longitudinal labour market data.

Gerard Wiggers is an economist with the Dutch Ministry of Health. His current research interest is mainly in the field of health economics.

Foreword

R. Asplund, P.J. Sloane and I. Theodossiou

The European Low-Wage Employment Research Network (LoWER) is a thematic network set up in 1995 on the Causes of Social Exclusion, and part of the Targeted Socio-Economic Research (TSER) programme of the European Commission. It brings together university researchers from different EU countries, who have been working on low pay, minimum wages, wage structures and wage inequalities. The overall aim of LoWER is to generate improved socio-economic knowledge on low-wage employment as a mechanism of social exclusion with the aim of providing better insights into ways of tackling the problem.

The first LoWER Conference on the Problems of Low-Wage Employment was held in Bordeaux on 31 January – 1 February 1997. The conference covered a number of issues including that of low earnings mobility. This book contains relevant contributions on this issue by conference participants of LoWER and invited speakers.

We are most grateful to the organizing committee under Steve Bazen, the invited keynote speakers Stephen Nickell and François Bourguignon, the other conference participants and the European Commission, which financed the operation of the LoWER network. We also want to express our gratitude to Petri Rouvinen for his excellent typesetting assistance.

Further details on the activities of LoWER may be obtained on the world-wide web at the following address: *http://www.eco.rug.nl/lower*.

Rita Asplund
Peter Sloane
Ioannis Theodossiou

INTRODUCTION

Low Pay and Earnings Mobility

1. Methodological and Econometric Issues in the Measurement of Low Pay and Earnings Mobility

P.J. Sloane and I. Theodossiou

1 INTRODUCTION

Earnings inequality rose in several OECD countries during the 1980s, most notably in the USA and the UK, and this has given rise to increased analysis by economists of those workers who are considered to be low paid. It is generally recognized that the causes of low pay are multifarious and particularly that life-cycle effects play an important role. This naturally leads on to the question of earnings mobility, for it matters whether particular individuals or groups are trapped in low-paid segments of the labour market or whether low pay is for many workers merely a transient phenomenon. Yet, as Buchinsky and Hunt (1996) observe, the measurement of earnings mobility has not received as much theoretical attention as has the measurement of earnings inequality and there is no real consensus on what is the most appropriate measure. But even on the question of low pay itself there is little agreement on how the phenomenon should be measured, perhaps because economic theory does not provide any clear guidance on the matter.

2 MEASUREMENT ISSUES

Broadly speaking there are two choices in judging whether an individual or group is low paid. First, one may define low pay in absolute terms given by a minimum acceptable standard of living or poverty level. Second, one may define low pay as a relative concept by focusing on the wage distribution or the dispersion of earnings. Using the former approach is particularly problematical in the context of international comparisons as one must allow for differences between exchange rates and purchasing power parities. It may also be difficult to fix on a figure which would leave sufficient numbers of low-paid workers across countries to make analysis meaningful, given the wide disparity in real incomes which exists in Europe. It is presumably for such reasons that all studies contained in this volume use relative definitions of low pay. This itself is not without its complications. For instance, there may be a wide disparity in real earnings across countries amongst those who are defined as low paid, so that one is not comparing like with like.

The measurement of pay itself gives rise to a number of difficulties. Should earnings be measured on an hourly, weekly, monthly or annual basis? Should the measure be limited to full-time, year round workers or include part-time or part-year workers? These problems are magnified when the focus is on earnings mobility. As Atkinson et al. (1992) note earnings may vary because of piece-rates or bonuses, short-time or overtime working, raising the question of whether or not the definition of low pay should be confined to basic pay. Earnings variations may also be of a short-term nature because of seasonal factors, suggesting that the definition should focus on annual earnings. However, relatively few data sets contain information on annual earnings. Earnings may rise without any change in worker inputs as a result of an annual wage adjustment and we may feel that this is a more appropriate indicator of an improvement in the position of the worker, particularly when the increase is positive in real terms. Again earnings may alter as a result of a job change with the same or a new employer and some of these changes may be involuntary. It is clear that an understanding of the reasons for earnings mobility is crucial if we are to draw appropriate inferences about whether workers are better or worse off as a consequence of it. Contributors to this book include variously hourly, weekly, monthly and annual earnings in order to measure low pay.

There is equal diversity in the low-pay cut-off chosen by the various contributors. Keese, Puymoyen and Swaim, Sloane and Theodossiou, and Stewart and Swaffield elect for two-thirds of median earnings, while McKnight prefers the so-called European decency threshold of 68 per cent of the mean and Lucifora two-thirds of the mean. Asplund, Bingley and Westergård-Nielsen, Eriksson, and Gregory and Jukes define the low paid simply in terms of those in the lowest quintile of the earnings distribution while Contini, Filippi and Villosio use the third decile to differentiate between the low and the high paid.

Finally there are two studies analysing occupations. Arai, Asplund and Barth focus on the occupational status of individuals in the lowest wage decile. Van Opstal, Waaijers and Wiggers compare the earnings of low- and high-skilled workers, defined on the basis of formal educational attainment.

This lack of uniformity of approach, common across the literature, complicates comparisons across the various countries.[1] Its significance depends on how sensitive explanations of low pay are to the precise definition adopted.[2] We do, on the other hand, have a number of studies examining the same countries which enables us to examine the extent to which these different definitions influence the findings.

3 ESTIMATING EARNINGS MOBILITY

Dickens (1997) notes that there are two basic characteristics of a changing earnings distribution. First, how close or far apart individuals are in their level of earnings. Second, to what extent the ranking of individuals alters from one period to the next. One may define a mobility measure as

$$M = \frac{2\sum_{i=1}^{N}\left|F(w_{it}) - F(w_{is})\right|}{N} \tag{1.1}$$

where $F(w_{it})$ and $F(w_{is})$ are the cumulative distribution functions for earnings in year t and s, respectively, and N is the number of individuals. The mobility measure is in this case twice the average absolute change in the percentile ranking between the two years. It has a minimum value of zero and a maximum value of one. Correspondingly, if earnings in the two years are independent, the mobility index has a value of 0.66.

It is possible to go a step further than this and distinguish between permanent and transitory components of earnings change. Thus, Friedman and Kuznets (1954) developed a permanent earnings model in which

$$w_{it} = X_{it} + u_{it} \tag{1.2}$$

where w_{it} equals the earnings of the *ith* individual at time t, X_{it} equals the permanent component of earnings and u_{it} equals the transitory component, representing chance factors. As Gittleman and Joyce (1996) note, for mobility to rise there should be a faster increase in the variance of the transitory component than in the permanent component. The standard practice is to average an individual's earnings over several years to obtain an estimate of permanent earnings and then to compare these averages over different time periods. One can then compute a set of transitory components for each individual – that is, the deviation of an individual's earnings from his or her mean earnings – in order to determine whether the variance of these deviations has altered across time periods. Using such an approach for the USA

Gottschalk and Moffitt (1994) showed that transitory movements in earnings had been responsible for between one-third and one-half in the variance of earnings from the 1970s to the 1980s. However, if the wage used in an inequality measure is an average of several years earnings it is known that inequality will fall as it reflects the mobility of individuals through the earnings distribution. Thus Buchinsky and Hunt (1996) estimate that inequality measured over a two-year period is between 7.2 per cent and 14.8 per cent lower than the average inequality in the two years. For a five-year period the reduction in inequality is between 13.5 per cent and 23.5 per cent.

Long-run earnings inequality may be represented by a Galtonian regression towards the mean model which, unlike the above, assumes that earnings, w_{it}, in successive time periods are not independent of one another. Let

$$w_{it} = \beta w_{it\text{-}1} + u_{it} \qquad (1.3)$$

where u_{it} is a stochastic variable and β measures the extent of regression towards the mean, with values close to one indicating very limited mobility and those close to zero suggesting rapid regression towards the mean. As Atkinson et al. (1992) note, there are a number of assumptions implicit in this model including population homogeneity, time homogeneity, the first-order Markov assumption that earnings at time t are independent of earnings at any period before $t-1$ and that the stochastic terms are uncorrelated over time and over individuals. If, for example, it is believed that there is labour market segmentation with different groups exhibiting different types of behaviour in different segments it will be necessary to relax at least some of these assumptions.

A common approach to identifying earnings mobility over time, and one used by several authors in this volume, is to classify earnings into discrete ranges and estimate the probability of transitions between these ranges. The probability that an individual in class i in period h moves into class h in period $t+1$ can be written as P_{ih} and the matrix P with elements P_{ih} such that $\Sigma_h P_{ih} = 1$ is the transition matrix (see Atkinson et al. 1992). At its simplest one could adopt a two-way classification which differentiates between low-paid and not-low-paid employees so that the transition matrix becomes

$$P = \begin{vmatrix} p_{11} & p_{12} \\ p_{21} & p_{22} \end{vmatrix}, \qquad (1.4)$$

where $0 < p_{ih} < 1$ and $\Sigma_h p_{ih} = \Sigma_h p_{2h} = 1$. If there is a high degree of mobility the off-diagonal elements will be large and if the same individuals tend to remain low paid over time the off-diagonal elements will be close to zero. This may be measured by the immobility ratio or the average jump (see for instance Lucifora in this volume). For the USA Buchinsky and Hunt (1996) find that the variability over time of the transition probabilities are significantly larger for wages than for annual earnings. This implies that the number of hours worked changes in the reverse direction to changes in wages (i.e. workers adjust their hours of work to compensate for changes in relative wages). They also find that there is much more stability in the transition probabilities for more educated and more experienced workers and that given education and experience, the staying probabilities are less variable at the higher than at the lower quintiles.

4 DATA ISSUES

Longitudinal data are essential for the estimation of earnings mobility. These may be either retrospective or panel and each has particular problems of its own. The use of event history data overcomes some of the problems of cross-section and panel data, but suffers from the potential problem of recall error. Indeed Horvath (1982) has pointed out that recall bias may be present in retrospective surveys as short as one year. This could be a problem particularly in the case of earnings which are distorted by inflation.

There is no doubt that panel data offer considerable advantages in the estimation of earnings mobility and use of them has been made by several contributors to this volume. Thus Asplund, Bingley and Westergård-Nielsen make use of Statistics Denmark administrative records and Confederation of Finnish Industry and Employers records, Gregory and Jukes of New Earnings Survey Panel data and Sloane and Theodossiou and Stewart and Swaffield of the British Household Panel Survey. Both Lucifora and Contini, Filippi and Villosio use a longitudinal data set drawn from the Italian Administrative Social Security (INPS) archives. In this case the panel of workers enables one to observe individual and firm characteristics simultaneously. Eriksson has a data set containing some 500 000 individuals drawn from the quinquennial Finnish Population Censuses. Finally, for the Netherlands van Opstel, Waaijers and Wiggers made use of the Social and Economic Panel (SEP) which contains information on wage levels for a panel of households over a number of years. The length of time analysed varies from two years up to twenty.

Panel data sets raise a number of problems. First, the data only become available over a number of years and the number of observations over time may be relatively limited. Second, there is the problem of attrition, which will cause the size of the panel to decline over time and possibly result in attrition bias. As Atkinson et al. (1992) note a loss of say 5 to 10 per cent per annum in the sample size will have a substantial cumulative impact on the proportion of the original sample remaining in the panel. A major advantage of panel data sets is, however, the ability to control for unobservables by the use of fixed effects models. Let us suppose

$$w_{it} = X_i a + Y_{it} b + u_{it} \qquad (1.5)$$

where X represents a vector of personal characteristics, which are fixed over time such as gender, race and most education, and Y represents a vector of time varying characteristics such as marital status and job and residential location and u_{it} the error term. In addition

$$u_{it} = Z_t + z_i(t) + v_{it} \qquad (1.6)$$

where Z_t, is a set of variables common to all individuals in the panel at time t affecting earnings (w_{it}), $z_i(t)$ is the unobserved systematic earnings determinants and v_{it} is a pure transitory term. Such fixed effects models using panel data allow the investigator to control for systematic individual characteristics and unobserved simultaneity biases influencing earnings equation (1.5).

There are, however, a number of econometric problems in using panel data. As Stewart and Swaffield observe, 'the satisfactory modelling of the transition probabilities into and out of low pay is not straightforward'. The first issue concerns the initial conditions problem. That is, conditioning on someone being initially low paid and then modelling the probability of him or her moving out of low pay in the next period will result in selection bias if being initially a low-paid employee is not exogenous. In much applied work two assumptions for the initial conditions are used: (1) the initial conditions are truly exogenous, and (2) the process is assumed to be in equilibrium. In general, a fully satisfactory solution to the initial conditions problem appears to require a full model for the process that influences an individual's probability of being observed in the state in question.

A second complication arises from the fact that we must take into account not only movements into and out of low pay but also movements into and out of employment, so that neglecting exits to non-employment will lead to an overstatement of upward mobility. Using the British Household Panel Study Gosling et al. (1997) find that men in the bottom quartile of the earnings distribution are almost three times as likely to move out of work in the twelve months following the first-wave interview as men in the top quartile and, though the effect for women is less strong, it is still substantial. This pattern is also found in this volume.

5 AN OVERVIEW OF THE VOLUME

This volume has a transparent story-line: it examines a wide variety of different approaches to investigating the issue of low pay and concludes with a chapter comparing the low-pay incidence in a number of OECD countries.

Part One, dealing with the mobility of low-paid workers over a medium-term horizon, begins with a paper on the Italian experience. In *Earnings Mobility in the Italian Economy*, B. Contini, M. Filippi and C. Villosio investigate the upward mobility of low-pay workers over a four-year period as well as the downward mobility of high-paid workers over the same period. The authors attempt to overcome the initial conditions problem by dividing the sample into two sub-groups – manual and non-manual employees – and estimate the probability of transition by using logistic models. They find that earnings mobility in Italy is not high and manual workers, women and those employed in small firms face a high probability of being confined to low-paid jobs.

T. Eriksson, *Long-Term Earnings Mobility of Low-Paid Workers in Finland* (Chapter 3), examines the upward mobility of Finnish low-paid workers during a twenty-year period. He shows that most of the movement out of low-paid employment occurs during the first five years following the individual's entrance into a low-paid job. Importantly, low-paid workers have higher exit rates to the non-employment state compared to other groups. In investigating changing patterns of earnings mobility he finds that exit rates out of the low-paid category are lower over the 1980s compared to the earlier decade.

In Chapter 4, *Low-Wage Mobility in a Working-Life Perspective*, A. McKnight explores the working patterns of UK individuals in low-paid employment and compares them with those in higher-paid jobs. The study shows that for individuals in low-paid employment the number of spells in low-wage employment, and the number and duration of spells in unemployment reduce the probability that the current low-wage employment spell will end.

Part Two investigates issues of mobility over the short run. It begins with the chapter *Wage Mobility for Low-Wage Earners in Denmark and Finland*. R. Asplund, P. Bingley and N. Westergård-Nielsen investigate the year-to-year upward mobility of low-wage earners in Denmark and Finland. The authors take into account attrition biases, selectivity issues and unobservable heterogeneity and find that overall mobility for the low-wage earners exhibits a slight upward trend in Denmark and a clear downward trend in Finland, but only in the short run. They also find that the impact of individual characteristics on low-pay mobility is generally not substantial and very similar across the two.

In Chapter 6, *An Econometric Analysis of Low Pay and Earnings Mobility in Britain*, Sloane and Theodossiou assume the exogeneity of the initial condition and attempt to confront the problem of the nested nature of employment decisions faced by the individual worker. That is, workers are assumed to face first the alternative of being employed or not and, conditional on being in employment, the alternatives of being in a higher-paid job or a low-paid job. The authors use both a multinomial logistic regression and a nested bivariate model. They find a degree of mobility from low-paid to higher-paid jobs over a two-year period, though many of the low paid move into unemployment. Individual human capital endowments are important in assisting mobility into higher-paid jobs.

In Chapter 7, *The Earning Mobility of Low-Paid Workers in Britain*, M. Stewart and J. Swaffield trace low-paid earner mobility over a four-year period on a year-to-year basis. They attempt to deal with the problem of initial conditions by using a bivariate probit model with selectivity using parental variables as instruments on the assumption that these variables affect the probability of being in a low-paid job at a point in time, but do not affect the conditional transition probabilities into and out of low pay. Being male, education, recent training, size of the firm and trade unions appear to affect substantially workers' upward exit rate from low-paid employment. The authors also find a considerable persistence in low pay; particularly for those who have already been low paid for more than one period. Finally, those who are low paid are found to be more likely to move into non-employment.

Part Three deals with a number of studies which are not confined solely to mobility, but also take a more general approach in investigating influences which affect wage distribution and wage growth. In Chapter 8, *Low Pay, A Matter of Occupation*, M. Arai, R. Asplund and E. Barth investigate the incidence of low-paid employment in Finland, Norway and Sweden. The authors find that low-paid employment incidence is higher in occupations in which young or female workers are over-represented. The study also suggests that the age-wage profiles of those in low-paid employment are flatter than those employed in high-paid jobs. Interestingly, the authors, using a simulation approach, find that a worker in a low-wage occupation is likely to experience a much steeper age-wage profile if he or she were to have been employed in a high-wage occupation. Thus the authors argue that an individual's human capital or industry affiliation cannot adequately explain the observed wage differentials across occupations.

In *The Effects of Unemployment on Future Earnings: Low-Paid Men in Britain 1984–94* (Chapter 9), M. Gregory and R. Jukes explore the implications of unemployment for the individual. The authors address the following questions: does re-entry into the employed labour force cause a decline in an individual's wages earned prior to the last non-employment spell? Is any de-

cline permanent, and if so, how long does it last? Is it unemployment incidence or its duration which influences subsequent earnings? Are low-paid
workers more severely affected by unemployment than the remainder of the
labour force? According to the authors the experience of unemployment has a
substantial negative effect on subsequent earnings but the effect progressively decreases if the individual remains employed for more than two years.
However, long-term unemployment appears to have a long-lasting effect on
the earnings capability of the individual, although this effect seems to be least
for the low paid.

In Chapter 10, *Working Poor? An Analysis of Low-Wage Employment in
Italy*, C. Lucifora examines the evolution of low-wage employment in Italy
over the 1975–93 period and investigates which groups in the labour force
are more likely to suffer from a high- or low-wage employment incidence,
and which individual characteristics of both workers and employers are more
frequently associated with low-wage employment. The results show that male
workers with higher educational attainment, those employed in large firms
and individuals located in the northern regions of Italy are less likely to earn
below the low-pay threshold. In the analysis of the dynamics of wages, using
longitudinal micro-data, it is shown that individuals who start from the lower
end of the earnings distribution are less likely to move higher up the earnings
ladder compared with those who start from higher positions.

In Chapter 11, R. van Opstel, R. Waaijers and G. Wiggers, *Wage Growth
of Low- and High-Skilled Workers in the Netherlands*, investigate the earnings profiles of low-skilled workers and compare them with those of their
higher-skilled counterparts. Their results show that low-skilled workers have
only a limited prospect of an upward earnings profile. In contrast, higher-
skilled workers experience a rapid and long-lasting increase in their earnings
profile. The authors also find that general training (as reflected in labour
market experience) rather than firm-specific training (as reflected in tenure in
the current firm) is the main contributor to an individual's earnings growth.

Finally in Part Four in the concluding chapter, *The Incidence and Dynamics of Low-Paid Employment in OECD Countries*, M. Keese, A. Puymoyen and P. Swaim present comparative evidence on low-paid employment
and earnings mobility for a number of OECD countries. They show that in all
countries low pay tends to be concentrated amongst low-skilled, inexperienced workers, females and the young. Low-pay incidence is particularly
high for females in Japan, Korea and Switzerland, for youths in Finland, and
for older workers in Japan and the UK. The authors argue that higher earnings inequality by no means ensures higher employment rates for low-skilled
workers. Furthermore, countries with higher inequality in earnings appear to
exhibit lower upward earnings mobility for low-paid workers. In all countries, the mobility prospects of low-paid workers are very diverse, with a

significant number remaining low paid or cycling between low pay and non-employment. This volume covers a wide range of issues on low-paid employment and from a wide range of perspectives. The reader can, therefore, gain an insight into the way in which labour market incentives and institutions affect both the incidence and duration of low-paid employment spells.

NOTES

1   Some authors do, however, compare different methods for the same country.
2   As Gosling et al. (1997) point out, the use of any low-pay threshold gives rise to a problem of 'wobble' around the threshold. If the threshold cuts through a dense part of the earnings distribution such that a large proportion of observations are just above and just below the threshold relatively small movements in wages will move individuals across the threshold in either direction.

REFERENCES

Atkinson, A.B., F. Bourguignon and C. Morrisson (1992), *Empirical Studies of Earnings Mobility*, Switzerland, Chur.: Harwood Academic Publishers.
Buchinsky, M. and J. Hunt (1996), *Wage Mobility in the United States*, National Bureau of Economic Research, Working paper no. 5455, July.
Dickens, R. (1997), *Caught in a Trap? Wage Mobility in Great Britain: 1975–1994*, Centre for Economic Performance, Discussion Paper no. 365, September.
Friedman, M. and S. Kuznets (1954), *Income from Independent Professional Practice*, New York: National Bureau of Economic Research.
Gittleman, M. and M. Joyce (1996), 'Earnings Mobility and Long-Run Inequality: An Analysis Using Matched CSP Data', *Industrial Relations*, 35(2), pp. 180–96.
Gosling, A. et al. (1997), *The Dynamics of Low Pay and Unemployment in Early 1990s Britain*, Institute for Fiscal Studies.
Gottschalk, P. and R. Moffitt (1994), 'The Growth of Earnings Instability in the US Labor Market', *Brookings Papers on Economic Activity*, no. 2, pp. 217–54.
Horvath, F. (1982), 'Forgotten Employment: Recall Bias in Retrospective Data', *Monthly Labor Review*, 105(3), pp. 40–43.

PART ONE

Low-Paid Employment: The Long-Run Horizon

2. Earnings Mobility in the Italian Economy [1]

B. Contini, M. Filippi and C. Villosio

1 INTRODUCTION

In recent years the distribution of earnings has become more dispersed in most European countries. Italy, too, has experienced an increase in earnings dispersion, even if inequality seems to be lower than in countries like the USA and the UK (OECD 1996).

There are different reasons that explain why at any point in time differences in individual earnings are observed. According to human capital models, in fact, individual earnings grow over time due to training and on the job experience. On the other hand, personal characteristics such as education, ability or family background may determine individual differences in earnings.

An issue somewhat different from the one addressed above concerns individual lifetime inequality. Cross-sectional inequality does not tell us anything about individual inequality. This depends on individual earnings mobility, i.e. the extent to which individuals move up or down the earnings distribution. From a welfare point-of-view it is important to assess the permanent or transitory nature of inequality: the question is whether low pay is a transitory event of a worker's life, as predicted by human capital models, or whether it is a permanent phenomenon.

This chapter focuses on the persistence in low pay and analyses whether a type of 'poverty trap' can be defined. We are particularly interested in investigating whether some groups of workers are more likely to persist in low-paid jobs, and in establishing the features that increase the probability of workers with high earnings moving down the wage distribution. To do this we estimate a logit model of the probability of persisting in the low-pay bracket and of the probability of moving down from the high-pay bracket after five years, assuming that the initial condition is exogenous.[2] This is a reasonable assumption although not a completely innocuous one; as will be explained, we try to take into account the 'initial condition problem' by dividing the population into two subgroups made up of manual and non-manual workers.

The chapter is organized as follows: section 2 illustrates the data set used; section 3 presents some structural characteristics about low-paid workers; section 4 analyses in some detail the different issues regarding earnings mobility. First we present some measures of earnings mobility, then we estimate a model of the probability of persisting in low-paid jobs and of the probability of moving down from high-paid jobs. Finally we calculate the probability of earnings mobility for different groups of workers. Section 5 concludes.

2 THE DATA

The analysis of earnings mobility is possible when individual wage profiles can be observed. Analyses of individual lifetime inequality in Italy are made feasible by the availability of a longitudinal data set drawn from the Administrative Social Security (INPS) archives. It is a panel of workers which allows us to observe both individual and firm characteristics simultaneously. For each calendar year 1986–91, the Social Security forms of employees born on 10 March, June, September and December of any year were selected. In this way, a sequence of random samples of the population of employees is formed (sampling ratio 1:91). Each yearly sample includes approximately 100 000 workers. Using available identifiers (fiscal and social security codes), individual longitudinal data are generated for each worker. The firm's longitudinal records are then accessed for each worker in the sample and the employer's attributes (code of economic activity, total number of employees) are linked to the employee.

Our interest here is the transition from low to high pay and vice versa, over a period of five years. For this reason our analysis is restricted to workers employed both in 1986 and 1990 (55 598 full-time workers).

There are different ways to define a low-pay threshold. The main difference is between absolute and relative measures. Absolute measures seem to be more appropriate when studying poverty levels; relative ones can be better used when addressing issues concerning the risk of social exclusion (OECD 1996). In this chapter we define low-paid workers as those individuals whose earnings fall in and below the third decile of the wage distribution, and high-paid workers if their earnings fall in and above the eighth decile. By our definition, therefore, the overall number of low-paid sample workers is equal to that of high-paid workers.

Table 2.1   Annual wage distribution in the sample in 1986 and 1990
(thousand lira)

	1986	1990
N	55 598	55 598
D9/D1	2.01	2.34
D5/D1	1.35	1.40
D9/D5	1.49	1.66
Mean	20 910	23 830
Median	19 531	21 403

Figure 2.1   Annual wage distribution in the sample in 1986 and 1990 –
earnings in 1986 currency (thousand lira)

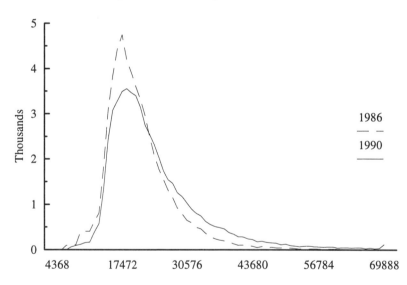

Workers can have low earnings in one period of time, usually one year, either because they are in a low-paid job or because they have worked for a small number of days. Our focus here is on the characteristics of low-paid jobs and of workers who fill those jobs. For this reason in the following analysis we use the daily wage to calculate the annual wage the individual would have earned if he had worked the entire year.[3] In this way we do not consider differences among workers in the number of days worked.

Table 2.1 shows the sample wage distribution in 1986 and 1990. It is clear that over five years the dispersion in the wage distribution has increased considerably, especially in the upper part of the wage distribution. Earnings for high-paid workers relative to the median (D9/D5) have increased by 19 percentage points; the dispersion in the earnings of low-paid workers (D5/D1) has increased by 10 percentage points. This is not surprising as we restrict the analysis only to workers employed both in 1986 and 1990.

3 LOW-PAID WORKERS: STRUCTURAL CHARACTERISTICS

Individual earnings can differ among workers according to personal characteristics such as education, training and location, and firm characteristics such as industry and firm size. As shown in Table 2.2 both individual and firm characteristics play an important role in determining the presence in the lower or in the upper tail of the wage distribution.

Table 2.2   *Descriptive statistics of low- and high-paid workers in 1986*

	low-paid N°	high-paid N°	low-paid frequencies	high-paid frequencies
AGE <30	9 753	2 500	49.22	12.62
AGE 30-40	3 255	6 522	20.50	37.24
AGE >40	3 535	8 018	18.38	41.68
MEN	9 613	14 620	23.13	35.17
WOMEN	7 066	2 060	50.36	14.68
MANUAL WORKERS	13 178	7 209	35.30	19.31
NON-MANUAL WORKERS	3 501	9 471	19.16	51.84
NORTH-WEST	6 062	7 607	25.66	32.19
NORTH-EAST	4 868	2 387	40.06	19.64
CENTRE	3 122	4 882	25.99	40.64
SOUTH	1 856	1 253	33.68	22.74
ISLANDS	771	551	33.62	24.03
MANUFACTURING	10 001	8 860	30.48	27.00
CONSTRUCTION	1 141	1 449	32.59	37.50
SERVICES	5 537	6 371	19.69	25.00
FIRM SIZE<=20	9 947	2 291	50.44	11.62
FIRM SIZE 20-500	5 859	6 475	27.00	29.84
FIRM SIZE >500	1 013	7 995	7.14	56.39
CHANGED EMPLOYER BETW. '86 AND '90:	6 174	3 101	39.73	19.96
QUITS	5 188	2 562	31.00	15.40
LAYOFFS	986	539	5.90	3.20

The incidence of low pay is higher among young people, women, manual workers and in the north-east of Italy. One-half of workers aged less than 30 are found to be in the bottom tail of the wage distribution, compared to 20 per cent of older workers; one out of two women is low paid, while only 23 per cent of men are in the low-pay bracket. Low pay is less concentrated in the service sector than in construction and manufacturing. Firm characteristics are also significant factors in determining the wage distribution; as is well known, workers in small firms have lower wages than those employed in medium and large firms.

Looking at the relationship between mobility and wages (Table 2.2, CHANGED EMPLOYER), in line with other findings (e.g. Contini et al. 1996, Flinn 1986), we find that workers in the lower tail of the wage distribution are much more mobile than those in the upper tail.

The data do not allow us to determine whether movers originate from quits or layoffs. One preliminary way to separate them is to look at whether the firm in which the mover was previously employed has closed in the same period in which the worker has moved. In that case most probably, the employee has been laid off. Otherwise we cannot be sure of the nature of the movement. For simplicity we will call *layoffs* the movements in which the firm has closed in the same month or the month after the workers has left the firm and *quits* the others.[4] Therefore, while layoffs are almost 'certain' events, quits are less identifiable.

One problem that can arise when using administrative archives is that mobility is overestimated because the legal transformations of firms are recorded as firm closures. To avoid this when calculating worker mobility, we do not consider movements originated by the legal transformations of firms to be such (spurious flows).

4 EARNINGS MOBILITY

4.1 Measurements of Earnings Mobility

The first way to look at earnings mobility is to analyse the transition matrix between years. Table 2.3 shows the transition probabilities between different pay brackets. The probability of being low paid is much higher for those who were low paid five years earlier: of those workers who were low paid in 1986, 66 per cent are still low paid in 1990, and only 34 per cent move out of the low-pay bracket. On the other hand, the probability of persisting in high-paid jobs for people who were already high paid is even higher: 76 per cent of the workers who were high paid in 1986 remain high paid five years later, and only 24 per cent move down in the wage distribution.

Table 2.3   Transition matrix between low and high pay, 1986–90

	1990		
1986	Low pay	Not low pay	Total
Low pay	11 002 (66%)	5 677 (34%)	16 679
Not low pay	5 678 (15%)	33 241 (85%)	38 919
	High pay	Not high pay	Total
High pay	12 736 (76%)	3 944 (24%)	16 680
Not high pay	3 943 (10%)	34 975 (90%)	38 918

As shown by the table, Italy and France are similar. In Italy and the UK, the correlation coefficient between wages in the two years increases with age.

Table 2.4 shows the correlation coefficients between wages in t and $t+5$ in Italy and in some other countries. As shown by the table, Italy and France are similar. In Italy and the UK, the correlation coefficient between wages in the two years increases with age.

Table 2.4   Correlation coefficients between W_t and $W_{(t+5)}$ [5]

Country	Age groups								
	20-25	25-30	30-35	35-40	40-45	45-50	50-55	55-60	All ages
Britain	0.21				0.81				
USA			0.58			0.75		0.63	0.70
France			0.72	0.84	0.82	0.83	0.84		
Italy	0.35	0.59	0.72	0.79	0.82	0.83	0.82	0.83	0.76

The immobility ratio calculated on the basis of the distribution of wages in 1986 and 1990 in Italy is 0.66. It represents the percentage of people staying in the same class or in the adjacent decile in the two years. The value of 0.66 has to be compared with the value of 0.28, which is the value of the immobility ratio if there were perfect mobility (i.e. the probability of each individual staying in a particular cell does not depend on the cell she/he was in previously).[6]

All these measures seem to suggest that earnings mobility in Italy is not very high. In the following paragraphs we analyse the characteristics (both of the individual and the firm) that reduce or increase earnings mobility for workers in the lower and upper part of the wage distribution.

4.2 Determinants of Earnings Mobility

The Model
A logit model is estimated to analyse the effects of individual and firm characteristics and the role of individual mobility in determining the probability of moving up or down in the wage distribution after five years. Our focus here is on identifying first whether being low paid is a persistent event for some groups of workers. Our analysis shows that there are some features that increase the probability of remaining in the bottom part of the wage distribution. Second we want to investigate whether individual mobility has some relationship with mobility in terms of earnings.

The model is estimated separately for the two tails of the wage distribution in order to single out the different behaviour in earnings mobility of high- and low-paid workers. For workers in the bottom tail of the wage distribution (i.e. deciles 1, 2 and 3) the dependent variable y is a binary variable taking the value of one if the worker is still in the bottom tail of the wage distribution after five years, and the value of zero otherwise. Similarly, for workers in the upper tail of the wage distribution (deciles 8, 9 and 10) the dependent variable takes the value of one if the individual has moved down to a lower decile five years later, and the value of zero otherwise. Thus, the model identifies the probability of low-paid workers persisting in low pay five years later, given individual and firm characteristics, and the probability of high-paid workers leaving the upper deciles.

Defining λ_1 and λ_2, respectively, as the low- and high-pay threshold (third and eighth decile), we have

Low-paid workers:

$$Y_1 = 1 \ \textit{if} \ (w_{i,1986} \leq \lambda_1 \ \textit{and} \ w_{i,1990} \leq \lambda_1) \qquad (2.1)$$
$$Y_1 = 0 \ \textit{otherwise}$$
$$P(Y_1 = 1) = f(x_i \beta_1)$$

High-paid workers:

$$Y_2 = 1 \ \textit{if} \ (w_{i,1986} \geq \lambda_2 \ \textit{and} \ w_{i,1990} < \lambda_2) \qquad (2.2)$$
$$Y_2 = 0 \ \textit{otherwise}$$
$$P(Y_2 = 1) = f(x_i \beta_2)$$

where $w_{i,t}$ are individual earnings at time t, x_i is a vector of individual and firm characteristics and β_1, β_2 the associated coefficients.

Such different specifications of the dependent variable for the two equations make it easier to read the results: a positive sign in the estimated coefficient in both equations means a 'bad event'. In fact, it means that such a variable increases the probability of a low-paid worker remaining in the lower part of the wage distribution, and increases the probability of a high-paid worker experiencing a deterioration in his or her condition.

The vector of the independent variables x_i contains:

- individual characteristics: gender, age (linear and quadratic terms), occupation (manual and non-manual workers), career advancement (transitions from manual occupations to non-manual or managerial occupations, and transitions from non-manual to managerial positions during the 1986–90 period), individual mobility (dummy for quit and layoff), length of unemployment spells (if movers, split for quits and layoffs);
- firm characteristics: geographical locality of workplace (north-west, north-east, centre = benchmark, south and islands), economic activity (manufacturing = benchmark, services, construction), firm size (the log of the number of employees of the firm).

As mentioned before, here we take the initial status to be exogenous.

The Results
Table 2.5 reports the estimated coefficients of the model and the standard errors. The χ^2 statistic tests the joint effect of the explanatory variables included in the model.[7] The value reported shows that individual and firm characteristics are statistically significant in determining the probability of persisting in the low tail of the wage distribution and moving out of the high tail.

The results are straightforward. Consider the following features: being a manual worker in manufacturing, being a woman, being a worker in small firms; in the bottom tail of the wage distribution these features reduce the probability of an upward move; in the upper tail of the distribution, on the other, hand the same characteristics increase the probability of a downward move.

Young workers benefit more from escaping from low-paid jobs than older ones, but they are more likely to move down from high-paid jobs than the older workers. Workers in the construction sector[8] have a high probability of an upward move if low paid, but they have a lower probability of persisting in the upper tail of the wage distribution if high paid. The same happens to workers in the north of Italy, while for southern workers it is very easy to move down from high-paid jobs. Not surprisingly occupational upgrading (CAREER ADVAN.) increases the probability of moving towards higher deciles and of persisting in high-paid jobs.

Table 2.5   Logit estimation

Variable	(1)			(2)		
	Prob (low paid in 1986 and low paid in 1990)			Prob (high paid in 1986 and low paid in 1990)		
	Parameter Estimate	Standard Error	Pr >Chi- Square	Parameter Estimate	Standard Error	Pr >Chi- Square
INTERCEPT	1.1104	0.2104	0.0001	1.4266	0.3764	0.0002
AGE	-0.0427	0.0123	0.0005	-0.1386	0.0193	0.0001
AGE^2/100	0.0656	0.0175	0.0002	0.1590	0.0244	0.0001
WOMEN	1.1690	0.0411	0.0001	1.2097	0.0718	0.0001
MANUAL	1.1195	0.0503	0.0001	2.1020	0.0531	0.0001
NORTH-WEST	-0.4222	0.0512	0.0001	0.2649	0.0558	0.0001
NORTH-EAST	-0.1409	0.0536	0.0086	0.1452	0.0729	0.0464
SOUTH	0.0105	0.0687	0.8788	0.5642	0.0844	0.0001
ISLANDS	-0.0360	0.0918	0.6950	0.6473	0.1191	0.0001
CONSTRUC.	-0.8621	0.0689	0.0001	0.1839	0.0723	0.0110
SERVICES	-0.1074	0.0435	0.0136	-0.7037	0.0523	0.0001
LOG FIRM SIZE	-0.2182	0.0097	0.0001	-0.2055	0.0092	0.0001
CAREER ADVAN.	-0.8018	0.0939	0.0001	-1.3450	0.1191	0.0001
QUIT	-0.6675	0.0668	0.0001	0.1284	0.1067	0.2289
LAYOFF	-0.4881	0.5018	0.3307	4.5228	1.1263	0.0001
UNEMPL_Q.	0.0067	0.0019	0.0004	0.0231	0.0035	0.0001
UNEMPL_L.	-0.0038	0.0112	0.7356	-0.0693	0.0248	0.0052
N° obs	16 590			16 652		
Y=1	10 957			3 928		
Y=0	5 633			12 724		
-2 Log Likelihood	19 028			13 348		
χ^2 (16 DF)	2 128.7			4 538.2		
Concordant	1			1		
Discordant	0.280			0.161		
Tied	0.003			0.002		

These results confirm not only that manual workers, women and workers in small firms represent the majority of low-paid workers, but also that they find it difficult to escape from low-paid jobs, while for these same groups of workers mobility out of high-paid jobs is much higher.

Another interesting result comes from the analysis of the relation between individual mobility and earnings mobility. As previously explained, we roughly discriminate among movers on the basis of layoffs and quits, depending on whether the original firm has closed in the same period of worker movement or not. The associated coefficients show that employer changes originating from 'quits' decrease the probability of persisting in low-paid jobs, while movements originating from 'layoffs' are not significant in determining upward moves. On the other hand, for high-paid workers, employer changes defined as 'quits' do not affect their earnings mobility, but people laid off have a higher probability of moving down from high-paid jobs. These results are in line with the distinction made between quits and layoffs: as expected, quitters benefit from employer changes. For workers who have been laid off, however, employer changes do not affect their earnings mobility if they are low paid, but their conditions worsen if they are high paid.

Finally periods of unemployment negatively affect the earnings profile of workers. The variables UNEMPL_Q and UNEMPL_L represent the number of months of absence from the labour market for, respectively, 'quitters' and 'laid offs', as defined above. There is a high probability that these are unemployment spells.[9] The associated coefficient shows that, for 'quitters', the length of unemployment spells increases the probability of low-paid workers persisting in the bottom tail of the distribution, and of high-paid workers worsening their condition; for 'laid off' workers unemployment spells are not significant in the lower part of the distribution, while for high-paid workers they seem to reduce the probability of a downward move. This last result seems surprising. It may depend on the imperfect ranking of layoffs or on the incomplete elimination of spurious movements.

We have already noticed elsewhere[10] that the length of unemployment spells between successive jobs has a negative effect on the earnings profile. This result supports the idea that unemployment duration results in a stigma on those who are involved, and runs against the idea of wait unemployment, associated with a profitable search for better opportunities.

4.3 Manual vs Non-Manual Workers

These models take the initial condition (low-pay or high-pay status in 1986) to be exogenous. This means that it is assumed that persistence in the low-pay bracket or exit from the high-pay bracket is entirely due to the observed explanatory variables. If there is correlation across time between the unobservables, then a problem of sample selection can arise, as we select those who were low paid (high paid) in 1986, and resulting estimations can be biased.

Stewart and Swaffield (1997) present different estimates of the probability of persisting in low pay under the assumption of exogenous and endogenous initial status. Their results show that imposing the initial condition as exogenous leads to the estimated effects on the conditional probability of remaining low paid being overstated.

If persistence in low pay is mainly due to the initial low-pay status, then we would expect the characteristics that increase the probability of persisting in low pay not to be significant in the probability of leaving the high-pay bracket. Our analysis shows that there are some features that significantly increase both the probability of persisting in low pay and of exit from high pay; they are gender, age, firm size and occupation. The first three characteristics are surely exogenous. The only problem comes with occupation which is strictly correlated with education.

Table 2.6   Logit estimation for manual workers

Manual workers	(1) Prob (low paid in 1986 and low paid in 1990)			(2) Prob (high paid in 1986 and low paid in 1990)		
Variable	Parameter estimate	Standard error	Pr >Chi-square	Parameter estimate	Standard error	Pr >Chi-square
INTERCEPT	1.7104	0.2334	0.0001	3.2935	0.3267	0.0001
AGE	-0.0424	0.0139	0.0023	-0.1631	0.0174	0.0001
AGE^2/100	0.0630	0.0197	0.0014	0.1983	0.0224	0.0001
WOMEN	1.3160	0.0487	0.0001	1.3309	0.1151	0.0001
NORTH-WEST	-0.4573	0.0619	0.0001	0.2138	0.0605	0.0004
NORTH-EAST	-0.1950	0.0635	0.0021	0.2658	0.0742	0.0003
SOUTH	-0.0886	0.0780	0.2556	0.3599	0.0791	0.0001
ISLANDS	0.0526	0.1057	0.6187	0.2939	0.1079	0.0064
CONSTRUC.	-0.8713	0.0811	0.0001	-0.1485	0.0623	0.0171
SERVICES	-0.0997	0.0521	0.0558	-0.7551	0.0640	0.0001
LOG FIRM SIZE	-0.1810	0.0119	0.0001	-0.2069	0.0100	0.0001
CAREER ADVAN.	-0.7546	0.1017	0.0001	-1.1668	0.1168	0.0001
QUIT	-0.6428	0.0812	0.0001	0.4481	0.0999	0.0001
LAYOFF	0.1554	0.6218	0.8027	3.3994	1.0067	0.0007
UNEMPL_Q.	0.0064	0.0022	0.0039	0.0103	0.0029	0.0003
UNEMPL_L.	-0.0134	0.0134	0.3187	-0.0641	0.0227	0.0048
N° obs	11 128			11 168		
Y=1	6 793			3 643		
Y=0	4 335			7 525		
-2 Log Likelihood	13 326			12 098		
χ^2 (16 DF)	1 468.6			1 855.9		
Concordant	1			1		
Discordant	0.283			0.247		
Tied	0.003			0.003		

A problem with our data is the lack of information on the individual's education. In order to improve the control of differences in the initial conditions, we have estimated models (1) and (2) separately for manual and non-manual workers, each relative to their own wage distribution. Tables 2.6 and 2.7 show the results for the two groups of workers. The main differences between non-manual and manual workers may be summarized as follows:

1. Industry: non-manual employees in the service sector are more likely to persist in low-paid jobs. On the contrary, being a manual worker in the construction sector reduces the probability of persisting in the low tail of the wage distribution.[11]

Table 2.7   Logit estimation for non-manual employees

Non-manual workers	(1) Prob (low paid in 1986 and low paid in 1990)			(2) Prob (high paid in 1986 and low paid in 1990)		
Variable	Parameter estimate	Standard error	Pr >Chi-square	Parameter estimate	Standard error	Pr >Chi-square
INTERCEPT	1.6213	0.4884	0.0009	1.4067	0.7574	0.0633
AGE	-0.0364	0.0298	0.2229	-0.0876	0.0373	0.0189
$AGE^2/100$	0.0777	0.0444	0.0798	0.1002	0.0454	0.0274
WOMEN	0.9411	0.0698	0.0001	0.8545	0.0923	0.0001
NORTH-WEST	-0.2308	0.0966	0.0169	-0.2804	0.0801	0.0005
NORTH-EAST	-0.1111	0.1057	0.2936	-0.3229	0.1122	0.0040
SOUTH	0.3100	0.1565	0.0477	0.0961	0.1581	0.5433
ISLANDS	-0.0738	0.1871	0.6934	-0.1010	0.2318	0.6632
CONSTRUC.	-0.2443	0.1631	0.1341	-0.0929	0.1753	0.5962
SERVICES	0.2495	0.0760	0.0010	-0.3815	0.0718	0.0001
LOG FIRM SIZE	-0.1226	0.0160	0.0001	-0.0986	0.0141	0.0001
CAREER ADVAN.	-2.4659	0.8770	0.0049	-4.0698	1.0049	0.0001
QUIT	-1.2223	0.1261	0.0001	-0.1857	0.1862	0.3187
LAYOFF	-0.4229	1.2041	0.7254	-0.6486	2.8941	0.8227
UNEMPL_Q.	0.0205	0.0041	0.0001	0.0217	0.0065	0.0008
UNEMPL_L.	0.0157	0.0309	0.6113	0.1181	0.1400	0.3989
N° obs	5 463			5 474		
Y=1	4 233			1 169		
Y=0	1 230			4 305		
-2 Log Likelihood	5 336			5 383		
χ^2 (16 DF)	501.1			279.3		
Concordant	1			1		
Discordant	0.307			0.355		
Tied	0.005			0.008		

2. Firm size: the effects due to firm size are in line with the previous findings (the probability of persisting in low-paid jobs and of moving out of high-paid jobs decreases as the firm size increases), but this effect is stronger for manual than for non-manual employees. Manual workers employed by large firms experience a notable increase in the probability of improving their condition.

3. Individual mobility: among both groups of workers mobility positively affects the probability of an upward move, but the effect is stronger among non-manual employees. As before, the coefficient associated with layoffs is not significant. In the upper part of the wage distribution, mobility is not significant for non-manual employees, while it increases the probability of a downward move for manual workers. Moreover, for manual workers the coefficient associated with layoffs is greater than that associated with quits.

4. Unemployment spells: periods spent in unemployment for low-paid workers have a significant but small effect on manual workers, the effect being stronger for non-manual employees. Among the high-paid workers, unemployment spells increase the probability of a downward shift in the wage distribution for both manual and non-manual employees.

The above findings reflect the substantial difference that exists in the earnings profiles of the two groups of workers. Manual workers experience a flat wage profile, mostly fixed and with little upgrading, especially among the low skilled. Hence, job changes have a minor effect on their wage profile. Moreover, unemployment spells do not affect the earnings mobility of manual workers, provided they are back on the job by the end of the observation period. On the other hand, a career interrupted by periods spent in unemployment reduces the earning prospects of non-manual employees.

4.4 Probabilities of Earnings Mobility

The use of a logistic distribution allows us to calculate and compare the earnings mobility probabilities for some typical individuals.[12] We define a benchmark case and then compare the effect of various factors on each. The results are shown in Tables 2.8 and 2.9. The probabilities are calculated using the coefficients of the model with manual and non-manual employees together.

The benchmark case concerns a young worker (aged 30), in manufacturing, employed by a small firm (20 employees), located in the north-west, with no career advancement and no employer changes.

Table 2.8 examines the influence of individual and firm characteristics on the probability of persisting in low pay and moving from high pay. It shows first of all the strong difference that exists between manual and non-manual employees: the probability of persisting in low-paid jobs and the probability of leaving high-paid jobs are much higher for manual than for non-manual workers. In the benchmark case the probability of persisting in low-pay status is about 61 per cent for a manual worker and 34 per cent for a non-manual employee; on the other hand, the probability of exit from high pay is 70 per cent for manual and 24 per cent for non-manual employees.

Table 2.8   Mean predicted probabilities of persisting in low pay and moving from high to low pay – individual and firm characteristics

Worker characteristics: (all employed by firm located in north-west, with no career advancement):	Low paid: probability of persisting in low pay	High paid: probability of downward move	Low paid: probability of persisting in low pay	High paid: probability of downward move
	Manual workers		Non-manual workers	
1. Young (aged 30) male, in manuf., employed by a small firm (20 employees), stayer	0.61	0.61	0.34	0.16
2. Old (aged 50) male, in manuf. employed by a small firm (20 employees), stayer	0.66	0.56	0.39	0.13
3. Young (aged 30) female in manuf. employed by a small firm (20 employees), stayer	0.84	0.84	0.63	0.39
4. Young (aged 30) male, in manuf. employed by a large firm (500 employees), stayer	0.44	0.45	0.20	0.09

The second row of the table shows the effect of age: old workers are more likely to persist in low-paid jobs, but they are less likely to leave high-paid jobs than the younger workers. Women (third row), especially if they are manual workers, have a small chance of escaping from low-paid jobs. The last row shows the effect of firm size: the probability of persisting in low-paid jobs is decidedly low if the worker is employed by a large firm rather than a small firm.

Table 2.9 shows the effect of different patterns of individual mobility on the probability of upward and downward moves in the wage distribution. We find that for a young manual worker in manufacturing the probability of persisting in the low-paid category is reduced by 16 percentage points if he or she quits and moves directly into a new job. But if he or she spends some months in unemployment searching for a new position, then the probability of persisting in low-paid jobs increases. The longer the spell, the higher the potential loss. If a worker in the upper part of the wage distribution is laid off (i.e. the firm has closed in the same period in which the worker moves) then without doubt (probability of 0.99 for manual and 0.95 for non-manual employees) he or she moves down in the distribution.

Table 2.9   Mean predicted probabilities of persisting in low pay: stayers and movers

Worker characteristics: all aged 30, male, employed by small firm (20 employees) in manufacturing, located in north-west, with no career advancement:	Low paid: probability of persisting in low pay	High paid: probability of downward move	Low paid: probability of persisting in low pay	High paid: probability of downward move
	Manual workers		Non-manual workers	
1. Stayer	0.61	0.61	0.34	0.16
2. Quits and takes up a new job without any unemployment spell	0.45	0.64 *	0.21	0.18 *
3. Quits and spends 6 months in unemployment	0.46	0.67 *	0.22	0.20 *
4. Quits and spends 12 months in unemployment	0.47	0.70 *	0.22	0.22 *
5. Is laid off and takes up a new job without any unemployment spell	0.49 *	0.99	0.24 *	0.95

Note: * = not significant.

5 CONCLUSIONS

Earnings mobility in Italy is not very high. The probability of being low paid is two times higher for those who were low paid five years earlier and the probability of being high paid is three times higher for workers who were high paid.

A multivariate analysis shows that manual workers, women and workers in small firms are not only more likely to be in low pay in any one period, but are also more likely to persist in low pay and to exit from high pay. Young workers are more likely to be in low pay in one period, but they are at less of a disadvantage in escaping from low-paid jobs than older ones; on the other hand they are more likely to move down from high-paid jobs than the older workers.

Movers benefit from employer changes, but if they are laid off, then employer changes do not affect their earnings mobility if they are low paid. However, their conditions worsen if they are high paid. The length of unemployment spells between jobs has a negative effect on the earnings profile, running counter to the idea of wait unemployment.

In order to improve the control of differences in the initial conditions, separate analyses are made for manual and non-manual employees. The analysis shows that there is a strong difference in the earnings careers of manual and non-manual employees: the former experience a flat wage profile, mostly fixed and with little upgrading. Hence, job changes have a minor effect on their wage profile and unemployment spells have little effect on their earnings mobility, provided they are back on the job by the end of the observation period. Non-manual employees, however, benefit from employer changes, but periods spent in unemployment reduce their earnings prospects.

NOTES

1   This research was partially carried out thanks to a MURST grant (40 per cent – 1995) through the Dipartimento di Economia, Università di Torino. We would like to thank seminar participants in Bordeaux, Firenze and Perugia for useful discussions.
2   A similar analysis was also conducted by Sloane and Theodossiou (1996).
3   Of course the effective annual wage and the calculated one are the same if the worker has worked all year.
4   Compared to a previous version of the study we use here a more restrictive definition of individual layoffs. By doing this we can single out more precisely those movements that are probably involuntary, but simultaneously we widen the quit category.
5   Data for the other countries is reported in Atkinson et al. (1992). *Britain*: data refer to males only, data start in 1963; variable is logarithm of annual earnings. *USA*: for young workers the data refer to male household heads; data start in 1971; variable is average hourly earnings, correlations averaged. For older workers the data refer to white males; data start in

1965; variable is annual earnings; correlations averaged. *France*: data refer to males; data start in 1950; variable is annual earnings.

6   See Atkinson et al. (1992).

7   The -2 Log Likelihood statistic has a chi-squared distribution under the null hypothesis that all explanatory variables in the model are zero.

8   This result needs to be read with caution: much employment in construction is in fact casual. We see here mostly the lucky segment.

9   Here we can only observe individuals who have not been on the regular payroll for a certain period of time. We cannot record with certainty that these are periods of unemployment. They can represent periods spent in self-employment, in the irregular economy or in the public sector. The last possibility (a short period spent in the public sector) is very unlikely in the Italian economy: an occupation in the public sector is in general a lifetime job. Other estimates on the same data show that the likelihood of moving into self-employment is a little over 5 per cent of all separations. On the other hand the probability of entering the irregular economy may be high especially in the South, but mainly for those who have never been regularly employed before (this is not our case).

10 See Contini et al. (1996).

11 As previously noticed, here we observe only the regular part of the construction sector, while most of the occupation in that sector is irregular. These results may not hold for that kind of worker.

12 In the logit model $P(Y=1) = e^{\beta'x} / 1 + e^{\beta'x}$, where x are the individual characteristics and β the estimated coefficients.

REFERENCES

Atkinson, A.B., F. Bourguignon and C. Morrisson (1992), *Empirical Studies of Earnings Mobility*, London: Harwood.

Contini, B., C. Malpede and C. Villosio (1996*), Wage Dynamics and Labour Mobility in Italy*, University of Turin, Economic Department, Working paper no. 06/96.

Flinn C.J. (1986), 'Wages and Job Mobility of Young Workers', *Journal of Political Economy*, **94**(3), pp. S88–S110.

OECD (1996), *Employment Outlook*, Paris

Sloane P.J. and I. Theodossiou (1996), 'Earnings Mobility, Family Income and Low Pay', *The Economic Journal*, **106**, May, pp. 657–66.

Stewart M. B. and J.K. Swaffield (1997*), Low Pay Dynamics and Transition Probabilities*, University of Warwick, mimeo.

3. Long-Term Earnings Mobility of Low-Paid Workers in Finland [1]

T. Eriksson

1 INTRODUCTION

Some of the distinguishing characteristics of the Finnish labour market during the last couple of decades have been the internationally low degree of wage dispersion, a significant reduction in wage inequality in the 1970s and an internationally low incidence of low-paid employment (OECD 1996). In the second half of the 1980s earnings inequality rose sharply (Eriksson and Jäntti (1997)) and the current economic crisis has led to a discussion about the widening of pay differentials as a route to higher employment growth.

As in many other countries, earnings and income distribution in Finland, as well as changes therein, have been documented by several studies, but until recently, little attention has been paid to the evolution of individuals' earnings mobility. Pönttinen's (1983) study shows that social (class) mobility in Finland has been relatively high in international terms. Similarly, Björklund and Jäntti (1997) find that Finland's high degree of inter-generational earnings mobility with respect to income is an outlier from an international perspective. As for intra-generational mobility there are three studies, all using data from the 1980s and the early 1990s. Asplund et al. (1997) study the wage mobility of manufacturing employees in the 1980–94 period and find that upward mobility was quite high in the beginning of the period, declined steadily during the 1980s and fell considerably as a consequence of the deep economic crisis in the early 1990s. Lilja (1996) and Jäntti (1996) have examined the career and earnings mobility, respectively, of non-manual workers in the manufacturing sector in the same period, finding similar developments for this group, too.

The purpose of this chapter is to examine the earnings mobility of Finnish low-paid workers during the period 1970 to 1990. Most previous studies of earnings mobility in countries other than Finland have looked at most at a five-year time horizon. Our study is different in that we examine relatively long periods (up to twenty years) of individuals' career histories. The data set used is a large, nationally representative sample of the working-age population. In addition to the importance of assessing the nature and severity of the low-pay problem, a focus on the lower end of the earnings distribution is also motivated by the fact that most of the changes in overall earnings inequality have occurred below the median of the distribution. The questions we attempt to answer are as follows. How frequent are movements out of low-paid jobs? How do people move out of and into low-wage jobs? How important are movements out of employment and into unemployment, schooling, or home working? How does mobility evolve over longer periods of time (10, 15 or 20 years)? Are changes in the earnings distribution accompanied by changes in earnings mobility at the lower end of the distribution?

The remainder of the chapter is organized as follows. The next section provides a brief overview of the issues and earlier research. Section 3 describes the data set used. Sections 4 and 5 give the results concerning patterns of mobility and changes in mobility over time, respectively. We finish by offering some conclusions.

2 BACKGROUND AND EARLIER RESEARCH

As is well known, descriptions and analyses of inequality which are based on cross-sections of the earnings distribution may provide only a partial picture of the dynamics of inequality. Human capital theory and the vast literature on empirical earnings equations indicate that life-cycle aspects of earnings are important. Hence, an unchanged earnings distribution may very well conceal a high level of mobility, that is, a considerable portion of the labour moving up and down the distribution while leaving the overall earnings dispersion unaltered. Another example is that changes in inequality may be due to increases or decreases in transitory or permanent earnings components; see Gottschalk and Moffitt (1994) for an analysis. Only if the permanent component is important, is the change more likely to be of a long-run nature. A related issue is whether low pay is a permanent or a transitory state. Clearly if low pay is transitory, it can be considered as a stepping stone to more stable and better paid jobs. Although less recognized in the literature, low-paid employment can also be followed by a loose attachment to the labour market. In all three cases mentioned, we need to know more about the movements up and down the distribution.

Patterns of earnings mobility do not necessarily bear a relationship to trends and changes in inequality in cross-sections. An increase or a decrease can be consistent with increasing, unchanged or declining levels of inequality. But growing (decreasing) cross-sectional inequality will lead to greater (less) inequality in the long run unless it is offset by increasing (decreasing) mobility.

The bulk of earlier research on earnings mobility has been surveyed by Atkinson et al. (1992) (see also Gottschalk (1997)). Most of the available evidence derives from investigations of data sets from France, UK and the USA. They find that:

1. Earnings mobility increases with length of period studied. It should be noted, however, that only a few studies have followed representative samples over longer time periods (one notable exception being Björklund (1993)). The time horizon in most of the studies has been five years or less, which may be rather short.
2. Mobility is highest for young groups, because at early ages workers are more likely to be in positions in which they receive training or to be shopping around for the right jobs (Mincer and Jovanovic 1981). However, this is not found in a more recent study by Gustafsson (1994) for Sweden, nor by Gittleman and Joyce (1996) for the USA. Their results point to small, if any, differences in exit rates from low pay between age groups.
3. Earnings mobility seems to be relatively constant across countries; see e.g. OECD (1996, 1997).[2] Recently Gottschalk and Moffitt (1994) and Buchinsky and Hunt (1996) have shown that at least for the USA, constancy seems to be present also during periods of large changes in the cross-sectional earnings distribution in one country.
4. The earnings mobility of males is higher than for females. Atkinson et al. (1992) argue that men have higher mobility because they are more likely to be in manufacturing occupations with greater job mobility. Gustafsson (1994) found higher mobility among Swedish women than for men, whereas Gregory and Elias (1994) and Gittleman and Joyce (1996) arrive at the opposite conclusion for the UK and the USA, respectively.

More recent work – see Asplund et al. in Chapter 5 of this volume and Stewart and Swaffield (1997) – has been concerned with the modelling of individual transition probabilities into and out of low pay. In this chapter, however, we focus solely on aggregate transitions, leaving the analysis of individual probabilities on our future research agenda.

3 DATA DESCRIPTION

Our data come from the quinquennial censuses in Finland from 1970 to 1990. Statistics Finland has compiled a data file which contains all individuals who lived in Finland during one of the sample years. The data set analysed in this paper is obtained from a 10 per cent random sample of this data file (a little over 500 000 individuals) and is therefore representative of the whole population.

The data set contains for each sample year, that is, 1970, 1975, 1980, 1985 and 1990, information on a host of individual characteristics (age, gender, marital status, schooling, region, occupation and industry) along with earnings from work on an annual or monthly basis). Earnings from work equals taxable wage income that comprises all wages and salaries, fringe benefits and fees.[3] The data stem from tax assessments and exist for everyone who has paid income tax or who has filled in their income report to the tax authorities without having paid any taxes. In the analysis below we will be looking at monthly earnings. These have been obtained by using information about the number of months worked in the census years.

For each of the four first sample years we include in our data set persons who were wage earners in that year, had positive earnings and were between 15 and 64 years of age.[4] In each sample year the sample is divided into earnings quintiles for the wage earners.[5] These data sets for each sample year are next followed over the subsequent 5, 10, 15 or 20 year period to construct transition matrices for periods of different length. Transitions out of the population of wage earners are also recorded. Thus, in addition to transitions between earnings quintiles we also have records on transitions to retirement, self-employment, schooling, home working, unemployment, and out of the sample (due to death or emigration) states.[6] Due to the construction of the data set, we are also able to trace the states the persons in a quintile were in five years earlier.

As the data come from the censuses and are based on the records of the tax authorities we are able to avoid two central problems in the bulk of the earnings mobility literature: non-response (attrition) and measurement error. The attrition is important in this context as people whose incomes vary a lot are more difficult to follow (or to obtain responses from), which may lead to the underestimation of mobility. This is, however, not a problem here as the censuses cover the whole population. For the same reason measurement errors in earnings, which are especially critical for an analysis of earnings mobility, are likely to be very small as all information are from the tax registers which are of high quality. However, the information regarding the state a person was in when out of work is obtained from questionnaires and is thus self-reported. Moreover, as a person can have been in two or more of these states during the year (unemployed and in school, for example), the state reported refers to the main activity during the year.

4 MOBILITY OF LOW-PAID WORKERS: PATTERNS 1970–90

In the following we will be looking at parts of transition matrices focusing on the transitions out of the lowest quintile which we use as our measure of low pay. Thus in Tables 3.1, 3.2, 3.3, and 3.4 below we consider a quintile in a given year and see how it is distributed across the quintiles in the next 5, 10, 15 or 20 years. Those who move out of employment are recorded as well. We distinguish between three different out-of-employment states:

i. a category consisting of persons with a relatively close labour market attachment, that is, people in unemployment, self-employment or school,
ii. a category of people who, due to death, retirement or emigration, are likely to have left the labour force permanently, and
iii. a category in between, consisting mainly of housewives and other persons not in the labour force.

In addition to these transition figures we also report transition rates for a restricted sample of individuals who have been employed at both points in time (i.e., have not moved to any of the out-of-employment states). In the tables, these transition rates are set out in italics along with those for the whole sample.

Let us begin by looking at Table 3.1, in which the transition rates for the whole sample are given. Focusing first on the transitions during the five-year horizon, we may note that the proportion staying in the lowest quintile was lower in the 1970s than in the 1980s. In the 1970s a little over one-fifth of the bottom quintile still remained in the same quintile five years later, whereas the proportion had risen to one-third in the 1980s. The shares of those 'continuously' in employment that did not leave the first quintile are higher and have also increased in the 1980s compared to the preceding decade.

Although the portion staying in the bottom quintile is lowest for the 1970–5 period, the proportion moving up the earnings distribution was considerably lower than in 1975–80 or 1985–90. The upward moving proportion was also low in the first half of the 1980s. In both 1970–5 and 1980–5 the share of the lowest quintile moving out of employment was high and more especially the proportion withdrawing permanently from the labour force was greater.

Table 3.1   Mobility out of the bottom quintile, both sexes

a. 1970 to: =>	1975		1980		1985		1990	
Bottom quintile	0.216	*0.340*	0.257	*0.400*	0.186	*0.331*	0.144	*0.341*
2nd quintile	0.146	*0.230*	0.126	*0.196*	0.112	*0.199*	0.106	*0.251*
3rd quintile	0.117	*0.184*	0.110	*0.171*	0.104	*0.185*	0.096	*0.228*
4th or 5th q.	0.157	*0.246*	0.150	*0.233*	0.160	*0.285*	0.146	*0.346*
Out of employment	0.364		0.357		0.438		0.508	
thereof: unempl., self-empl., in schooling	0.132		0.099		0.099		0.111	
thereof: not in sample or retired	0.146		0.217		0.317		0.387	
thereof: home worker etc.	0.086		0.042		0.022		0.010	

b. 1975 to: =>	1980		1985		1990	
Bottom quintile	0.228	*0.277*	0.193	*0.260*	0.152	*0.229*
2nd quintile	0.348	*0.422*	0.259	*0.350*	0.228	*0.343*
3rd quintile	0.134	*0.163*	0.156	*0.210*	0.151	*0.227*
4th or 5th q.	0.114	*0.138*	0.134	*0.180*	0.134	*0.201*
Out of employment	0.176		0.258		0.335	
thereof: unempl., self-empl., in schooling	0.054		0.060		0.051	
thereof: not in sample or retired	0.078		0.179		0.272	
thereof: home worker etc.	0.044		0.019		0.012	

c. 1980 to: =>	1985		1990	
Bottom quintile	0.363	*0.480*	0.260	*0.390*
2nd quintile	0.192	*0.254*	0.171	*0.257*
3rd quintile	0.098	*0.129*	0.108	*0.162*
4th or 5th q.	0.104	*0.137*	0.127	*0.191*
Out of employment	0.243		0.334	
thereof: unempl., self-empl., in schooling	0.117		0.125	
thereof: not in sample or retired	0.098		0.193	
thereof: home worker etc.	0.028		0.016	

d. 1985 to: =>	1990	
Bottom quintile	0.329	*0.411*
2nd quintile	0.237	*0.296*
3rd quintile	0.116	*0.145*
4th or 5th q.	0.118	*0.148*
Out of employment	0.200	
thereof: unempl., self-empl., in schooling	0.053	
thereof: not in sample or retired	0.000	
thereof: home worker etc.	0.020	

Turning next to the consideration of whether there are differences in the transition rates between male and female workers, it should be noted that women are disproportionately represented among low-wage workers (see Table 3.A1 in the Appendix). The gender difference in the share remaining in the bottom quintile has changed during the period. As can be seen from Tables 3.2 and 3.3, female low-pay workers were less mobile than their male counterparts in the 1970s. During the 1980s women have been exiting low pay at approximately the same rate as men. Moreover, the degree of upward mobility has been higher among female low-wage workers in the 1980s.

Table 3.2   Mobility out of the bottom quintile, males

a. 1970 to: =>	1975		1980		1985		1990	
Bottom quintile	0.203	0.270	0.280	0.439	0.176	0.339	0.147	0.332
2nd quintile	0.151	0.201	0.072	0.113	0.064	0.123	0.056	0.126
3rd quintile	0.176	0.234	0.106	0.166	0.090	0.173	0.073	0.165
4th or 5th q.	0.222	0.295	0.180	0.282	0.190	0.365	0.167	0.377
Out of employment	0.247		0.362		0.481		0.557	
thereof: unempl., self-empl., in schooling	0.078		0.121		0.113		0.124	
thereof: not in sample or retired	0.169		0.241		0.368		0.433	

b. 1975 to: =>	1980		1985		1990	
Bottom quintile	0.210	0.256	0.229	0.296	0.144	0.235
2nd quintile	0.207	0.253	0.143	0.185	0.120	0.195
3rd quintile	0.180	0.220	0.160	0.207	0.130	0.211
4th or 5th q.	0.221	0.270	0.242	0.313	0.221	0.359
Out of employment	0.182		0.226		0.385	
thereof: unempl., self-empl., in schooling	0.073		0.070		0.095	
thereof: not in sample or retired	0.109		0.156		0.290	

c. 1980 to: =>	1985		1990	
Bottom quintile	0.373	0.523	0.263	0.407
2nd quintile	0.120	0.168	0.088	0.136
3rd quintile	0.091	0.128	0.137	0.212
4th or 5th q.	0.129	0.181	0.158	0.245
Out of employment	0.287		0.354	
thereof: unempl., self-empl., in schooling	0.163		0.130	
thereof: not in sample or retired	0.124		0.224	

d. 1985 to: =>	1990	
Bottom quintile	0.338	0.462
2nd quintile	0.143	0.196
3rd quintile	0.104	0.142
4th or 5th q.	0.146	0.200
Out of employment	0.269	
thereof: unempl., self-empl., in schooling	0.180	
thereof: not in sample or retired	0.089	

Another difference between the two decades is that in the 1970s, women exit low-pay employment more frequently than men by leaving employment altogether, whereas in the 1980s, the pattern has been the opposite. The proportion of low-pay female workers exiting to homework has fallen considerably at the same time as exits to out-of-employment states with a closer labour market attachment have increased in importance.

In addition to women, the bottom quintile contains a disproportionately large share of youths and only a very small share of elderly workers. Looking at the transition rates by age (set out in Table 3.4) is interesting as this may tell us something about the persistence – and hence severity – of low pay. A closer inspection of the table reveals that the differences across age groups in the share remaining in the lowest quintile were rather small in the 1970s (save for the over 50 years of age group). Both in 1970 and 1975, about a quarter of the low paid in each age group continued to be so five years later.

At the same time as the level of the share of stayers grew in the 1980s, the differences between age groups also increased somewhat (again the oldest category is an exception), and now the share of young people remaining in the low-pay group was 10 percentage points lower than in the 35–49 years category. It can be noted that Gustafsson (1994) has also found a rather weak relationship between income mobility and age for Sweden. However, this is not a phenomenon specific to the Nordic countries, as Gittleman and Joyce (1996) did not find mobility decreasing with age in the USA either.

Table 3.3   *Mobility out of the bottom quintile, females*

a. 1970 to: =>	1975		1980		1985		1990	
Bottom quintile	0.293	*0.472*	0.224	*0.343*	0.203	*0.321*	0.166	*0.279*
2nd quintile	0.170	*0.274*	0.207	*0.317*	0.185	*0.292*	0.187	*0.315*
3rd quintile	0.082	*0.132*	0.117	*0.179*	0.127	*0.201*	0.131	*0.221*
4th or 5th q.	0.076	*0.122*	0.105	*0.161*	0.119	*0.188*	0.110	*0.185*
Out of employment	0.379		0.347		0.366		0.405	
thereof: unempl., self-empl., in schooling	0.066		0.071		0.071		0.069	
thereof: not in sample or retired	0.124		0.175		0.242		0.308	
thereof: home worker etc.	0.189		0.101		0.053		0.029	

b. 1975 to: =>	1980		1985		1990	
Bottom quintile	0.228	*0.284*	0.204	*0.273*	0.154	*0.229*
2nd quintile	0.381	*0.474*	0.290	*0.389*	0.264	*0.393*
3rd quintile	0.116	*0.144*	0.152	*0.204*	0.157	*0.234*
4th or 5th q.	0.079	*0.098*	0.100	*0.134*	0.097	*0.144*
Out of employment	0.196		0.254		0.328	
thereof: unempl., self-empl., in schooling	0.049		0.059		0.043	
thereof: not in sample or retired	0.074		0.152		0.262	
thereof: home worker etc.	0.073		0.043		0.023	

c. 1980 to: =>	1985		1990	
Bottom quintile	0.356	*0.444*	0.258	*0.356*
2nd quintile	0.255	*0.318*	0.227	*0.326*
3rd quintile	0.103	*0.129*	0.127	*0.175*
4th or 5th q.	0.087	*0.109*	0.104	*0.143*
Out of employment	0.199		0.274	
thereof: unempl., self-empl., in schooling	0.075		0.077	
thereof: not in sample or retired	0.079		0.168	
thereof: home worker etc.	0.045		0.029	

d. 1985 to: =>	1990	
Bottom quintile	0.324	*0.385*
2nd quintile	0.293	*0.348*
3rd quintile	0.123	*0.146*
4th or 5th q.	0.102	*0.121*
Out of employment	0.158	
thereof: unempl., self-empl., in schooling	0.066	
thereof: not in sample or retired	0.058	
thereof: home worker etc.	0.035	

Table 3.4 Mobility out of the bottom quintile by age groups

a. 1970, 15-24 years to: =>	1975		1980		1985		1990	
Bottom quintile	0.234	0.307	0.213	0.268	0.201	0.252	0.185	0.238
2nd quintile	0.180	0.237	0.177	0.222	0.166	0.208	0.169	0.218
3rd quintile	0.150	0.197	0.169	0.212	0.165	0.207	0.157	0.202
4th or 5th q.	0.197	0.259	0.237	0.298	0.265	0.333	0.265	0.342
Out of employment	0.239		0.204		0.203		0.224	

a. 1970, 25-34 years to: =>	1975		1980		1985		1990	
Bottom quintile	0.281	0.356	0.363	0.478	0.294	0.424	0.277	0.426
2nd quintile	0.168	0.213	0.143	0.188	0.140	0.202	0.140	0.215
3rd quintile	0.126	0.160	0.104	0.137	0.101	0.146	0.099	0.152
4th or 5th q.	0.214	0.271	0.149	0.197	0.159	0.228	0.134	0.207
Out of employment	0.211		0.241		0.306		0.350	

a. 1970, 35-49 years to: =>	1975		1980		1985		1990	
Bottom quintile	0.256	0.406	0.396	0.653	0.230	0.574	0.125	0.613
2nd quintile	0.144	0.228	0.082	0.135	0.064	0.160	0.032	0.157
3rd quintile	0.102	0.162	0.062	0.102	0.048	0.120	0.022	0.108
4th or 5th q.	0.129	0.204	0.066	0.110	0.059	0.146	0.025	0.122
Out of employment	0.369		0.394		0.599		0.796	

a. 1970, 50-65 years to: =>	1975		1980		1985		1990	
Bottom quintile	0.077	0.520	0.091	0.771	–	–	–	–
2nd quintile	0.028	0.189	0.010	0.085	–	–	–	–
3rd quintile	0.021	0.142	0.008	0.068	–	–	–	–
4th or 5th q.	0.022	0.149	0.009	0.076	–	–	–	–
Out of employment	0.852		0.882		0.100		0.100	

b. 1975, 15-24 years to: =>	1980		1985		1990	
Bottom quintile	0.225	0.261	0.208	0.242	0.181	0.218
2nd quintile	0.405	0.454	0.324	0.367	0.311	0.407
3rd quintile	0.135	0.151	0.200	0.138	0.164	0.215
4th or 5th q.	0.129	0.150	0.171	0.199	0.183	0.221
Out of employment	0.137		0.141		0.170	

b. 1975, 25-34 years to: =>	1980		1985		1990	
Bottom quintile	0.235	0.263	0.220	0.249	0.181	0.237
2nd quintile	0.405	0.454	0.324	0.367	0.311	0.407
3rd quintile	0.135	0.151	0.200	0.227	0.164	0.215
4th or 5th q.	0.119	0.133	0.138	0.156	0.108	0.141
Out of employment	0.106		0.118		0.236	

b. 1975, 35-49 years to: =>	1980		1985		1990	
Bottom quintile	0.262	0.348	0.189	0.344	0.085	0.321
2nd quintile	0.315	0.419	0.205	0.373	0.102	0.385
3rd quintile	0.092	0.122	0.084	0.153	0.049	0.185
4th or 5th q.	0.082	0.109	0.072	0.131	0.029	0.109
Out of employment	0.249		0.450		0.735	

b. 1975, 50-65 years to: =>	1980		1985		1990	
Bottom quintile	0.136	0.430	0.112	0.479	0.056	0.496
2nd quintile	0.129	0.408	0.080	0.342	0.039	0.345
3rd quintile	0.023	0.073	0.019	0.081	0.008	0.071
4th or 5th q.	0.028	0.089	0.023	0.098	0.010	0.088
Out of employment	0.684		0.766		0.887	

(continued on the next page)

Table 3.4   Mobility of the bottom quintile by age groups (continued)

c. 1980, 15-24, to: =>	1985		1990	
Bottom quintile	0.348	*0.398*	0.253	*0.298*
2nd quintile	0.266	*0.304*	0.237	*0.278*
3rd quintile	0.132	*0.151*	0.157	*0.184*
4th or 5th q.	0.128	*0.146*	0.204	*0.240*
Out of employment	0.126		0.149	

d. 1985, 15-24, to: =>	1990	
Bottom quintile	0.289	*0.324*
2nd quintile	0.301	*0.337*
3rd quintile	0.156	*0.175*
4th or 5th q.	0.147	*0.164*
Out of employment	0.107	

c. 1980, 25-34, to: =>	1985		1990	
Bottom quintile	0.362	*0.438*	0.284	*0.357*
2nd quintile	0.211	*0.256*	0.214	*0.269*
3rd quintile	0.124	*0.150*	0.144	*0.181*
4th or 5th q.	0.129	*0.156*	0.154	*0.193*
Out of employment	0.174		0.204	

d. 1985, 25-34, to: =>	1990	
Bottom quintile	0.322	*0.385*
2nd quintile	0.250	*0.299*
3rd quintile	0.133	*0.159*
4th or 5th q.	0.132	*0.157*
Out of employment	0.163	

c. 1980, 35-49, to: =>	1985		1990	
Bottom quintile	0.465	*0.623*	0.253	*0.417*
2nd quintile	0.139	*0.186*	0.237	*0.390*
3rd quintile	0.063	*0.084*	0.157	*0.259*
4th or 5th q.	0.080	*0.107*	0.203	*0.334*
Out of employment	0.253		0.393	

d. 1985, 35-49, to: =>	1990	
Bottom quintile	0.406	*0.536*
2nd quintile	0.190	*0.251*
3rd quintile	0.077	*0.102*
4th or 5th q.	0.085	*0.111*
Out of employment	0.242	

c. 1980, 50-65, to: =>	1985		1990	
Bottom quintile	0.267	*0.748*	0.095	*0.772*
2nd quintile	0.045	*0.126*	0.015	*0.122*
3rd quintile	0.020	*0.056*	0.007	*0.057*
4th or 5th q.	0.025	*0.070*	0.006	*0.049*
Out of employment	0.643		0.877	

d. 1985, 50-65, to: =>	1990	
Bottom quintile	0.293	*0.711*
2nd quintile	0.074	*0.180*
3rd quintile	0.018	*0.044*
4th or 5th q.	0.027	*0.065*
Out of employment	0.588	

The fact that young workers account for a disproportionately large share of the bottom quintile, of course, reflects low pay being linked to life-cycle patterns of pay. However, a non-negligible part of the low paid are not at the beginning of their careers. The probabilities of moving out of the low-pay quintile are of about the same size across age groups and, as can be seen from Table 3.A3 in the Appendix, the gender and age composition of those remaining in the bottom quintile, even as long as ten years later, is very similar to that of the bottom quintile itself.[7] Thus, although a considerable proportion of those leaving low pay are young – about 50 per cent in the 1970s and one-third in the 1980s – a relatively high share of the young (20 to 30 per cent) also remain low paid five years later.

As is borne out by Tables 3.1, 3.2, 3.3 and 3.4, for most of the individuals in the bottom quintile in a particular year, low pay is merely a temporary state. But for some people, low pay is a permanent state and their share of the bottom quintile increased in the 1980s. Who faces a higher probability of remaining in low-paid jobs? In the 1980s, male low-paid workers had exit rates from the bottom quintile of the same magnitude as women. During the preceding decade they had been higher. Except for the old workers who have very low exit rates, the exit rates differ only little between age groups during most of the period studied. At the end of the period 1985–90, however, the differences grew, and now the 35–49 year olds faced a clearly higher probability of remaining in a low-paid job than the 15–24 year or 25–34 year olds.

In characterizing low-wage employment it is not only important to look at where these persons are moving to, but also to see where they come from. Table 3.A1 in the Appendix sheds some light on this issue. We can see that there is a fairly stable pattern over the years. About two-thirds have been either out of employment or already in the bottom quintile five years ago. Of those in employment at both points of time, about half had also been low paid five years earlier. Downward mobility is also important. Thus about 12 to 17 per cent of the persons in the bottom quintile in the 1980s came from the three upper quintiles.[8]

As can be seen from the tables, neglecting exits to non-employment leads to an overstatement of upward mobility.[9] Accounting for transitions to out-of-employment is particularly important with respect to the low paid, as they are more likely to exit into non-employment than those further up the earnings distribution. This can be seen from Table 3.A2 in the Appendix, which by way of example, shows the mobility of the third quintile in 1975 and 1985. The transition rates to non-employment are considerably lower than those found for the bottom quintile in the same years. The difference grows further as we compare them to the fourth and fifth quintiles (not shown).

5 EVOLUTION OF MOBILITY

In this section we consider two questions. Firstly, how does the picture of low pay and the earnings mobility of the people with low pay change as we successively extend the time horizon? Secondly, has the earnings mobility of the bottom quintile been stable over time, or have there been changes in mobility accompanying the changes in inequality?

So, let us first return to Tables 3.1, 3.2, and 3.3, in which the exit rates for different time horizons are set out. Beginning with the whole sample, we can see that the share remaining in the bottom quintile falls as the time horizon is extended to 10 years and falls further somewhat for horizon lengths of 15 and 20 years. Most of the exits from the low-pay category take place during the first five years and compared to them the further changes are relatively small.[10] The same holds also when we look at men and women separately or restrict attention to those who were employed in both comparison years. As for upward mobility we may note a corresponding pattern; the proportion in the second quintile declines further, whereas the other quintiles change only marginally as the length of the observation period is increased.

The decline in the share staying in the lowest quintile is smaller when we consider only those who remain employed. This is worth noting since many studies of earnings mobility have restricted the attention to the continuously employed, such as for example OECD (1996), and have thus overstated the probability of moving up the distribution.

Trends in mobility are particularly interesting in view of the changes in cross-section earnings inequality, as increases (decreases) would tend to off-set the impact of increasing (decreasing) annual inequality on longer-run inequality, whereas a decrease (increase) would do the opposite. As has already been noted, the levels of mobility out of low pay are lower in the 1980s than in the 1970s. This pertains to the five-year horizon we examined in the previous section. Comparisons of the shares remaining in the bottom quintile after ten years (for which for obvious reasons we only have observations in the 1980s) also indicate a decline, albeit a considerably smaller one.

As documented by Eriksson and Jäntti (1997), wage dispersion in Finland decreased between 1970 and 1985 and increased between 1985 and 1990. The reduction in dispersion was especially large in the early 1970s; the 90/10 decile ratio fell from 1.46 to 1.24. During the following ten years the ratio fell further to 1.04, from which it rose to 1.13 in 1990. The 1970–5 reduction was due to a decline in dispersion on both sides of the median, whereas the major part of the decline in 1975–85 was due to a compression in the lower half of the distribution. The increase in 1985–90 was mainly due to a widening of differentials below the median. While changes in inequality in the 1970s were due both to changes in earnings dispersion between and within (age, education and industry) groups, movements in the 1980s have almost been entirely the result of within-group changes.

One of the key results in Table 3.1 is that the earnings mobility of low-wage employees was unchanged during the 1970s and then fell to lower levels in the 1980s. Now, as there are no data at our disposal from the 1960s, we cannot say whether mobility was higher or lower in the 1970s, and reinforced or off-set the tendency towards greater equality in the 1970s. As for the 1980s the fall in mobility, which had already begun in the first half of the decade when cross-sectional inequality was still declining, implies that the rise in inequality observed in the second half of the decade may actually be larger than it appears and that long-run inequality will increase.

The trends differ between demographic groups. The decrease in mobility is smaller for women and is increasing with age. This is worth noting in view of the finding that within-group inequality has risen in just about every gender-age group in the 1980s. Our results indicate that long-run inequality has increased especially for men and older workers. As explained by Gittleman and Joyce (1996), the decline in mobility is consistent with permanent (but not transitory) factors like shifts in demand for skills explaining the rise in earnings dispersion. This is somewhat puzzling as there have been only rather small changes in returns to education and experience in the 1980s (Eriksson and Jäntti 1997).

6 CONCLUSIONS

We have documented the development of earnings mobility for low-paid workers over a twenty-year period, looking at longer time horizons than usual. We find that most of the low paid move out of low-paid employment during the following five years. After that, some further upward mobility or movements out of employment occur, but they are significantly smaller in magnitude. A somewhat surprising finding is that, except for the oldest age group, the exit rates do not differ much across demographic groups. The low paid exit non-employment more frequently than other groups of employees. Neglecting this leads to an overstatement of their upward mobility.

During the period studied there has been a number of changes in earnings mobility. In the 1980s the gap in upward mobility between female and male low-paid workers closed. In the 1970s men had higher exit rates. At the same time the share of low-paid women exiting the bottom quintile to non-employment was decreasing. Finally, the overall earnings mobility of the low-paid category fell in the 1980s compared to the 1970s. The decline is larger for men, adults and old workers. The trends in mobility have not moved in such a way as to offset the recent increase in cross-section inequality. Thus, long-run inequality is likely to have increased.

NOTES

1   I am grateful to Larjos Parkatti for help with the data.
2   Of course this implies that when comparing cross-sectional inequality across countries it is not necessary to adjust for differences in mobility.
3   In every year, high incomes, i.e. the top percentile, are top-coded. In place of the actual incomes for these, Statistics Finland has imputed the actual average earnings above the top code cut-offs. The sample sizes are: 1970: 177 086, 1975: 150 066, 1980: 234 690, 1985: 252 969, and 1990: 205 072 individuals.
4   The first year in the data set is somewhat problematic. All variables except earnings refer to 1970. Earnings information is available for 1971. We only include individuals who were in the labour force in 1970 and who had positive earnings in 1971. Hence, some persons who entered the labour force in 1971 are erroneously omitted from the data set. Naturally, the main consequence for the analysis in this paper is that the first transitions we observe come from a shorter period.
5   The data set was originally set up in terms of deciles. Corresponding tables with results for the deciles show that the lowest decile, which is an alternative measure of low pay, as a rule

has a lower level of mobility than the second decile. However, to save space, only the results for quintiles are presented.

6 Only a few studies – see e.g. the recent study by Buchinsky and Hunt (1996) – have examined data sets which include observations of zero earnings.

7 The same holds for the 1980 bottom quintile.

8 To what extent the downward mobility is permanent or transitory has to be assessed by extending the analysis to cover more than only comparisons over pairs of years.

9 Thus, for example, the picture of earnings progression among the low-paid painted in OECD (1996), which is based on samples of individuals who had been full-time wage earners in both years 1986 and 1991 is in all likelihood an all too rosy one.

10 It should, of course, be noted that we are only observing how many of the 'original' quintile, in 1970, say, are in the bottom quintile ten years later, 1980. We do not know from the tables whether or not these persons were also in the bottom quintile in 1975.

REFERENCES

Asplund, R., P. Bingley and N. Westergård-Nielsen (1997), *Wage Mobility in the Danish and Finnish Private Sectors, 1980–1994*, paper presented at the 1997 EALE conference in Århus.

Atkinson, A., F. Bourguignon and C. Morrisson (1992), *Empirical Studies of Earnings Mobility*, Chur: Harwood Academic Publishers.

Björklund, A. (1993), 'A Comparison Between Actual Distributions of Annual and Lifetime Income: Sweden, 1951–89', *Review of Income and Wealth*, **39**, pp. 377–86.

Björklund, A. and M. Jäntti (1997), *Intergenerational Mobility of Economic Status: Is the United States Different?*, paper presented at the 1997 American Economic Association meeting in New Orleans.

Buchinsky, M. and J. Hunt (1996), *Wage Mobility in the United States*, NBER working paper no. 5455.

Eriksson, T. and M. Jäntti (1997), 'The Distribution of Earnings in Finland 1971–1990', *European Economic Review*, **41**, pp. 1736–79.

Gittleman, M. and M. Joyce (1996), 'Earnings Mobility and Long-Run Inequality: An Analysis Using Matched CPS Data', *Industrial Relations*, **35**, pp. 180–96.

Gottschalk, P. (1997), 'Inequality, Income Growth, and Mobility: The Basic Facts', *Journal of Economic Perspectives*, **11**, pp. 21–40.

Gottschalk, P. and R. Moffitt (1994), 'The Growth of Earnings Instability in the U.S. Labor Market', *Brookings Papers on Economic Activity*, **2**, pp. 217–72.

Gustafsson, B. (1994), 'The Degree and Pattern of Income Immobility in Sweden', *Review of Income and Wealth*, **40**, pp. 67–86.

Jäntti, M. (1996), *Teollisuuden toimihenkilöiden liikkuvuudesta Suomessa: palkkaluokka- ja toimipaikkojen vaihdot 1980–1992*, Helsinki: Palkansaajien tutkimuslaitos tutkimuksia 63.

Gregory, M. and P. Elias (1994), 'Earnings Transitions of the Low Paid in Britain, 1976–91: A Longitudinal Study', *International Journal of Manpower*, **15**, pp. 170–88.

Lilja, R. (1996), *Toimihenkilöura Suomen teollisuudessa*, Helsinki: Elinkeinoelämän Tutkimuslaitos B 117.

Mincer, J. and B. Jovanovic (1981), 'Labor Mobility and Wages' in S. Rosen (ed.), *Studies in Labor Markets*, Chicago: University of Chicago Press.

OECD (1996), *Employment Outlook*, Paris.

OECD (1997), *Employment Outlook*, Paris.

Pönttinen, S. (1983), *Social mobility and social structure: a comparison of Scandinavian countries,* Helsinki: Societas Scientiarum Fennica, Commentationes Scientiarum Socialium 20.

Stewart, M. and J. Swaffield (1997), *Low Pay Dynamics and Transition Probabilities,* University of Warwick, working paper.

APPENDIX

Table 3.A1   The bottom quintile, some characteristics

Bottom quintile in year:	1970	1975	1980	1985
Proportion females	0.390	0.753	0.552	0.633
Age:15-24	0.484	0.561	0.461	0.311
Age: 25-34	0.135	0.174	0.205	0.371
Age: 35-49	0.304	0.212	0.296	0.219
Age: 50-64	0.077	0.053	0.038	0.099
5 yrs earlier in: Bottom q.	n.a.	0.309	0.301	0.343
5 yrs earlier in: 2nd q.	n.a.	0.264	0.137	0.153
5 yrs earlier in: 3rd to 5th q.	n.a.	0.122	0.214	0.175
5 yrs earlier in: Out of empl.	n.a.	0.305	0.348	0.329

Table 3.A2   Mobility of the third quintile, 1975 and 1985

	1975:				1985:			
To:	1980		1985		1990		1995	
Bottom quintile	0.055	0.062	0.063	0.079	0.069	0.099	0.091	0.101
2nd quintile	0.114	0.128	0.101	0.127	0.093	0.134	0.140	0.156
3rd quintile	0.356	0.399	0.267	0.335	0.214	0.308	0.361	0.403
4th or 5th q.	0.368	0.412	0.365	0.458	0.320	0.460	0.305	0.340
Out of employment	0.107		0.204		0.304		0.103	

Table 3.A3   Characteristics of stayers from the 1975 bottom quintile

Characteristic	In bottom quintile 1975	Still in bottom quintile 1980	Still in bottom quintile 1985
Females (%)	0.753	0.781	0.809
Age in '75 (%): 15-24	0.561	0.547	0.600
Age in '75 (%): 25-34	0.174	0.177	0.193
Age in '75 (%): 35-49	0.212	0.242	0.208
Age in '75 (%): 50-65	0.053	0.033	–

4. Low-Wage Mobility in a Working-Life Perspective [1]

A. McKnight

1 INTRODUCTION

Whilst there has been long-running interest in the causes and consequences of low-wage employment this topic has recently come to the fore following quite dramatic changes in the income distribution (and in particular the earnings distribution) in many countries over the last two decades. The main features of this change in the United Kingdom has been first a narrowing in the mid-1970s and then a widening of the earnings distribution. This widening of earnings differentials has been common across many OECD countries, although the extent to which earnings distributions have widened has varied. The United States is perhaps the extreme case where real wages at the lower end of the distribution have actually fallen (OECD 1996). The UK has seen wages at the lower end of the distribution increase only marginally over the period 1985–95. Other countries have not seen such a significant widening of these distributions although international comparisons in this area must be viewed with caution. The trends in earnings inequality have sparked concern about changes in low-wage employment as the widening of the distribution in the UK appears to have been driven by stagnant wage growth at the bottom of the distribution rather than changes at the top.

While the relative position of the low paid and the number of workers who fall into this category are a matter for concern, a number of studies have gone on to examine whether low-paid employment is a temporary phenomenon or whether there is evidence of persistence. These studies have revealed a combination of both significant upward mobility alongside considerable inertia for other groups of workers. Further studies have gone on to identify the characteristics of 'movers' and 'stayers'. This chapter adopts a new approach, exploiting an event history data set, the Family and Working Lives

47

Survey (FWLS), to map both the evolution of low-wage employment over time and to estimate what factors affect the probability of an individual exiting a spell of low-wage employment.

The first section is descriptive and looks at the quality of the earnings information in the FWLS. This is followed by the introduction to the age cohort analysis and presentation of age/employment profiles for the five age cohorts studied in this paper. The working lives of individuals who were in low-wage employment at the end of 1994 or beginning of 1995, when the survey was conducted, are compared with individuals not in low-paid employment in the same period. This type of descriptive analysis makes it possible to observe whether individuals who were in low-wage employment at the time the survey data were collected had experienced important differences in their work histories compared with higher-paid workers.

If low-wage employment is a temporary experience for individuals then there is less cause for concern than a situation where individuals who enter low-wage employment are unlikely to leave it. Although the FWLS does not contain historical records of individual earnings, a 'proxy' for low-wage employment has been constructed using information on occupations. Using Labour Force Survey (LFS) data the average earnings of full-time employees within each occupational group[2] are used to rank occupations and identify low occupational wage groups with average gross weekly earnings less than 68 per cent of the mean (The Council of Europe Decency Threshold). This approach was verified via an analysis of occupational earnings differentials, after controlling for age and region of residence, along with the proportion of employees within an occupation who are low paid. The identification of low occupational wage groups was conducted separately for males and females, resulting in a relative concept of low pay.

From the lifetime occupational histories provided by each individual in the survey, the mapping between occupations and low pay provides an historical record of movements into and out of low-wage occupations. In the first part of the chapter, cohort analysis of these movements is undertaken by measuring the average proportion of an age group in low-wage occupations in every month of the cohort's work history. Cohort analysis makes it possible to map the evolution of low occupational wage experience of individuals born in different time periods in addition to exploring time period effects. In addition, a measure of persistence in low-wage occupations is obtained by examining the proportion of individuals in low-wage employment who have been in a particular spell of low-wage employment for three years or longer.

The second section explores mobility out of low-wage occupations in a number of ways. Particular emphasis is placed on the relationship between unemployment and low occupational wage employment. Econometric techniques are used to examine whether spells and duration of unemployment increase the likelihood of an individual exiting a spell of low occupational wage employment.

2 THE DATA

The analysis is conducted using an event history data set from a household survey conducted in the United Kingdom in 1994/95. The survey collected information on respondents 'current circumstances' (employment, housing, family, benefits, geographical location), 'background' information about each respondent (parental social class and level of education) and detailed historical information relating to six main areas of their lives.[3] This study draws on the retrospective information collected on employment, known as work histories. Individuals were asked to record dates of events relating to employment, unemployment and spells spent out of the labour force. For each period of employment supplementary information was collected on employment status, occupation, industry, trade union membership and establishment size. In addition to changes of employer, changes in occupation whilst remaining with the same employer were recorded, creating a fairly systematic record of all occupations held. Work histories were collected from the point an individual left compulsory education to the date (1994/95) of the interview.

Use of event history data overcomes some of the problems associated with cross-sectional and panel data but comes with its own unique problem; recall error. The extent to which recall errors affect the validity of event history data is still not well understood and may cast some doubt on the reliability of information about events that took place some time before the interview. A recent paper (Elias 1997) has highlighted the discrepancies between unemployment rates calculated using event history data compared with those recorded in cross-sectional surveys, such as the LFS, which collect information at a point in time. The main finding appears to be that spells of unemployment are not recalled at all well after two or three years, thereby biasing the data towards the recollection of long duration unemployment (and even long duration unemployment is under-recorded). This was found to be a particular problem for women, who appear to reclassify spells of unemployment into inactivity, and older age groups.

2.1 Low-Wage Individuals in the Family and Working Lives Survey

The quality of the earnings information in the FWLS is assessed by comparing it with two national surveys most frequently used for the analysis of earnings; the New Earnings Survey (NES) and the LFS.

The NES is an approximate 1 per cent sample of employees, with earn-ings information provided by their employers. The employers of individuals with the relevant National Insurance number are identified via the Pay-As-You-Earn (PAYE) tax system. Hence, some employees earning below the threshold for payment of tax may not be included, in cases where no record of their tax payment and national insurance numbers exist. This results in a significant under-representation of individuals earning low wages and those in part-time employment. [4]

In 1993 the LFS started to collect earnings information from the out-rotating element of the survey. As this is a household survey there is no lower limit associated with the identification of individuals via tax records, but there is always some question over the reliability of self-reported earnings, particularly for those in the highest earnings bands.

Figure 4.1   Gross weekly earnings distributions of male employees, LFS, FWLS and NES 1994/95

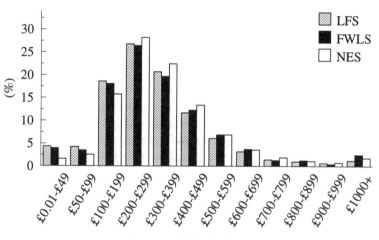

Gross weekly earnings bands

Figures 4.1 and 4.2 show, for males and females respectively, the earn-ings distributions of employees in the LFS, FWLS and NES for the period 1994/95. The under-representation of low-wage individuals in the NES is clearly apparent. The LFS records 15 per cent of female employees in the £0–49 earnings band, in contrast to 8 per cent in the NES. Similarly, males with low levels of weekly earnings are under-represented in the NES com-pared with the LFS, although the problem is less stark as fewer males are in part-time employment.

The distribution of gross weekly earnings in the FWLS is close to that observed in the LFS. The differences are not great and could be explained in terms of the timing of the survey, differences in question design, etc. This evidence suggests that the earnings information in the FWLS is fairly reliable and that low-wage employees have been captured by the survey.

Figure 4.2   Gross weekly earnings distributions of female employees, LFS, FWLS and NES 1994/95

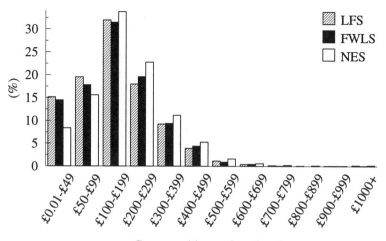

Gross weekly earnings bands

2.2 Work Histories of Individuals in the Family and Working Lives Survey

The work history information has been reconstructed into a calendar time file making it possible to characterize each month of a respondent's working life in terms of their employment status. Work history information was collected from 8 650 individuals. Removing those with incomplete histories reduced the sample to 8 373. Preliminary investigation indicates that this reduction has not led to any significant bias. In this section the proportion of respondents in employment is mapped over time, breaking the sample down by gender and five age cohorts (16–24, 25–34, 35–44, 45–54, 55–64), where age is defined at the date of the survey.

Figures 4.3 and 4.4 show the profile of labour force participation by age for the five age cohorts, for males and females respectively. Employment comprises of employees and the self-employed. These charts show the proportion of the age/gender cohort which was in employment at each age as the cohort ages. There are clear differences in the experience of males relative to females over the life cycle. The gradual entry of females into the labour market is soon followed by withdrawal during years of family formation, then re-entry until the cohort reaches retirement age. For females the proportion of the cohort in employment peaks between the age of 17 and 20 for all cohorts. For males employment rates are consistently higher and do not follow the 'M-shaped' participation profile characteristic of older females. The cohorts have experienced changes in the economy and the labour market at different ages and different members of the cohort are exposed to these at different ages due to aggregation of work histories. This may lead to variations in the response to such changes.

Comparisons across the age cohorts show lower activity rates amongst the younger cohorts during the years of labour market entry. This is likely to be associated with higher school staying on rates and greater participation in higher and further education. With the exception of the 55–64 age cohort, the age/employment profiles for males (Figure 4.3) show successively lower employment rates for younger age cohorts at every age since entering the labour market. The lower proportion in employment between the ages of 16 and 22 can be explained in terms of an increased proportion participating in education.

The pattern for males shows a dramatic change between the high rates of labour force participation of the two older age cohorts (35–44 and 45–54) between the age of 16 and 19 and the much lower rates found amongst the two younger age cohorts (16–24 and 25–34). The difference between these two groups is around 30 per cent. It is the lower employment rates beyond this age for the younger cohorts that are the most perplexing. Some of the difference may be explained in terms of the economic cycle, recall error and increased participation in education at all ages, but it would appear that a trend exists that younger male age cohorts are characterized by declining employment rates. The dip in the participation rate of the oldest cohort between the age of 17 and 26 is likely to be associated with World War II. The early 1990s recession could help explain very rapid (and perhaps early) decline in the participation rate of the 55–64 cohort and the 'dip' in the 16–24 cohort between the age of 18 and 24. It would appear that the male 25–34 cohort made the most gains over this period with increasing labour force participation over a period in which other cohorts experienced declines. The 35–44 cohort appears to have the steepest descent in participation rates at the end of the period.

For females (Figure 4.4) the younger cohort have successively higher employment rates during the years of family formation than their older counter-

Figure 4.3   Age/employment profiles of males by age cohort

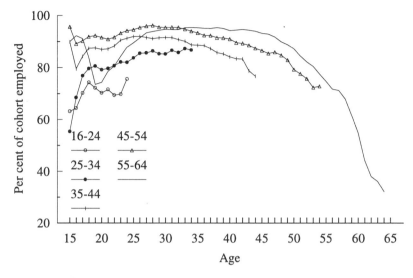

Source: Family and Working Lives Survey, 1994/95

Figure 4.4   Age/employment profiles of females by age cohort

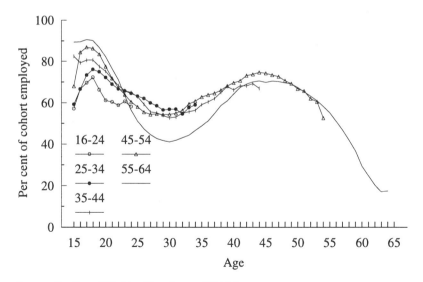

Source: Family and Working Lives Survey, 1994/95

parts, supporting recent evidence of trends towards higher rates of employment during the years of family formation (Harkness 1996), although the trend appears to have been checked by the early 1990s recession.

The focus of this study is the experience of low-paid individuals and therefore it is interesting to pose the question: have individuals in low-wage employment at the time of the survey experienced significantly different working lives than those earning above a low-wage threshold? Figure 4.5 compares the employment rates of employees earning below the third decile point of the earnings distribution (represented by the black shaded area) with those earning above this level (represented by the line). These charts map the evolution of employment, the proportion of the cohort in employment in each month, for each age cohort over time. It is worth noting that as these individuals had to be in employment at the time of the survey their work histories will not be representative of a sample of individuals at a point in time, which would include individuals in unemployment and those out of the labour force. To improve statistical reliability, information has been censored where there were less than 100 observations in a month. As a greater proportion of each cohort is employed above the low-pay threshold the result is that this series tends to start at an earlier date.

The comparison of work histories of males (left-hand column) who were in low-wage employment at the time of the survey with higher-paid males shows that the low-wage males had lower employment rates over time than higher-paid males. The black line representing the employment rates of higher-paid males is always above the shaded area representing the employment rates of lower-paid males. This is the case for all five age cohorts. While there is some doubt about the reliability of recalled spells of unemployment there is no reason to suspect that this will differ between these two groups. This means that comparisons are likely to be more reliable than concentrating on the actual employment rates observed.

The right-hand column of charts reveals a contrasting experience for low-wage females compared with higher-paid females. The employment rates over time are not only lower for those in low-wage employment, at the time of the survey, but a greater proportion of this group withdrew from the labour market during years of family formation and, on average, stayed away longer. This pattern is particularly prominent for younger age cohorts. The employment rate of 25–34 year old females in higher-paid employment has continued to rise up to the survey date, while the low paid experienced an accentuated dip in employment rates. This may be a combination of both lower-paid jobs being taken by 'women returners' and higher-paid women maintaining their contact with the labour market, combining a career with raising children. In a study of highly qualified women Corti et al. (1995) found such a

Figure 4.5 **Work histories of males and females in low-wage employment at the time of the survey and those in better-paid employment, for five age cohorts**

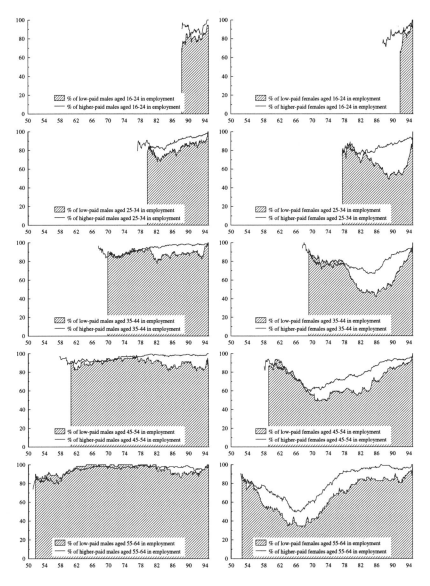

Source: Family and Working Lives Survey, 1994/95

pattern existed amongst females with higher level qualifications. Stewart and Greenhalgh (1984) found evidence that women who experience interruptions in their work experience earn substantially less on average than women who do not. Women earning higher wages face greater opportunity costs, are more able to finance childcare and more likely to take only minimum time out of the labour market. The low-paid women, who have taken more time out of the labour force will have accumulated less work experience and may have seen their skills depreciate. Consequently low paid women may be in receipt of lower wages as a result of extended periods out of the labour force.

3 OCCUPATION AS A PROXY FOR LOW-WAGE EMPLOYMENT

The distribution of average earnings by occupation shows a wide degree of dispersion. Part of this dispersion is undoubtedly the result of compositional differences between the groups; for example, in an occupation group dominated by young people, the relative wages will appear low even though the wage for these young people may be in line with the wages other young people earn. It will be shown in this section, however, that after controlling for region of residence and age, there exists a substantial variation in occupational earnings differentials. This relationship between occupations and earnings and its apparent stability over long periods of time makes occupation a suitable proxy for low-wage employment when earnings information is not available. A classification of Low Occupational Wage (LOW) groups has been devised from a study of occupational earnings differentials using a number of sources of information on occupational earnings.

The stability of this relationship between earnings and occupations has previously been exploited in a number of studies. Nickell (1982) used the mean earnings within each occupation group to rank occupations to create an occupational hierarchy. This occupational hierarchy was used to investigate the determinants of an individual's position in the hierarchy and to determine factors and events that led to occupational 'success'. Nickell was interested in looking at occupational success *per se* and not at the low-wage group in particular so he makes no distinction between different positions on the occupation hierarchy.

Elias and Blanchflower (1989) used occupational earnings as an indicator of the relative economic well-being of individuals. They used work history information in the National Child Development Survey (Sweep 4) to look at the relationship between occupational position, family background, ability and work history. They used the median earnings of the occupational group in which an individual was employed in or from their previous employment, for those who were not in employment at the time of the survey, to describe an individual's relative labour market position. Greenhalgh and Stewart (1985) similarly used the average earnings in occupational groups to measure occupational status and mobility using an event history data set.

The classification of low-wage employment using occupation as a proxy is devised from a variety of information sources on occupational earnings and occupational earnings differentials. All the main data sources used classified occupational information according to the *Standard Occupational Classification* (SOC), information at the minor group level of this classification (77 occupational groups)[5] was used. Earnings information was used from the LFS and seven quarters of this survey were pooled to increase the sample size (Spring 1993 to Autumn 1994). The earnings data used were gross weekly earnings for full-time employees. It must be borne in mind that the effect of defining low pay relative to the mean of male and female wages separately is that low-paid females defined in this way will, on average, be earning significantly less than males. This study explores low pay relative to 'own sex' average earnings. The reasons behind the observed differentials are not explored further here; low pay is defined in terms of the 'norms' within each group.

3.1 Construction of the Low Occupational Wage (LOW) Classification

The definition of low pay is in some sense arbitrary and many different definitions of low pay exist in the literature. The definition of low pay adopted is the Council of Europe Decency Threshold, set at 68 per cent of the mean gross wage. Average earnings in occupational minor groups were ranked in ascending order and occupations with average earnings less than 68 per cent of the gross weekly wage were defined as low-wage occupations (Figures 4.6 and 4.7). However, average earnings ignore compositional differences between occupational groups and without controlling for factors such as age and region of residence low-wage occupational groups may be identified which are dominated by young, inexperienced workers, or concentrated in regions which have lower regional wage differentials. In order to identify low-wage occupational groups after taking these factors into account, individual earnings equations were estimated including the necessary control factors together with a set of occupation dummy variables representing the minor group categories. The coefficients on the occupation dummies were transformed into percentage earnings differentials relative to a reference occupational group.[6] Ranking the differentials in ascending order made it possible to examine the rank moves of occupation groups after controlling for other factors. These differentials show that even after controlling for age and region of residence there exist wide differentials in earnings attributable to

The Long-Run Horizon

the occupation in which an individual is employed. This analysis prompted the inclusion of some additional occupations into the low-wage group and exclusion of some which had moved up the distribution. The black columns denote the occupation groups identified by the low-wage classification scheme.

Figure 4.6   *Ranked average gross weekly earnings of male full-time employees by SOC minor groups (£)*

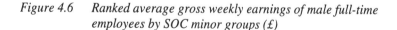

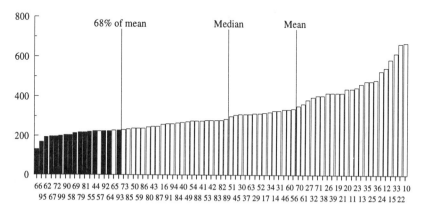

Source: Labour Force Surveys, Spring 1993 – Autumn 1994

Figure 4.7   *Ranked average gross weekly earnings of female full-time employees by SOC minor groups (£)*

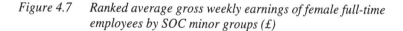

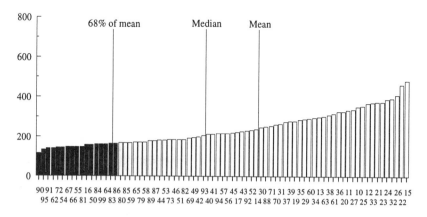

Source: Labour Force Surveys, Spring 1993 – Autumn 1994

A further check was carried out by calculating the proportion of full-time employees in an occupational minor group with earnings less than 68 per cent of the gross mean wage (without controls). Figures 4.8 and 4.9 chart these percentages for males and females respectively. It can be seen, for example, that around 75 per cent of male full-time employees in minor group

Figure 4.8   *Percentage of males in full-time employment whose earnings are below 68 per cent of the male gross mean wage*

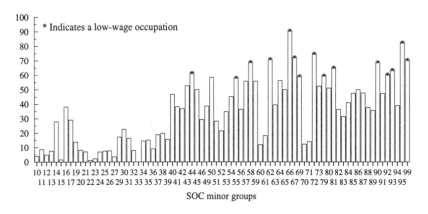
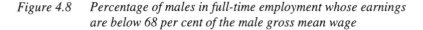

Source: Labour Force Surveys, Spring 1993 – Autumn 1994

Figure 4.9   *Percentage of females in full-time employment whose earnings are below 68 per cent of the male gross mean wage*

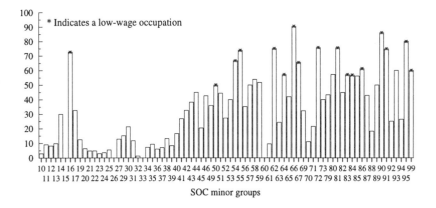

Source: Labour Force Surveys, Spring 1993 – Autumn 1994

72 (Sales Assistants and Check-out Operators) are earning less than 68 per cent of the mean gross wage and that 90 per cent of female full-time employees in minor group 66 (Hairdressers, Beauticians and Other Related Occupations) are similarly low paid. All the minor groups included in the classification scheme have over 50 per cent of low-wage employees.

When the sets of low-wage occupations were identified it was apparent that approximately two-thirds of the occupational categories were common between males and females. In the light of this an attempt was made to develop one group of low-wage occupations. However, this was rejected as it was felt that the compromises involved were too great to justify. It does appear that there are some occupational groups where, even after taking into account the lower average wage that females receive, females earn significantly less than their male counterparts (even in a relative sense). The different patterns of employment across occupations between males and females would also make one classification scheme of low pay inappropriate.

Table 4.1 shows the composition of the low-wage classification for males and females, describing the constituent minor occupational groups.

Table 4.1   *The SOC minor groups defined as low occupational wage groups*

	Males		Females
44	Stores and despatch clerks, storekeepers	16	Managers in farming, horticulture, forestry and fishing
55	Textiles, garments and related trades	50	Construction trades
58	Food preparation trades	54	Vehicle trades
62	Catering occupations	55	Textiles, garments and related trades
64	Health and related occupations	62	Catering occupations
66	Hairdressers, beauticians and related occupations	64	Health and related occupations
67	Domestic staff and related occupations	66	Hairdressers, beauticians and related occupations
69	Personal and protective service occupations nec	67	Domestic staff and related occupations
72	Sales assistants and check-out operators	72	Sales assistants and check-out operators
79	Sales occupations nec	81	Textiles and tannery process operatives
81	Textiles and tannery process operatives	83	Metal making and treating process operatives
90	Other occupations in agriculture, forestry and fishing	84	Metal working process operatives
92	Other occupations in construction	86	Other routine process operatives
93	Other occupations in transport	90	Other occupations in agriculture, forestry and fishing
95	Other occupations in sales and services	91	Other occupations in mining and manufacturing
99	Other occupations nec	95	Other occupations in sales and services
		99	Other occupations nec

3.2 How Well Does the LOW Classification Work?

The low-wage classification thus far has been defined in terms of full-time employees, but it is clearly the case that both part-time employees and the self-employed are likely to make up a significant proportion of the low paid. This means that any classification must be able to identify these groups. This section applies the LOW classification and evaluates its ability to identify the low paid by comparing the earnings distributions of those identified by the classification scheme as low paid with the rest of the working population in the LFS and the FWLS.

Identifying low-wage individuals by assigning them to a low-wage group according to the typical earnings received in their occupation results in the inclusion of individuals with earnings above the low-pay threshold and the exclusion of others who receive low pay due to the typical earnings of their occupation. To test how well the proxy measure of low pay identifies low-wage individuals the actual earnings distribution of the low-wage group identified is compared with all those excluded from this group. Table 4.2 shows the distribution of earnings from the LFS and the FWLS for these two groups.

Table 4.2   *Earnings distributions showing the comparison between individuals identified as being in LOW employment with those not in LOW employment (column %)*

£	Labour Force Survey, Spring 1994				Family and Working Lives Survey			
	Males		Females		Males		Females	
	LOW	not LOW	LOW	not LOW	LOW	not LOW	LOW	not LOW
0-49	14.3	2.2	27.1	6.1	12.6	3.5	29.4	7.4
50-99	16.6	3.6	31.0	9.2	11.6	1.9	30.9	11.1
100-149	19.9	6.8	22.6	12.9	17.9	4.7	22.5	13.4
150-199	22.4	11.1	11.3	17.4	22.7	9.6	10.9	18.0
200-249	11.5	14.9	3.9	14.2	17.4	12.3	3.8	13.9
250-299	6.4	13.2	2.1	12.1	5.8	14.5	1.2	13.1
300-349	6.0	13.1	1.2	9.4	5.8	12.8	0.8	7.9
350-399	0.9	9.1	0.3	6.3	2.9	10.3	0.2	6.0
400-449	0.9	7.1	0.3	4.9	1.9	8.8	0.0	4.9
450-499	0.3	5.3	0.0	2.8	1.0	6.2	0.2	1.8
500+	0.7	13.7	0.0	4.7	0.5	15.4	0.0	2.5
100%	*669.0*	*3 898.0*	*1 589.0*	*3 096.0*	*207.0*	*1 266.0*	*521.0*	*1 083.0*

The earnings distribution of females in the LFS who are classified to LOW employment is heavily skewed towards the lower end of the distribution in comparison with the rest. The modal group is £50–99 gross weekly earnings. The first three earnings bands account for over 80 per cent of all those classified to LOW compared with around 28 per cent for those who are not (for whom the modal earnings group is £150–199). Males classified to LOW have a modal earnings group of £150–199 (illustrating the higher earnings of males relative to females), with approximately 73 per cent in or below this earnings band. For males not classified to LOW around 24 per cent are in this band or below and the modal group is £200–249. Overall 15 per cent of males and 34 per cent of females in employment were identified as being in low occupational wage employment.

Data from FWLS for females shows a similar picture with earnings of the LOW group concentrated at the lower end of the distribution, with the modal groups (31 per cent) in the second earnings band (£50–99 per week gross pay). Like the LFS not all individuals in the first band (£0–49 per week) are picked up by the classification. A similar picture is apparent for males. Once again it is the fourth earnings band (£150–199) which contains the largest proportion of LOW individuals, even though the earnings distribution for males is centred further up the earnings distribution than for females. Overall 14 per cent of males and 33 per cent of females in employment were identified as being in low occupational wage employment.

4   THE EVOLUTION OF LOW OCCUPATIONAL WAGE (LOW) EMPLOYMENT

The evolution of low occupational wage employment is mapped using the occupational detail in the work histories to show the proportion of individuals working in low-paid occupations at different points in their working lives. What we are interested in looking at is whether the proportion of respondents working in LOW employment has changed over time for all age groups (structural effects) and whether the proportion of those in employment who are working in LOW employment shows distinctive patterns between age cohorts (cohort effects) and over the life cycle (life-cycle effects), i.e. do individuals start in LOW employment and then move up the occupation hierarchy into better-paid jobs and what proportion remain in this group as the cohort ages? As labour market experience is so different for males and females this analysis has been carried out separately for each. This enables us to see the effect of increased levels of labour market participation of women, to identify life-cycle effects and how this may have changed.

Figure 4.10 shows the proportion of employment in each gender/age cohort made up of LOW employment. The LOW employment rate is indicated by the black line. In addition, the proportion of employment made up of long duration LOW employment is shown; identified as spells of LOW employment lasting 36 months or longer. The general pattern for both males and females is one where a significant proportion of young people enter low-wage occupations in their first jobs with the share diminishing as the cohort ages. The higher rates at labour market entry are likely to result from a combination of deferred entry of more able young people, who continue in further and higher education and enter the labour market with better-paid jobs, bringing the LOW employment rate down, together with movement up the occupation hierarchy as the cohorts gain experience. It is clear from these charts that a substantial proportion of employment, especially for women, is made up of low occupational wage employment in later years of their working life, showing that low-wage employment is by no means concentrated amongst new entrants to the labour force.

The experience of the different cohorts reveals that a greater proportion of young people entering employment went into low-wage occupations in recent years compared with older age cohorts. This may partly be explained by an increase in staying on rates at school and higher participation rates in further and higher education, resulting in the less able and lower-skilled individuals finding employment (although it is known that a significant proportion are on government training schemes or unemployed). In addition the increase in young people contributing towards the financing of education through employment income might provide an explanation, as these jobs tend to be low paid. It is perhaps heartening to note that the majority who find employment are not in low-wage occupations.

Males in the 16–24 and 25–34 cohorts show an initial increase in the proportion in LOW employment. In fact the proportion for the 16–24 age cohort has not started to decline by the time of the survey. In the 35–44 age cohort the initial decline is followed by an increase.

The most striking feature of the evolution of female LOW employment is the much higher proportion in all age cohorts than that recorded for males. As each cohort ages the proportion in LOW employment decreases over time and then begins to rise. This dip is likely to be associated with the higher probability of low-skilled mothers exiting from the labour force during the years of family formation, leaving women who delay having children climbing further up the occupation hierarchy, and higher qualified women who are more likely to maintain contact with the labour market over this period. As women return to the labour market the proportion employed in low-wage occupations increases again and remains high. Like males the proportion of the 16–24 age cohort appears higher than the earlier cohorts (with the possible exception of the 55–64 cohort) but rather than increasing over the observed time period the proportion declines. The 25–34 age cohort shows a dramatic decline over the first 12 years in the labour market from around 60 per cent to 25 per cent, after which the proportion starts to increase. The older age cohorts show that after approximately 20 years in the labour market the proportion in LOW employment stabilizes, showing very little fluctuation, around 30 per cent for the 35–44 and 45–54 age cohorts and 35 per cent for the 55–64 age cohorts.

The likelihood of individuals who enter low occupational wage employment remaining there for a significant period of time can be measured in a number of ways. The approach adopted here looks at the persistence of LOW employment by expressing the proportion of individuals in LOW employment

Figure 4.10   Evolution of the percentage of employment in low-wage occupations

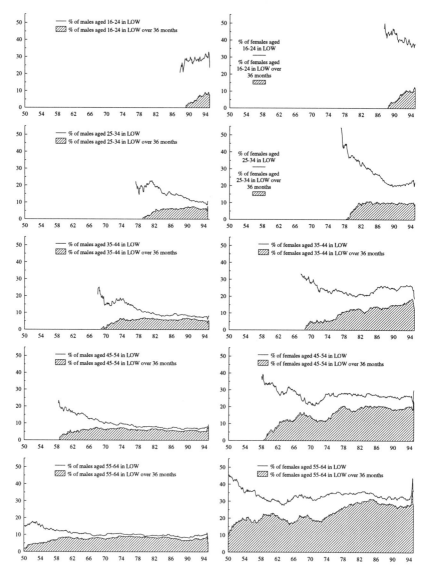

Source: Family and Working Lives Survey, 1994/95

who have been continuously employed in a low-wage occupation for three years or longer. During this period an individual may have changed jobs, but this must not have led to a move out of a low-wage occupation. This measure of long duration LOW employment is represented in Figure 4.10 by the black shaded area for each age cohort and for males and females separately. These charts reveal that, particularly for the older age cohorts, nearly all of LOW employment is of long duration. During the early years of labour market experience the durations appear shorter but as tenure increases the durations appear to increase. This pattern is common across all age cohorts.

Such a high share of long duration LOW employment shows that this type of employment is by no means temporary for many people and cannot be regarded as a step on the ladder up the occupational hierarchy for many of those who find this type of employment. These charts show considerable persistence in low occupational wage employment.

It should be noted that, as occupations have been used as a proxy for low-pay, individuals remaining in an occupational group may have experienced earnings progression, as there exists a distribution of earnings within occupations. Alongside this earnings for most groups have increased in real terms over the last two decades, but less so for the lowest paid.

5 MOBILITY OUT OF LOW OCCUPATIONAL WAGE EMPLOYMENT

The work history information collected in the FWLS can be thought of as a series of episodes that make up an individual's working life. A working life is made up of spells in employment, unemployment and periods not in the labour force (not in LF). Applying the low occupational wage classification scheme further distinguishes between periods in low-wage employment and periods which are not. This produces four potential types of episode and an additional type for periods of employment where the occupational type is not known.

For *completed* spells it is possible to characterize each spell by an origin and destination state. Table 4.3 shows each completed spell defined in this way for males and Table 4.4 for females.

By definition, a completed spell cannot have the same destination as the origin state and therefore there are no observations on the diagonal. These tables show row percentages. The first row shows the percentage of all completed episodes of LOW employment, followed by rows showing episodes of not-in low employment ending in LOW employment (not-LOW), employment but with unknown occupation (emp not known), unemployment (unemp) and out-of the labour force (not in LF). The final column gives the total number of completed spells of LOW employment. For males this is 1 560 and females 3523, showing greater changes in state experienced by females compared with males. This appears to be driven by the considerable number of moves made by females into and out of the labour force; 35 per cent of all destinations of completed spells for females were out of the labour force (the figure for males is 20 per cent). Overall the average number of completed spells for females is 3.2 with a lower average for males at 2.4.

Table 4.3   Origin and destination states of completed spells for males (row percentages)

| | Destination | | | | | |
Origin	LOW	not LOW	emp not k	unemp	not in LF	Total (=100%)
LOW		45.3	8.4	21.4	24.9	1 560
not LOW	15.5		15.3	32.6	36.5	3 027
emp not known	11.3	53.2		15.0	20.5	1 127
unemp	21.2	63.1	9.3		6.4	1 429
not in LF	18.2	60.7	12.3	8.8		1 796
Total	*13.7*	*36.9*	*10.6*	*18.4*	*20.3*	*8 939*

Table 4.4   Origin and destination states of completed spells for females (row percentages)

| | Destination | | | | | |
Origin	LOW	not LOW	emp not k	unemp	not in LF	Total (=100%)
LOW		24.7	8.9	11.3	55.1	3 523
not LOW	14.6		12.4	11.0	62.0	4 371
emp not known	18.3	38.9		7.0	35.8	1 598
unemp	35.0	43.7	8.7		12.7	1 113
not in LF	36.1	48.7	11.0	4.1		4 585
Total	*19.6*	*27.7*	*9.6*	*7.8*	*35.3*	*15 190*

While females show a greater proportion of moves out of the labour force, males are more likely to move from employment into unemployment. Males also appear more likely to experience upward mobility by moving from low occupational wage employment into higher-paid occupations, making up 45 per cent of all moves from low-wage employment. The figure for females is much lower at 25 per cent. The completed spells do not reveal a greater probability of a spell of low-wage employment ending in a spell of unemployment than non-LOW wage employment. For males a greater proportion of non-LOW employment spells end in unemployment than LOW employment spells, but this is mainly a consequence of the high proportion of spells in LOW employment ending in non-LOW employment. Approximately one-fifth of all completed spells of unemployment for males end in low-wage employment. For females over one-third of completed unemployment spells end in LOW employment and 36 per cent of moves from out of the labour force are into low-wage occupations.

The analysis that follows makes use of the spells of low occupational wage employment including those which are incomplete. This means that an individual may contribute more than one spell of low occupational wage employment. As low-wage employment has been defined in a relative sense the analysis is conducted separately for males and females.

6 THE PERSISTENCE OF A SPELL OF LOW-WAGE EMPLOYMENT: EVIDENCE OF CUMULATIVE INERTIA

Event history data can be used to explore whether low-wage employment forms a trap from which it is difficult for an individual to exit. Persistence of low-wage employment can be due to a number of factors: the level of skill attained by an individual, age, region of residence, social origin or labour demand. In addition, an episode of low-wage employment may itself affect the probability of a spell ending. There may exist cumulative inertia by which the longer an individual remains in a spell of low-wage employment the less likely is he or she to leave. Alternatively, employees may be reluctant to recruit those persons who have a longer history of low-wage employment to higher-paid jobs. Historical working patterns may also affect the probability of a spell ending, such as the cumulative time spent in low-wage employment and the number of spells. It has been shown elsewhere that even after controlling for individual heterogeneity the cumulative effect of low-wage employment and unemployment can affect an individual's housing tenure, increasing the likelihood of living in social rental accommodation (McKnight and Elias 1997). It is also of interest to explore the relationship between unemployment and low-wage employment to see whether the length of time spent unemployed and the number of spells of unemployment affect the exit probability.

A logistic regression is used to model the probability of a spell of LOW employment ending, given that the individual is in a spell of LOW employment, and to estimate the effect of various explanatory variables on this probability. Some variables are time varying (duration, etc.) and some are time constant (age cohort, social origin). As an individual must be in a spell of LOW employment the risk set is made up of all spells of low-wage employment and therefore all those at 'risk' of a spell ending. The hazard rate is the probability that an event will occur at a particular time (month) to an individual given that the individual is at risk at that time. The dependent variable in such an analysis is a 'zero-one' variable, zero indicating that an individual is in a spell of low-wage employment in a given month and one indicating that a spell of low-wage employment has ended in a given month.

Examining the exit probabilities of all spells of low-wage employment in this way does not discriminate between those spells which end in upward mobility, exiting from the labour force or unemployment and those which are 'right censored'.[7] The point of interest here is whether duration of low-wage employment effects the exit probability, thereby indicating some sort of cumulative inertia. The analysis of different destinations is expected to form a separate study.

Like any type of duration analysis this study faces the usual problem of observed and unobserved individual heterogeneity. The inclusion of historical working patterns goes some way to control for heterogeneity, but even so some of the relationship between duration and exit probabilities is likely to be due to differences in individuals' characteristics. If the exit probability declines as a spell of low-wage employment lengthens, this may be due to either:

−   *sorting*
    individuals of low ability remain in a spell longer. Higher ability individuals who enter low pay exit after shorter periods;
−   *or true state dependence*
    the experience of low pay reduces the probability of an individual exiting as the spell lengthens as a direct result of the experience of low pay.

The probability of a spell of low-wage employment ending is estimated using a logistic regression

$$\log\left[\frac{P(y=1)}{1-P(y=1)}\right] = \beta_0 + \beta_1(t) + \sum_{k_1=1}^{K_1}\beta_{k_1}x_{k_1} + \sum_{k_2=1}^{K_2}\beta_{k_2}x_{k_2} + \sum_{k_3=1}^{K_3}\beta_{k_3}x_{k_3} \tag{4.1}$$

where k_1 relates to personal characteristics such as age at time of survey, highest qualification or social origin and the k_2 variables to the 'current' spell, that is the duration of the spell and the k_3 variables contain historical information including number of spells, cumulative duration of LOW employment, number of spells and cumulative duration of unemployment and employment tenure.

The variables relating to an individual's personal characteristics, duration variables and historical variables will only partially determine the probability of exiting any spell of low-wage employment. Ideally information on the sector of employment, additional information on the establishment, other events such as education and training and the economic cycle are likely to affect the probability of a particular spell ending. It is envisaged that additional work will involve building such variables and incorporating them into the model. For the time being only a time trend (month) is included which is entered linearly and so is unable to pick up fluctuations over time.

Results are presented for two models. Model A includes the level of highest qualification while Model B contains education in addition to the social class of the individuals' parents when they were 16 (see Table 8.A1 in the Appendix for a description of the classification). While education and social class background are likely to be correlated, this set of variables was included in order to examine whether there exists persistence in low pay across generations, after controlling for education and other characteristics. If this hypothesis is true then we would expect to find that a lower social class background is associated with a reduced probability of exiting a spell of LOW employment. Additional analysis (not shown here) revealed that social class background had the greatest influence on whether an individual began a spell of LOW employment. Lower social classes were associated with an increased likelihood of entering a spell of LOW employment.

The model was estimated separately for two age groups, 16–24 and 25–49. The 16–24 age group was modelled separately, as it is well known that young people, for a number of reasons, change jobs more frequently than older workers. The second age group was limited to 49 years of age or less, as it was shown in Figures 4.3 and 4.4 that labour force participation falls sharply after this age. As a result the factors affecting exit from a spell of LOW employment are likely to be affected by changes in the participation rate.

7 SUMMARY OF FINDINGS

Examining first Model A results for males (Table 4.5) aged 16–24, the probability of a spell of LOW employment ending is dependent on the highest level of qualification. Relative to having less than an O level (or equivalent) qualification the probability of a spell ending is greater for more qualified males. As many of the males in this cohort will have had little labour market experience it is not surprising that the work history variables are mainly insignificant. However, the cumulative length of time spent in unemployment positively influences the likelihood of exiting a spell of LOW employment. When social class background is included (Model B) fewer education variables are significant. The possession of a first degree or A level (or equivalent qualification) no longer has a significant effect on the exit probability compared with males who have less than an O level qualification. Social class background appears to be important; if an individual's parents were in classes C1 or E there is a negative effect on the likelihood of exiting a spell of LOW relative to class A. The cumulative effect of time spent unemployed continues to have a positive influence.

The Long-Run Horizon

Table 4.5   Estimates of the logit model of the probability of a spell of low-wage employment terminating, by age cohort, for males

	16-24				25-49			
	Model A		Model B		Model A		Model B	
	Coeff.	S.E.	Coeff.	S.E.	Coeff.	S.E.	Coeff.	S.E.
Constant	-6.832	2.762 *	-6.601	2.829 *	-2.577	0.616 *	-2.107	0.716 *
Month	0.004	0.004	0.005	0.005	-0.002	0.001	-0.002	-0.001 *
Personal characteristics								
Age at date of survey								
16-19	ref		ref					
20-24	0.399	0.267	0.422	0.278				
25-29					ref		ref	
30-34					-0.159	0.118	-0.156	0.121
35-39					-0.331	0.165 *	-0.370	0.167 *
40-44					-0.637	0.232 *	-0.689	0.235 *
45-49					-0.667	0.300 *	-0.734	0.303 *
Highest qualification								
Higher degree	2.450	0.652 *	1.729	0.766 *	0.600	0.433	0.389	0.454
Degree	0.891	0.369 *	0.555	0.412	1.014	0.153 *	0.910	0.159 *
A level	0.585	0.302 *	0.346	0.337	0.471	0.125 *	0.374	0.131 *
Intermediate	0.639	0.315 *	0.557	0.327 *	0.261	0.138 *	0.228	0.141
O level	0.565	0.269 *	0.581	0.286 *	0.046	0.080	0.004	0.082
Lower than O level	ref		ref		ref		ref	
Social grade of parent								
A			ref				ref	
B			-0.432	0.529			-0.018	0.297
C1			-0.575	0.558			-0.157	0.297
C2			-1.047	0.564 *			-0.372	0.293
D			-0.731	0.579			-0.319	0.295
E			-1.557	0.709 *			-0.148	0.334
Not working			-0.826	0.654			-0.207	0.334
Not known			-1.089	0.821			-0.245	0.398
Characteristics of the spell of LOW employment								
Duration of spell (LOW)	0.001	0.020	0.006	0.021	-0.005	0.003 *	-0.005	0.003 *
Dur. of spell (LOW) sq	-1.0E-04	2.0E-04	-1.0E-04	2.0E-04	1.8E-05	9.3E-06 *	1.7E-05	9.3E-06 *
Historical variables								
Cumul. duration in LOW	-0.010	0.016	-0.011	0.016	-0.006	0.002 *	-0.006	0.002 *
Spells in LOW empl.	0.188	0.226	0.205	0.242	0.177	0.067 *	0.170	0.067 *
Employment tenure	-8.2E-05	0.007	-0.004	0.007	0.001	0.001	0.002	0.001
Cumulat. unemployment	0.022	0.012 *	0.025	0.012 *	6.0E-05	0.004	2.0E-04	0.004
Spells of unemployment	-0.047	0.266	0.027	0.281	0.131	0.060 *	0.143	0.061 *
n	5 505		5 505		46 799		46 799	
Model Chi-Square	53.30		64.85		330.81		342.58	
Degrees of freedom	14		21		17		24	

Note: * denotes statistically significant at the 5 per cent significance level; 'ref' indicates the reference category in a set of dummy variables; S.E. indicates standard error of the estimated coefficient.

Work history variables for males aged 25–49 are more important. In Model A both the duration of a spell of LOW employment and the cumulative time spent in LOW employment negatively affect the likelihood of exiting a spell. A significant negative coefficient on the variable representing the length of the spell in LOW employment indicates a reduced probability of the spell ending as this length increases. A positive coefficient on the square of this coefficient indicates that this occurs at an increasing rate as the duration increases, thereby providing evidence of cumulative inertia. This suggests that the longer spells of LOW employment are associated with reduced exit probabilities (even after controlling for the level of education). However, at this stage it is not possible to say whether this is due to true state dependence or individual heterogeneity. The number of previous spells of LOW employment and unemployment positively influence the likelihood of a spell ending suggesting a high turnover relationship between low-wage employment and unemployment for some individuals. Including social class background (Model B) appears to have little effect. None of these variables are significant and the overall pattern is unchanged. This result suggests that social class background of older males has little impact on whether they leave a spell of LOW employment, after controlling for their level of education. Work histories and other personal characteristics appear to play a greater role.

Females in the younger age group (Table 4.6) in the model without social class background (Model A) show some interesting results relating to their level of education. Relative to a lower than O level qualification a highest qualification between O and A levels has a negative effect on the probability of exiting a spell of LOW employment. In contrast a degree level qualification has a positive effect. It is not clear what the correct interpretation of these estimates should be. One explanation is that higher qualified women are more likely to experience shorter spells of LOW employment while women with the lowest level of qualification are the most likely to exit the labour force in this part of the life cycle than females with O level or intermediate level qualifications. Social class background (Model B) does not appear to have a significant effect for young females (16–24).

In the 25–49 age group of females education positively affects the probability of exiting a spell of LOW employment relative to women with very low levels of education. Results from the historical variables show that the cumulative time spent in LOW employment has a negative effect on the exit probability. In addition both the number of spells of LOW employment and unemployment increase the likelihood of exiting a spell of LOW employment. Social class background (Model B) has a significant effect for these older females; relative to the two highest class categories the likelihood of exiting a spell of LOW employment is reduced for all other known classes. Education and work history variables remain important. The negative coefficients on the age group variables relative to the youngest age group (25–29) are likely to be associated with the higher rates of withdrawal of women during these ages shown in Figure 4.4.

Education and social class origin affect the probability of a spell of low-wage employment ending. Social class origin appears to be most important for older females (25–49), less so for males. Information relating to the current spell of LOW employment and work history variables indicates two main features. First, as the duration of a spell of low-wage employment increases the probability of the spell ending decreases at an increasing rate for males aged 25–49. Cumulative time spent in low-wage employment over an individual's working life also reduces the probability of exiting, although this is less important for young males with limited work histories. Second, individuals who have experienced a higher number of spells of low-wage employment and unemployment (for the older age cohort) face a higher probability of a spell of low-wage employment ending.

Table 4.6   Estimates of the logit model of the probability of a spell of low-wage employment terminating, by age cohort, for females

	16-24 Model A Coeff.	S.E.	16-24 Model B Coeff.	S.E.	25-49 Model A Coeff.	S.E.	25-49 Model B Coeff.	S.E.
Constant	-8.095	2.023 *	-8.940	2.124 *	-3.242	0.276 *	-2.709	0.366 *
Month	0.007	0.003 *	0.008	0.003 *	-0.001	0.001	-0.001	5.0E-04 *
Personal characteristics								
Age at date of survey								
16-19	ref		ref					
20-24	0.557	0.208 *	0.653	0.214 *				
25-29					ref		ref	
30-34					-0.175	0.073 *	-0.182	0.073 *
35-39					-0.224	0.090 *	-0.249	0.091 *
40-44					-0.380	0.113 *	-0.402	0.114 *
45-49					-0.498	0.135 *	-0.528	0.136 *
Highest qualification								
Higher degree	1.594	1.178	1.845	1.181	0.422	0.418	0.320	0.421
Degree	0.499	0.254 *	0.385	0.284	1.014	0.127 *	0.932	0.130 *
A level	-0.095	0.233	-0.206	0.252	0.560	0.085 *	0.488	0.088 *
Intermediate	-0.562	0.249 *	-0.627	0.259 *	0.177	0.111	0.150	0.112
O level	-0.412	0.184 *	-0.411	0.194 *	0.104	0.053 *	0.082	0.055
Lower than O level	ref		ref		ref		ref	
Social grade of parent								
A			ref				ref	
B			0.560	0.414			-0.167	0.245
C1			0.450	0.415			-0.417	0.239 *
C2			-0.003	0.405			-0.436	0.236 *
D			0.305	0.415			-0.485	0.237 *
E			0.538	0.442			-0.560	0.252 *
Not working			0.490	0.441			-0.472	0.258 *
Not known			1.178	0.674 *			-0.494	0.316
Characteristics of the spell of LOW employment								
Duration of spell (LOW)	0.022	0.015	0.022	0.015	0.001	0.002	0.001	0.002
Dur. of spell (LOW) sq	-6.2E-05	1.0E-04	-5.0E-05	1.0E-04	-6.8E-07	7.3E-06	-1.3E-06	7.3E-06
Historical variables								
Cumul. duration in LOW	-0.023	0.013 *	-0.021	0.013	-0.004	0.001 *	-0.003	0.001 *
Spells in LOW empl.	0.535	0.181 *	0.506	0.181 *	0.165	0.041 *	0.164	0.041 *
Employment tenure	-0.009	0.007	-0.011	0.007	-0.003	0.001 *	-0.003	0.001 *
Cumulat. unemployment	0.019	0.014	0.017	0.014	-3.0E-04	0.002	-0.001	0.002
Spells of unemployment	-0.048	0.221	-0.021	0.221	0.114	0.053 *	0.124	0.053 *
n	9 487		9 487		102 794		102 794	
Model Chi-Square	64.52		81.12		502.74		518.61	
Degrees of freedom	14		21		17		24	

Note:
* denotes statistically significant at the 5 per cent significance level; 'ref' indicates the reference category in a set of dummy variables; S.E. indicates standard error of the estimated coefficient.

These results reveal persistence of low-wage employment and the identification of a greater number of spells in unemployment. A greater number of spells of low-wage employment is associated with an increased probability of a spell of low-wage employment ending. This indicates a less stable pattern of labour market attachment for this group of workers.

8 CONCLUSIONS

This study of low-wage employment has revealed a number of key characteristics associated with the working lives of individuals in low-wage employment. Identifying a set of low-wage individuals in a cross section ignores important work history differences between these individuals and those who are in better-paid jobs. It was shown that low-wage males had experienced lower employment rates over their working lives and pronounced differences were evident in the work histories of low-wage females compared to those in higher wage employment. The low-wage females were more likely to have spent time out of the labour market during years of family formation than the higher-paid women and these spells were of longer duration.

The construction of a 'proxy' classification of low-wage employment based on occupation made it possible to exploit the work history data. In the absence of retrospective information on earnings, the occupation-based classification was used to classify spells of employment into high and low-wage employment. This made it possible to map the evolution of low-wage employment over time by age cohort. The main observations were the much higher rates of low-wage employment found amongst females and a rise in low-wage employment for the younger age cohorts for both sexes. Defining long-duration low-wage employment as that which lasts for three years or longer it was shown that a substantial proportion of low-wage employment was made up of long spells, particularly for the older age groups.

A logistic regression was used to explore for potential cumulative inertia. Although at this stage it is not possible to distinguish between true state dependence and heterogeneity, these early results reveal that the probability of a spell of low-wage employment ending is reduced as the duration of a spell of low-wage employment increases and as the cumulative duration over an individual's working life increases. An interesting result revealed by this analysis is that the number of spells in low-wage employment, unemployment and the duration of unemployment all increase the probability of a spell of low-wage employment ending, after controlling for level of education and social class origin, thereby identifying a less stable pattern of labour market attachment for this group of workers. It was shown for older women (25–49) that the probability of exiting a spell of LOW employment was influenced by their social class origin, even after controlling for their level of education and differences in their work histories.

NOTES

1   Special thanks are due to Peter Elias for helpful and encouraging comments throughout the preparation of this chapter. In addition I am grateful to Mary Gregory and participants of the European Low-wage Employment Research Network conference in Bordeaux, January 1997, for their comments and suggestion. This research was partly funded by the Department of the Environment, Transport and the Regions.
2   77 Minor Groups (2-digits) of the *Standard Occupational Classification* (SOC).
3   Event histories were collected for employment, marital status, children, education and training, housing and benefits.
4   Recent evidence reveals that there has been an increase in the number of records submitted for individuals below the threshold since the introduction of computerized payroll systems. However, caution must be applied to these data as they are likely to be biased towards those employed in large establishments where computerization is more likely.
5   Initially a more detailed occupation level was considered (371 occupation groups). However, small sample sizes meant that for a number of occupational groups these estimates were not statistically robust.
6   The occupational earnings differentials can be found in Figures 4.A1 and 4.A2 in the Appendix.
7   Right censored spells are spells which are incomplete at the date of the survey.

REFERENCES

Corti, L., H. Laurie and S. Dex (1995), *Highly Qualified Women*, Sheffield: Employment Department, Research Series 50.

Elias, P. (1997), *Who forgot they were unemployed?*, University of Essex: Working Papers of the ESRC Research Centre on Micro-social Change no. 97–19.

Elias, P. and D. Blanchflower (1989), *The Occupations, Earnings and Work Histories of Young Adults – Who gets the good jobs?*, Department of Employment, Research Paper 68.

Greenhalgh, C.A. and M.B. Stewart (1985), 'The Occupational Status and Mobility of British Men and Women', *Oxford Economic Papers*, **37**, pp. 40–71.

Harkness, S. (1996), 'The Gender Earnings Gap: Evidence from the UK', *Fiscal Studies*, **17**(2), pp. 1–36.

McKnight, A. and P. Elias (1997), 'Unemployment, Low Wage Employment and Housing Tenure', in *Housing, Family and Working Lives*, Coventry: University of Warwick, Institute for Employment Research.

Nickell, S.J. (1982), 'The Determinants of Occupational Success in Great Britain', *Review of Economic Studies*, **49**, pp. 45–53.

OECD (1996), *Employment Outlook*, Paris, July.

Stewart, M.B., and C.A. Greenhalgh (1984), 'Work History Patterns and the Occupational Attainment of Women', *Economic Journal*, **94**, pp. 493–519.

APPENDIX

Figure 4.A1 *Occupational earnings differentials of male full-time employees, after controlling for age and region of residence*

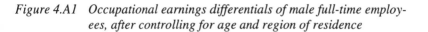

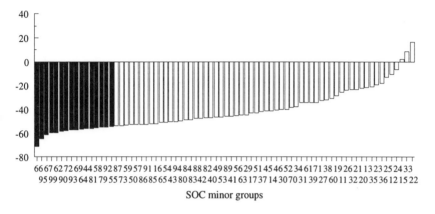

SOC minor groups

Source: Labour Force Survey, Spring 1993 – Autumn 1994

Figure 4.A2 *Occupational earnings differentials of female full-time employees, after controlling for age and region of residence*

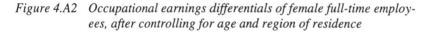

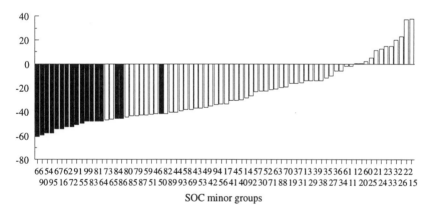

SOC minor groups

Source: Labour Force Survey, Spring 1993 – Autumn 1994

Table 4.A1   Classes of occupational groups

Class	Occupational groups
A	Professionals and senior managers in business or commerce or top-level civil servants.
B	Middle management executives in large organizations. Principal officers in local and civil service. Top managers or owners of small business concerns, educational and service establishment.
C1	Junior managers, owners of small establishments and all others in non-manual positions.
C2	All skilled manual workers and those manual workers with responsibility for other workers.
D	All semi-skilled and unskilled manual workers, apprentices and trainees to skilled workers.
E	Casual workers and those without a regular income.

PART TWO

Low-Paid Employment: The Short-Run Horizon

5. Wage Mobility for Low-Wage Earners in Denmark and Finland[1]

R. Asplund, P. Bingley and N. Westergård-Nielsen

1 INTRODUCTION

A number of studies of wage mobility have shown that the mobility of wage rates of wage earners is actually much larger than commonly thought (OECD 1996). Part of this mobility is found to be related to normal life-cycle mobility where individuals start at some point after having completed full-time education, and move upward until the end of their working career. Life-time inequality is thus created by someone dropping behind in the race for the 'normal' upward mobility. Another part is related to factors that individuals themselves (or policy makers) can influence, including attachment to the labour market, child care, type of work etc. Several results (e.g. Asplund et al. 1996) show that general human capital such as education and experience are important determinants of where people are observed in the wage distribution. Upward wage mobility, in turn, is found to be associated with higher education, less unemployment, less experience and the absence of changes in occupation and industry. Furthermore, high individual mobility is noted to be compatible with unchanged overall wage dispersion as measured by Gini coefficients.

This chapter investigates the year-to-year mobility of wages for two private-sector samples of low-wage earners in Denmark and Finland. Unlike previous work in this field we are estimating a model for the change in percentile rank in the wage distribution for each individual. Furthermore, we adjust for sample selection bias due to attrition and only looking at those persons who have ever been in the lowest quintile. One of the problems with previous estimations has been that they do not adjust for the fact that a substantial attrition happens from the lowest and highest wage deciles. The adopted model also attempts to control for unobserved heterogeneity among the observed persons. Furthermore, the model also distinguishes between different levels of mobility.

Especially for policies toward the low-wage earners it is important to identify factors that make it more likely that a person will drop behind in the race for lifetime upward mobility and thus become a low-wage earner. On the other hand it is also crucial to identify groups of individuals for whom low mobility is only a temporary phenomenon. These findings have consequences for policies concerning minimum wage setting and job creation schemes. The traditional political concern is related to a static perception of those at the low end of the wage distribution and neglects the fact that many actually move upward in the wage distribution if they get started on a work career.

The chapter deals with two countries, Denmark and Finland, and seeks to identify commonalities and differences in what makes people upwardly or downwardly mobile in these two countries. The study focuses exclusively on the upward and downward mobility for individuals who at some point in time have been in the lowest quintile of the wage distribution, i.e. among the lowest 20 per cent. In contrast to previous studies for Denmark and Finland (Bingley et al. 1995, Asplund and Bingley 1996) analysing wage mobility among (all) deciles of the wage distribution, here we quantify the degree of mobility and consider this relative to each individual's starting position in the wage distribution. Only movements exceeding a threshold of 1 per cent in either direction are considered as mobility. The main advantage of this approach is that we avoid problems of treating situations where people are very close to a quintile threshold equal to situations where they are far from the threshold.

Another point to mention is that in this study we are exclusively dealing with wage rates and not income or earnings. The main problem with the latter measures is that they also involve a labour supply decision which may be considered to be endogenous. However, many studies still use income or earnings because of shortcomings in data availability and the desire to implement standard estimation techniques for balanced panel data.

2 PREVIOUS STUDIES

A recent comprehensive survey of empirical studies of earnings mobility is found in Atkinson et al. (1992). (See the Introduction to this volume.) A selected number of studies of individual mobility are briefly discussed below to illustrate some of the different approaches that have been used.

2.1 Measures

As outlined in the Introduction to this volume, several methods of measuring mobility have been proposed. If focusing on a raw transition matrix, it is natural to count the proportion of immobile observations on or near the diagonal. Similarly one can count the periods the observed individuals stay below some threshold income of interest (part of the analyses of Gottschalk 1982, and Lillard and Willis 1978). Quantifying the size of individual transitions over longer time periods may be informative, and one can calculate the average absolute cell jump. Cells of the transition matrix have been variously defined: money earnings (Hart 1976), income relative to the mean (Thatcher 1971).

Inflation of nominal income means, however, that absolute transitions are observed also without any relative changes. The alternative is to look at the individuals' relative position in the distribution, whereby the relative position can be calculated using e.g. quintiles or deciles. Mobility is then measured as movements between one decile/quintile in time t to another decile/quintile in time $t+1$.

This method has the virtue of being in accordance with the tradition of income distribution studies. In particular, being an order statistic it is robust to outliers. This is important especially when considering hourly wages constructed from earnings over hours because hours are prone to measurement error. For policy purposes those at the bottom end of the wage distribution are of greatest interest, and it is obvious that outliers are grouped at the extremes of the distribution. Temporary and part-time workers, for instance, are commonly found among the low-wage earners, one reason being that measurement errors in hours are most likely to occur for these individuals. Obviously a large proportion of measurement error shows up also among those (outliers) transiting many deciles in a single period. The imprecisely calculated wage rate for many samples may therefore motivate broad grouping.

Measures of individuals' relative positions are, though, open to the criticism that income ranges are closer towards the middle of the distribution, meaning that even a small 'push' may be sufficient to contribute to the mobility. In fact, investigation of the distribution of transitions originating around the wage decile thresholds using Danish data points to some degree of grouping when focusing on movements out of a decile during a single year (Bingley et al. 1995). This effect is much less severe when analysing transitions over a longer period of time because the changes in decile are more stable in the longer run; the potential grouping problem seems almost to disappear when investigating a four-year period.

From a normative perspective it is interesting to link mobility and lifetime inequality. Mobility may be seen as the degree to which annual inequality differs from lifetime inequality, where lifetime inequality is calculated as the weighted (according to proportion of lifetime incomes) average of individual annual inequalities (e.g. Shorrocks 1978). The measurement of inequality literature (recently surveyed in Lambert 1993) puts forward a variety of single index summary measures, such as the Gini coefficient, Theil index, square of coefficient of variation, indices giving a coefficient conditional on a choice of parameter and partial orderings such as Lorenz curves. However, lifetime averages of these measures often fail to agree on unique rankings (as shown in Shorrocks 1981). Classes of dominance criteria analogous to the static inequality literature have yet to be developed in the context of income mobility (see Atkinson et al. 1992).

There are essentially two ways to proceed if one is interested in inequality indices over different time periods. First, for shorter panels estimate dynamic earnings equations and use these to simulate lifetime earnings trajectories (see Lillard 1977 for an example). Second, use longer panels which can be approximated for example to the working lifetime (a good recent example is Björklund 1993) to calculate annual and longer-run inequality indices. Clearly, the former is more liable to measurement error and mean-reverting bias associated with being unable to predict well from individual-specific unobservables.

The majority of the literature uses measures of mobility which result from various stochastic specifications of changes in incomes or wages over time. McCall (1971) estimates a first-order Markov model for poverty transitions. Hart (1976) considers a simple Galton–Markov model of regression towards the mean. Schiller (1977) describes a ventile transition matrix. Shorrocks (1978) proposes a mobility index for transition matrices based on the convergence speed of a Markov chain. MaCurdy (1982) estimates a complex autoregressive moving average structure by quasi-maximum likelihood. These are all purely statistical models.

2.2 Models

A rich representation of earnings dynamics is obtained in models where the main focus is on earnings determinants. This specification allows for a distinction between permanent and transitory sources of mobility.

$$\log W_{it} = X_i \alpha + Y_{it} \beta + \upsilon_{it} \qquad (5.1)$$

$$\upsilon_{it} = \lambda_i + \nu_i(t - \bar{t}) + \varepsilon_{it} \qquad (5.2)$$

The logarithm of the real wage W_{it} of individual i in period t is assumed to be determined by permanent observed characteristics, X_i and Y_{it}. Unobserved individual attributes are captured by individual-specific terms in υ_{it}. The individual effect λ_{it} represents unmeasured characteristics like productivity that affect the level of earnings persistently and V_{it} represents unmeasured variables like learning ability which influence earnings growth. The variance term ε_{it} gives a measure of the true transitory component of earnings.

Lillard and Weiss (1979) is a study using this formulation with an added serial correlation in the error term. Berry et al. (1988) use PSID data for 1975–81 to examine the effect of plant closure on US earnings. It is found that mean earnings decrease and variance increases, but this effect diminishes over time since displacement. Gottschalk (1982) uses NLS data for 1966–75 to consider the above model but omits serial correlation and individual explanatory variables. This enables a minimal decomposition into permanent and transitory earnings. A poverty threshold is imposed and the number of periods individuals are below it is counted from actual observed and predicted permanent earnings. An ordered logit (using demographic controls) is estimated on the number of periods of non-transitory poverty. It is found that 43 per cent of individuals with low earnings in a random year had low earnings in all years of the study. This implies a great deal of permanency among the poor.

2.3 Attrition

Attrition bias may understate mobility as a result of focusing on those stable individuals staying within the sample. Keane et al. (1988) studied the movement of real wages over the business cycle using NLS-YM data for 1966–81. They found that failure to account for self-selection biased real wages procyclically. This is attributed to workers with a low permanent wage (associated with low education and high incidence of unemployment) as well as those with high transitory wages being more likely to lose employment in a recession.

Stewart and Swaffield in Chapter 7 of this volume, estimate poverty transitions on British data (BHPS). The focus of their study is on controlling for the potential endogeneity of sample attrition and the origins of the mobility process. This is, in fact, the only other study we are aware of that attempts to account for such issues which may otherwise seriously call into question the statistical generality of wage mobility estimation. Though unobserved individual heterogeneity is not controlled for in the Stewart–Swaffield study, it is something we do allow for and which we find to be important.

3 THE ECONOMETRIC FRAMEWORK

3.1 Chosen Measure of Mobility

In this study wage mobility is measured as the year-to-year change in the individual's percentile rank in the wage distribution. The idea thus is to rank all observations according to their hourly wage rate and subsequently measure the percentage change in rank between two points in time, in this case for a group of low-wage earners defined as those individuals who have ever been in the lowest quintile. This wage mobility measure has the benefit of combining the advantages of a relative measure with the fact that we avoid problems linked to the use of wage thresholds.

3.2 Selectivity Bias

Any attempt to identify determinants of individual mobility within the wage distribution over time will face two potential sources of selectivity bias. First, the results may be influenced by a potential sample selection bias due to panel attrition, i.e. to mobility being observed only for those who have a positive wage both in the starting and the destination year. Even in the best panel data sets, a certain number of individuals will leave the sample due to natural causes, unemployment or retirement. Alternatively they may become self-employed. These individuals falling outside the estimation sample may be of interest in their own right, e.g. in representing people with a weak attachment to the labour market. Hence, focusing merely on individuals having a positive wage in both periods, thus ignoring these exits, might seriously bias the results by understating both upward and downward wage mobility. This problem is important in the present study because we are in both countries relying on establishment-level data where people are most often observed within the same establishment or industry.

Second, ignoring the fact that the individuals' starting positions in the wage distribution depend on their background characteristics may lead to possible endogeneity bias. As mentioned earlier individuals might be observed in the lower end of the wage distribution at a given point in time due to a clearly transitory variation in their wages. For example, a young person with a high education may have temporarily accepted a low-wage job, although he would undoubtedly have been higher up in the wage distribution had he started in a 'normal' job. Most likely he will, therefore, quickly move upwards in the wage distribution. In contrast to most previous studies of individual wage mobility, the present study covers both types of selectivity.

3.3 Unobserved Heterogeneity

Unobserved heterogeneity is supposed to influence both mobility and attrition in different ways. First, it can be assumed that the individual will over time be hit by certain shocks from the surrounding economy or from the person himself. These might be job changes or changes in the local labour market or changes in family relations or some other factor that affects the productivity of the individual. Second, each individual will have some characteristics that are constant over time and that will influence the risk of leaving the sample or of being mobile. One example could be special skills or high ability. Such unobservables are in the present study accounted for in an error components framework as permanent heterogeneity as opposed to transitory noise.

3.4 The Econometric Model

The approach followed here is motivated primarily by concern for labour market policies. As a consequence, the gross hourly wage rate is the income concept of interest. The population of greatest relevance has a weak attachment to the labour market and is made integral to the adopted approach by estimating a limited error covariance matrix and simultaneously allowing for non-random attrition. The approach used is reduced form. In particular, using information on the individuals' background characteristics, the probability of moving from one quintile to another within the wage distribution is estimated simultaneously with the probabilities of having a positive wage both in the starting and the destination year and of belonging to a specific origin quintile. In other words, controls are imposed for potential sample selection bias as well as for potential endogeneity bias.

For all those who do not disappear from the sample in a given year we can observe wage mobility as a change in percentile rank. This is computed from the year-on-year difference in normalized ranks and divided into 41 categories. As a consequence we are estimating three simultaneous equations: a mobility equation that describes the changes in rank: an attrition equation that describes the probability that someone's wage is not observed in a period and an origin equation that determines the initial conditions of the mobility process. Further details of the econometric model can be found in the Appendix.

4 DATA

The Danish data are a representative 5 per cent sample of private-sector workplaces taken from Statistics Denmark administrative records. The time period covered is 1980–91. A worker is followed so long as (s)he is employed in a sampled workplace and one year before and after this attachment. The Finnish data originates from the Confederation of Finnish Industry and Employers (TT) records. This is a sample of every 15th worker employed in a member firm of the Confederation extending from 1980 to 1994. A worker is followed so long as (s)he is employed at an establishment of a member firm.

Danish private-sector workers are relatively mobile and consequently attrition is high in Denmark when using this data set. The observed attrition is clearly smaller in the Finnish data, which might be due to the fact that the member firms of the Confederation cover about 75 per cent of all workplaces within manufacturing and only a minor part of the more mobile service sector. The following description gives some idea about overall wage mobility.

Table 5.1   Mobility out of the lowest quintile (pooled data, percentage)

Denmark 1981–91							
Number of persons ever seen		1st	2nd	3rd	4th	5th	Sum
in the first quintile	54 085	65	22	7	4	2	100
in the second	42 632	0	55	30	12	3	100
in the third	32 265	0	0	57	34	9	100
in the fourth	25 986	0	0	0	66	34	100
in the fifth	20 663	0	0	0	0	100	100
Total	175 631	20	20	20	20	20	100
Finland 1980–94							
Number of persons ever seen		1st	2nd	3rd	4th	5th	Sum
in the first quintile	100 117	62	28	7	2	1	100
in the second	71 652	0	47	41	11	2	100
in the third	52 407	0	0	49	45	6	100
in the fourth	43 696	0	0	0	65	35	100
in the fifth	41 607	0	0	0	0	100	100
Total	309 479	20	20	20	20	20	100

First of all we have organized all individual hourly wage rates into quintiles. Table 5.1 shows, with the data pooled for all years investigated, how large a share of those who have ever been observed in the lowest quintile will also turn up in a higher quintile. Among the 54 085 observations of individuals in Denmark who have ever been in the lowest quintile, 65 per cent have persistently stayed in the 1st quintile, while 22 per cent have at some point in time also been in the 2nd quintile. Only 13 per cent have turned up in the 3rd or a higher quintile. This means that 35 per cent of all individuals who have ever been in the lowest quintile are also found in higher quintiles. The corresponding figure for Finland is 38 per cent.

The table further shows that in Denmark 45 per cent of those individuals who have had their lowest appearance in the 2nd quintile are actually also found in higher quintiles. For Finland this share is even higher at 53 per cent. The general tentative conclusion to be drawn is that the first quintile is more difficult to leave than the 2nd quintile. The final outcome, however, depends completely on how attrition is distributed across individuals.

Figure 5.1 reports the distribution of changes in individual percentile ranks between two consecutive periods. For both countries the distribution has a mean value around zero. While the distribution for Denmark is skewed

Figure 5.1   Wage mobility distribution

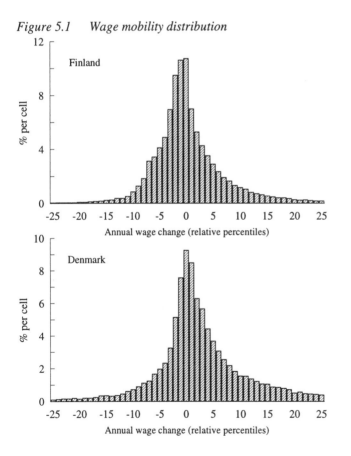

to the right with a positive median value to the right of zero, the distribution for Finland is more skewed to the left and has a negative median indicating that people in the Finnish sample are more likely to move downwards than upwards if they remain employed, all else equal. The explanation is that people in Finland tend to disappear from the bottom of the wage distribution, while attrition in Denmark to a larger extent happens from the upper end of the distribution.

The subsequent analysis will focus exclusively on the mobility for those who have ever been in the lowest quintile. Although there are a number of people who start out in higher quintiles before they 'visit' the lowest one, most individuals in the lowest quintile also start out here. Table 5.2 shows that in Denmark only some 10 per cent of all individuals ever observed in the lowest quintile start out higher up in the wage distribution, compared to 16 per cent in Finland (upper panel of Table 5.2). In order to simplify our model,

Table 5.2   Number of periods before and after being observed in the lowest quintile

Number of periods before first	DENMARK			FINLAND		
observed in lowest quintile	Frequency	Per cent	Cum. share	Frequency	Per cent	Cum. share
-14	–	–	–	39	0.04	0.04
-13	–	–	–	72	0.07	0.11
-12	–	–	–	127	0.13	0.24
-11	–	–	–	212	0.21	0.45
-10	20	0.04	0.04	320	0.32	0.77
-9	42	0.08	0.11	428	0.43	1.20
-8	76	0.14	0.26	542	0.54	1.74
-7	128	0.24	0.49	661	0.66	2.40
-6	194	0.36	0.85	793	0.79	3.19
-5	289	0.53	1.38	971	0.97	4.16
-4	439	0.81	2.20	1 203	1.20	5.36
-3	691	1.28	3.47	1 557	1.56	6.92
-2	1 098	2.03	5.50	2 280	2.28	9.19
-1	2 552	4.72	10.22	6 788	6.78	15.97
Number of periods after observed in lowest quintile						
1	8 957	16.56	61.41	15 908	15.89	50.66
2	5 933	10.97	72.38	10 728	10.72	61.38
3	4 185	7.74	80.11	8 175	8.17	69.54
4	3 093	5.72	85.83	6 553	6.55	76.09
5	2 323	4.30	90.13	5 229	5.22	81.31
6	1 761	3.26	93.38	4 309	4.30	85.62
7	1 339	2.48	95.86	3 520	3.52	89.13
8	1 019	1.88	97.74	2 858	2.85	91.99
9	753	1.39	99.14	2 316	2.31	94.30
10	467	0.86	100.00	1 868	1.87	96.17
11	–	–	–	1 432	1.43	97.60
12	–	–	–	1 090	1.09	98.68
13	–	–	–	791	0.79	99.47
14	–	–	–	526	0.53	100.00
Total	54 085	100	–	100 117	100	–

we have excluded these observations from the analysis. We are, in other words, only looking at those who are either staying within the 1st quintile or moving up (lower panel of Table 5.2).

Another dimension of the mobility measure is the time horizon over which it is measured, which allows us to explore how the short-run mobility depicted in Figure 5.1 is related to long-run mobility. Figure 5.2 repeats the exercise that was performed (from one year to the next) in Figure 5.1, for

Figure 5.2   *Wage mobility distribution over time among those who are for the first time observed in the lowest quintile*

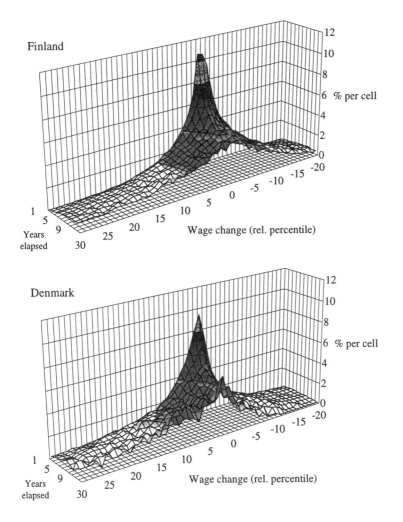

longer time intervals. The original figure is now at the back wall of the box, and as more years elapse between comparisons we move towards the front of the box. The result is that the distributions spread out. It is, however, remarkable that the mean remains of the same sign throughout, so the downward trend in overall mobility for Finland is maintained. Sampling variance increases as we consider years further apart (especially for Denmark) because of attrition from the sample plus the fewer combinations of available years as the number of years elapsed increase.

However, even these mobility distributions conceal churning in the wage distribution. In Figure 5.2 we are merely considering the end point of a process, and neglecting individual histories which may have been up and down along the way. We attempt to capture aspects of this in Figure 5.3. The upper part shows mobility trends. An individual could be said to have a mobility trend if, over a given time period, most moves were in the same direction. With random movement and the absence of any individual trends on average of those mobile, one-half of all moves would be in each direction. The immobile are not graphed, which explains why the sum of up and down moves is reduced to less than 100 per cent by the proportion of non-moves.

In Denmark upward mobility is from the outset more common than downward mobility, and this proves to be a trend with later moves in the same direction outnumbering the rest. For Finland, downward mobility is initially slightly more important. As the time horizon lengthens the proportion of moves up increases, and the proportion of moves down falls. Abstracting from business cycle effects as one does over the long period, simple life-cycle upward mobility remains, as is to be expected. Part of the reason is that we are increasingly neglecting all those persons who drop out of the sample. The graphs in Figure 5.3 nevertheless lead us to conclude that long-run trends are not necessarily apparent in the short run and indeed the evidence may be contradictory, as in the case of Finland. Short-run mobility measures may, as a result, be misleading.

The lower part of Figure 5.3 shows the persistence of individual wage mobility over time, i.e. the number of subsequent moves in the same direction as the time horizon lengthens. Random movement would give exponential decay in persistence. However, we observe that persistence declines much more slowly, obviously starting at the same point in time as in the upper part. As the time frame expands a lower proportion moves constantly in the same direction, but the reduction in this proportion falls as we consider longer periods. This suggests the existence of a group of persistent one-direction movers, which points to individual heterogeneity rather than state dependence.

These findings give an idea of the stability of progression of individuals through the wage distribution. After the first year the positive difference

Figure 5.3   *Trends (upper graph) and persistence (lower graph) in long-run wage mobility among those who are for the first time observed in the lowest quintile*

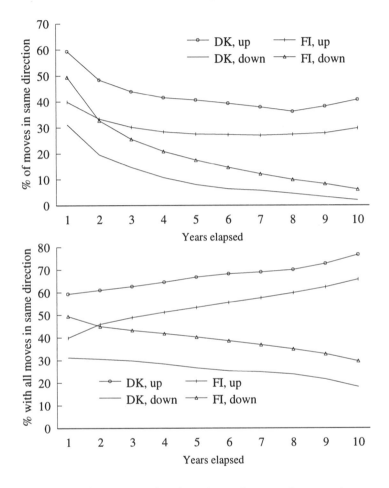

between persistent upward and persistent downward movers increases (up to a limit). Between 50 and 60 per cent of all low-wage earners have after 10 years experienced both moves up and down the wage distribution. For Denmark the long-run rate of persistent upward mobility is about 40 per cent, while it is about 30 per cent for Finland. These are individuals who always move up the wage distribution. The long-run downward persistence rate is lower: less than 8 per cent in Finland and even lower in Denmark. It is, however, not obvious that the process has stabilized after 10 years in Finland due to the unprecedented recession.

All of these effects are based on the hourly wage rates of the sample persons. This means that our findings may be biased by the fact that the attrition is not randomly distributed and that we are probably more likely to see people leave the sample from the lower end of the wage distribution than from the upper. In order to deal with this problem, we propose a statistical model that corrects for these factors and which can produce corrected estimates of mobility and its determinants.

5 ESTIMATIONS

Direct interpretation of the estimated parameters in an ordered model is not straightforward because marginal changes come through the different parts of the model as well as indirectly. Full estimates are nevertheless presented in Tables 5.A1 and 5.A2 in the Appendix to give an idea of sign, relative magnitude and significance.

Three equations are estimated jointly. The *origin quintile* equation can be thought of as a simple cross-section level of earnings function, except that the wage rate is split into ordered groups. Thus, a positive sign indicates a higher initial wage or higher starting quintile. The *attrition* equation is simply a binomial panel probit, and a positive sign indicates higher probability of leaving the sample. The *mobility* equation is of primary interest and is similar to a wage equation in first differences. Here, however, the percentile rank differences are split into groups, and all we may directly infer from a positive sign is that upward mobility is more likely than downward mobility. Simultaneity of origin and non-attrition are controlled for, and the mobility coefficients are consequently unbiased.

Consider first the origin equation. The estimates are entirely conventional for both countries regarding returns to human capital: quadratic age profile, positive return to longer education. Furthermore, there is a traditional occupational hierarchy and a large premium for men.

The attrition equation is an auxiliary catch-all function, since we do not specify out of sample destination. Accordingly, attrition captures a mix of transitions into retirement, study, self-employment, emigration, jobs outside the sampled firms and long-term unemployment. Theoretical priors regarding the net effects of explanatory variables are weak here. The coefficients are, however, remarkably similar for the two countries. Those with higher education, men and the young and the old are most likely to leave the sample (minimum attrition level obtained for the 40-year-olds in Finland and for the 45-year-olds in Denmark). The first three findings are due mainly to re-employment elsewhere, the latter to retirement and unemployment. Non-manual workers are the least likely to leave the sample in both countries.

The mobility function shows that low-wage males in both countries are more downwardly mobile than low-wage women. Mobility in Denmark is found to be negative quadratic in experience, measured as actual rather than the usual potential, as should be expected from the slope of a wage trajectory–experience profile. The maximum is found for 7.4 years. For Finland mobility is found to be more and more downward the longer experience, though the coefficient is rather small. Changes in occupation or skill group lead to upward mobility in both countries (though the effect is much larger in Finland) as these shifts are dominated by moves up the traditional occupational hierarchy. There is a wage mobility premium to geographical mobility in Finland, but not in Denmark. More education seems in Denmark to increase upward mobility, while this effect is weaker in Finland. Finance followed by manufacturing are the most upwardly mobile industries in Denmark. In Finland employees in the wood industry are most upwardly and construction workers most downwardly mobile. Wage mobility according to occupation in Denmark accords with the wage-levels skill hierarchy. In Finland, in contrast, non-manual workers are most upwardly mobile, but of these, technicians rather than managers are most upward mobile. Time controls show up very little for Denmark, but there is strong cyclicality for Finland, where upward mobility of low-wage earners is most important in economic upswings.

Table 5.3 reports the relationship between mobility and attrition which can be used to characterize the type of mobility in each industry. If mobility is accompanied by low attrition, it can be taken as an indication of improving work conditions, whereas downward mobility accompanied by high attrition indicates that people try to leave the industry because it is a declining sector. It can be seen that the high mobility is accompanied by relatively low attrition in metal, wood and paper for manual workers in Finland, whereas construction has downward mobility accompanied by higher attrition. The same pattern emerges for construction, trade and transport in Denmark. Only finance in Denmark shows upward mobility and low attrition. It is also remarkable, that manual workers in both countries seem to have lower mobility and more attrition. The same is also found for higher-level salaried employees.

Estimated variance and correlation terms are presented at the bottom of the two Appendix tables. All correlations, except one, are strongly significant, which indicates that endogeneity of origin and selectivity of nonattrition are important. Not taking this into account may bias the estimates of wage mobility.

Table 5.3   Summary of estimation results for the lowest quintile

Industry sector:	Finland				Denmark	
	Manual workers		Non-manual workers		All employees	
	Mobility	Attrition	Mobility	Attrition	Mobility	Attrition
Metal industry	0.14	-0.75	ref.	ref.	ref.	ref.
Wood industry	0.20	-0.72	0.07	0.15	-	-
Paper industry	0.34	-0.94	-0.01	-0.11	-	-
Construction	-0.08	0.00	-	-	-0.13	0.00
Other manufacturing	0.00	-0.11	-	-	-	-
Service sector	0.00	0.00	-	-	0.00	0.00
Trade	-	-	-	-	-0.15	0.07
Transport	-	-	-	-	-0.10	0.11
Finance	-	-	-	-	0.05	-0.13
Skill level:						
Skilled workers	-	-	-	-	0.11	0.06
Manual workers	0.00	0.58	-	-	-0.17	0.18
Clerical workers	0.06	-0.07	-	-	ref.	ref.
Upper non-manual	-0.06	0.00	-	-	-0.33	0.12

Notes: ref. refers to reference group in the estimations, and 0 indicates that the estimate is statistically insignificant.

Source: Tables 5.A1 and 5.A2.

Correlation between unobservables associated with mobility and those associated with attrition are of different sign for different components. In an error components framework, the individual effect can be thought of as a permanent effect related to individual unobservables, and the remainder error is simply a transitory component. Correlation between permanent unobservables is different to that between transitory unobservables. The permanent correlation $\rho_{\eta_{AM}}$ is positive indicating that in the long run, those unobservable characteristics that make you more likely to leave the sample also make you more upwardly mobile. In the short run the opposite is the case in Finland, as shown by a negative $\rho_{\varepsilon_{AM}}$, while the short-run effect is positive but insignificant in Denmark.

The net correlation (a sum of the two weighted according to group size), which would be estimated if the appropriate panel estimator was not implemented, is of indeterminate sign, and so sample selection may not be evident from pooled cross-sections of data. Unobservables associated with higher origin ($\rho_{\eta_{OM}}$) are positively correlated with upward mobility in both countries. In the case of people with lower wages this correlation appears to be about the same size in the two countries. This suggests the same attrition processes in the two data sets. But this need not be the case and is purely an empirical question.

6 DIAGNOSTICS AND SIMULATIONS

Mis-specification tests in models such as these are frought with difficulties. As a crude diagnostic check we eyeball the predictions to see how well they fit the data. Goodness-of-fit measures for the primary equation of interest, mobility, are presented in Figure 5.A1 in the Appendix. The profiles of the observed distribution histograms are immediately apparent. The expected per cent in each category is calculated from summing (across individuals) the predicted probabilities of being in each state. Exactly on top of these is the predictive distribution. So we fit the curve perfectly, but nevertheless may be misclassifying everyone thereunder. The proportion expected to be in the correct cell is just the predicted probabilities multiplied by the observed and then summed over individuals. The extent to which our model fits better than random assignment (weighted by the right proportions in the right cell) is given by the height by which this line lies above the observed. The standard deviation of these predictions is relatively unimportant until 5 and 3 cells out, respectively. It is apparent from studying the distributions that the predictions are doing worse for downward mobility than for upward.

Is this a good or a bad fit? We may conclude that the model is not grossly misrepresenting the data. Recall that we are addressing an awkward question of relative wage movements, and not levels. This is notoriously difficult; data are fitted among 41 cells, jointly with the attrition and origin dimensions.

7 CONCLUSIONS

In this chapter we have investigated the year-to-year wage mobility for low-wage Danish and Finnish workers using comparable data for the private sector in the two countries. A model is estimated that takes into account that persons not observed for two consecutive years may differ non-randomly from others, and taking also into account that it may not be random from which quintile each person originates. It has been proven that neglecting the selection issue arising from only including the persons who can be observed in two consecutive years introduces bias into the estimates.

Estimates of the mobility functions show large similarities between the two countries. The results indicate that men in the group of low-wage earners in both countries are relatively more downwardly mobile than low-wage women. It seems as if higher experience in itself is related to downward mobility. In Finland this tendency can, however, be offset by acquiring more occupation-specific skills or by moving to another region. In Denmark, changing region is not associated with upward mobility, while human capital tends to be more positively related to mobility and higher experience leads to upward mobility over the first seven years of a labour market career.

NOTES

1   Comments from the participants at the LoWER conference held in Bordeaux 31 January and 1 February are gratefully acknowledged. Financial support from *Danmarks Grundforskningsfond*.

REFERENCES

Asplund, R., E. Barth, C. le Grand, A. Mastekaasa and N. Westergård-Nielsen (1996), 'Wage Distribution Across Individuals', in E. Wadensjö (ed.), *The Nordic Labour Markets in the 1990's*, vol. I, part 2, Amsterdam: North–Holland.

Asplund, R. and P. Bingley (1996), *Wage Mobility in Finnish Industry in 1980–1994*, Helsinki: ETLA The Research Institute of the Finnish Economy, Series B 123.

Atkinson, A.B., F. Bourguignon and C. Morrisson (1992), *Empirical Studies in Earnings Mobility*, London: Harwood.

Berry, S., P. Gottschalk and D. Wissoker (1988), 'An Error Components Model of the Effect of Plant Closing on Earnings', *Review of Economics and Statistics*, **70**, pp. 701–7.

Bingley, P., N.H. Bjørn and N. Westergård-Nielsen (1995*)*, *Wage Mobility in Denmark 1980–90*, CLS Working Paper 95–10.

Björklund, A. (1993), 'A Comparison between Actual Distributions of Annual and Lifetime Income: Sweden 1951–89', *Review of Income and Wealth*, **39**(4), pp. 377–86.

Gottschalk, P. (1982), 'Earnings Mobility: Permanent Change or Transitory Fluctuations?', *Review of Economics and Statistics*, **64**(3), pp. 450–56.

Hart, P.E. (1976), 'The dynamics of earnings, 1963–1973', *Economic Journal*, **86**, pp. 551–65.

Keane, M., R. Moffitt and D. Runkle (1988), 'Real Wages over the Business Cycle: Estimating the Impact of Heterogeneity with Micro Data', *Journal of Political Economy*, **96**(6), pp. 1232–65.

Lambert, P. (1993), *The Distribution and Redistribution of Income*, Manchester University Press.

Lillard, L. (1977), 'Inequality: Earnings vs. Human Wealth', *American Economic Review*, **67**, pp. 42–53.

Lillard, L. and R.J. Willis (1978), 'Dynamic Aspects of Earnings Mobility', *Econometrica*, **46**(5), pp. 985–1012.

Lillard, L. and Y. Weiss (1979), 'Components of variation in panel earnings data: American scientists 1960–1970', *Econometrica*, **47**(2), pp. 437–54.

McCall, J.J. (1971), 'A Markovian model of income dynamics', *Journal of the American Statistical Association*, **66**, pp. 439–77.

MaCurdy, T.H. (1982), 'The Use of Time Series Processes to Model the Error Structure of Earnings in a Longitudinal Data Analysis', *Journal of Econometrics*, **18**(1), pp. 83–114.

OECD (1996), *Employment Outlook*, Paris.

Schiller, B. (1977), 'Relative earnings mobility in the US', *American Economic Review*, pp. 926–41.

Shorrocks, A.F. (1978), 'Income inequality and income mobility', *Econometrica*, **48**, pp. 613–25.

Shorrocks, A.F. (1981), 'The Measurement of Mobility', *Econometrica*, **46**(5), pp. 1013–24.

Thatcher, A.R. (1971), 'Year-to-year variations in the earnings of individuals', *Journal of the Royal Statistical Society*, Series A, **131**, pp. 374–82.

APPENDIX

Figure 5.A1   Goodness of fit

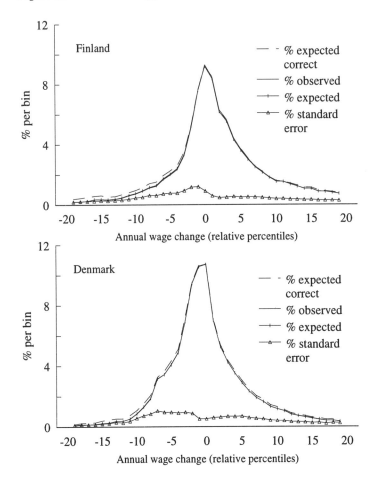

Table 5.A1　Danish panel wage mobility 1981–91: model estimates (standard errors in parentheses)

Variable	[EQN 'up'] Mobility		Attrition		Origin Quintile	
	Value	S. E.	Value	S. E.	Value	S. E.
Male	-0.0613	(0.0153)	0.0114	(0.0150)	0.7979	(0.0062)
Age/100		-	-10.1776	(0.3534)	1.7709	(0.0158)
Age2/1000		-	1.1219	(0.0462)	-0.2014	(0.0020)
Experience/10	0.0422	(0.0296)		-		-
Experience2/1000	-0.2681	(0.0708)		-		-
Δ Skill	0.0531	(0.0239)		-		-
Δ Region	-0.0897	(0.0984)		-		-
General	0.1565	(0.0251)	-0.2208	(0.0202)	-0.2056	(0.0109)
Vocational	0.1831	(0.0261)	-0.2516	(0.0211)	-0.0135	(0.0108)
College	0.2462	(0.0426)	-0.2643	(0.0432)	0.2887	(0.0161)
University	0.0250	(0.0493)	0.0741	(0.0461)	0.4699	(0.0153)
Construction	-0.1339	(0.0360)	0.0181	(0.0348)	0.1576	(0.0105)
Trade	-0.1492	(0.0168)	0.0670	(0.0171)	-0.3430	(0.0068)
Transport	-0.1032	(0.0363)	0.1055	(0.0365)	-0.3430	(0.0068)
Finance	0.0520	(0.0224)	-0.1285	(0.0235)	0.1634	(0.0091)
Services	-0.0329	(0.0208)	-0.0074	(0.0221)	-0.0659	(0.0090)
Manager	-0.3314	(0.0479)	0.1205	(0.0482)	0.9168	(0.0111)
Skilled	0.1055	(0.0254)	0.0631	(0.0243)	0.1468	(0.0083)
Unskilled	-0.1722	(0.0178)	0.1842	(0.0175)	-0.0472	(0.0078)
Other skill	-0.1945	(0.0205)	0.1720	(0.0190)	-0.1954	(0.0111)
Köbenhavn	-0.0017	(0.0238)	0.0879	(0.0246)		-
Frederiksborg	0.0015	(0.0287)	0.0208	(0.0302)		-
W. Sjöland	-0.0604	(0.0273)	-0.0027	(0.0293)		-
S. Jylland	0.0000	(0.0274)	-0.0504	(0.0294)		-
E. Jylland	-0.0145	(0.0249)	0.0145	(0.0263)		-
W. Jylland	0.0111	(0.0282)	-0.0689	(0.0302)		-
N. Jylland	-0.1012	(0.0290)	-0.0263	(0.0307)		-
1981	0.8353	(0.0620)	-1.1423	(0.0295)		-
1982	0.7755	(0.0615)	-1.1426	(0.0275)		-
1983	0.7861	(0.0640)	-1.2215	(0.0271)		-
1984	0.8556	(0.0602)	-1.1026	(0.0254)		-
1986	0.7239	(0.0575)	-1.0180	(0.0239)		-
1987	0.7070	(0.0582)	-1.0279	(0.0237)		-
1988	0.7455	(0.0597)	-1.0723	(0.0236)		-
1989	0.7849	(0.0593)	-1.0577	(0.0230)		-
1990	0.7836	(0.0558)	-0.9486	(0.0224)		-
(Year-81)/10		-		-	-0.0992	(0.0719)
(Year-81)2/100		-		-	0.0905	(0.1694)
(Year-81)3/1000		-		-	0.0065	(0.1101)
$\rho_{\varepsilon AM}$	0.1238 (0.0815)					-
$\rho_{\eta AM}$	0.2499 (0.0678)					-
$\rho_{\eta OM}, \rho_{\eta OA}$	0.3383	(0.0088)	0.0935	(0.0090)		-
$\sigma_{\eta A}, \sigma_{\eta M}$	0.6083	(0.0189)	0.0334	(0.0342)		-
Observations	29 762					
Log likelihood		-	-380 176			-

Table 5.A2   Finnish panel wage mobility 1980–94: model estimates
(standard errors in parentheses)

Variable	Equation					
	[EQN 'up'] Mobility		Attrition		Origin Quintile	
	Value	S. E.	Value	S. E.	Value	S. E.
Male	-0.0854	(0.0110)	0.0242	(0.0135)	1.1656	(0.0055)
Age/100	-		-11.8923	(0.3009)	1.6035	(0.0143)
Age2/1000	-		1.5170	(0.0392)	-0.1707	(0.0018)
Experience/10	-0.0769	(0.0237)	-		-	
Experience2/1000	0.0502	(0.0547)	-		-	
Δ Skill	0.5853	(0.0494)	-		-	
Δ Region	0.2608	(0.0308)	-		-	
Basic	0.0634	(0.0122)	-0.0634	(0.0150)	-0.6069	(0.0057)
Low secondary	0.0813	(0.0122)	-0.0634	(0.0150)	-0.6069	(0.0057)
College	0.0726	(0.0124)	-0.0924	(0.0150)	-0.4522	(0.0052)
Clothing	0.1196	(0.0589)	-0.0289	(0.0702)	0.5057	(0.0107)
Metal manual	0.1381	(0.0330)	-0.5427	(0.0257)	-0.2680	(0.0176)
Wood manual	0.2052	(0.0384)	-0.7469	(0.0254)	0.4825	(0.0169)
Wood non-manual	0.0707	(0.0395)	-0.7243	(0.0280)	0.2722	(0.0153)
Paper manual	0.3413	(0.0358)	0.1475	(0.0380)	-0.1411	(0.0183)
Paper non-manual	-0.0141	(0.0448)	-0.9437	(0.0307)	0.5832	(0.0175)
Construction	-0.0751	(0.0315)	-0.1083	(0.0381)	0.6570	(0.0180)
Others	-0.0194	(0.0311)	0.0402	(0.0378)	0.3439	(0.0175)
Services	-0.0027	(0.0199)	-0.1135	(0.0241)	0.5053	(0.0152)
Manual	-0.0607	(0.0264)	-0.0551	(0.0324)	0.1478	(0.0171)
Clerical	0.0603	(0.0372)	0.5828	(0.0306)	-1.3417	(0.0105)
Upper	-0.0636	(0.0201)	-0.0661	(0.0254)	-0.4176	(0.0075)
South	-0.0577	(0.0690)	0.0010	(0.0821)	1.3345	(0.0113)
1980	-0.1270	(0.0090)	-0.0039	(0.0114)	-	
1981	0.1917	(0.0450)	-0.9277	(0.0277)	-	
1982	0.0708	(0.0452)	-0.9551	(0.0264)	-	
1983	0.0322	(0.0461)	-1.0114	(0.0250)	-	
1984	-0.0588	(0.0450)	-0.9817	(0.0236)	-	
1986	-0.1049	(0.0427)	-0.9064	(0.0228)	-	
1987	-0.1102	(0.0419)	-0.8714	(0.0226)	-	
1988	-0.1606	(0.0423)	-0.8854	(0.0227)	-	
1989	-0.1868	(0.0399)	-0.7984	(0.0224)	-	
1990	-0.1406	(0.0385)	-0.7490	(0.0224)	-	
1991	-0.1041	(0.0361)	-0.6575	(0.0225)	-	
1992	0.0730	(0.0389)	-0.7402	(0.0240)	-	
1993	-0.3734	(0.0379)	-0.6943	(0.0246)	-	
(Year-80)/10	-		-		0.8690	(0.0423)
(Year-80)^2/100	-		-		-1.7864	(0.0728)
(Year-80)^3/1000	-		-		0.6930	(0.0348)
$\rho_{\varepsilon AM}$	-1.7864 (0.0728)				-	
$\rho_{\eta AM}$	0.2156 (0.0614)					
$\rho_{\eta OM}, \rho_{\eta OA}$	0.2857	(0.0066)	0.0850	(0.0080)	-	
$\sigma_{\eta A}, \sigma_{\eta M}$	0.7420	(0.0117)	0.0305	(0.0462)		
Observations	65 310					
Log likelihood	-810 924					

Econometric Framework

Wages are ranked separately for each country for each year, and the ranks are normalized to the unit interval. The position of an individual in her/his first year in the sample is divided into quintiles. These are determined by the following latent and observed Origin wage equations:

$$O_i^* = Z_i\omega + \eta_i^o \tag{5.3}$$

$$O_i = \begin{cases} 1 & if & O_i^* \leq 0.2 \\ 2 & if & 0.2 < O_i^* \leq 0.4 \\ 3 & if & 0.4 < O_i^* \leq 0.6 \\ 4 & if & 0.6 < O_i^* \leq 0.8 \\ 5 & if & 0.8 < O_i^* \end{cases}$$

where O_i^* is the latent variable corresponding to Origin quintile O_i for individual i. Z_i is a matrix of individual characteristics, ω is a corresponding vector of coefficients and η_i^O is a random error.

Each year a number of individuals leave the sample due to retirement, sickness, unemployment, re-employment in a non-sampled unit, self-employment, etc. Nothing is known about the reason for attrition from the Finnish data, and so for the purposes of comparison we ignore the distinction between exit states, which we know from the Danish data. Strictly, the problem is one of non-response in that individuals may return to the sample after some time outside, but we use the generic term attrition for convenience. The attrition process is assumed to be determined by the following latent and observed equations:

$$A_{it}^* = Y_{it}\gamma + \eta_i^A + \varepsilon_{it}^A \quad \forall \quad O_i = 1 \tag{5.4}$$

$$A_{it} = \begin{cases} 0 & if & A_{it}^* \leq 0 \\ 1 & if & A_{it}^* > 0 \end{cases}$$

where A_{it}^* is the latent variable corresponding to attrition from the sample A_{it} for individual i in year t. Y_{it} is a matrix of individual characteristics, γ is a corresponding vector of coefficients. ε_{it}^A and η_i^A are random errors, which may be thought of as respectively transitory and permanent components.

For all those who do not disappear from the sample in a given year we can observe their wage mobility. This is computed from the year-on-year difference in normalized ranks, and divided into 41 discrete categories. These are determined by the following latent and observed Mobility equations:

$$M_{it}^* = X_{it}\beta + O_i\delta + \eta_i^M + \varepsilon_{it}^M \quad \forall \quad A_{it} = 0, O_i = 1 \tag{5.5}$$

$$M_{it} = \begin{cases} -20 & \text{if} \quad M_{it}^* \le -0.195 \\ -19 & \text{if} \quad -0.195 < M_{it}^* \le -0.185 \\ \quad \cdots \\ -1 & \text{if} \quad -0.015 < M_{it}^* \le -0.005 \\ 0 & \text{if} \quad -0.005 < M_{it}^* \le +0.005 \\ +1 & \text{if} \quad +0.005 < M_{it}^* \le +0.015 \\ \quad \cdots \\ +19 & \text{if} \quad +0.185 < M_{it}^* \le +0.195 \\ -20 & \text{if} \quad 0.195 < M_{it}^* \end{cases}$$

where M_{it}^* is the latent variable corresponding to mobility M_{it} for individual i in year t. X_{it} is a matrix of individual characteristics, β is a corresponding vector of coefficients, O_i is an indicator of Origin quintile and δ is a corresponding coefficient. ε_{it}^M and η_i^M are random errors, which may be thought of as respectively transitory and permanent components.

Stochastic assumptions for the error terms are captured by the following variance-covariance matrix of a multivariate normal distribution:

$$V\begin{pmatrix} \varepsilon^M \\ \varepsilon^A \\ \eta^M \\ \eta^A \\ \eta^O \end{pmatrix} = \begin{pmatrix} 1 & \cdot & \cdot & \cdot & \cdot \\ \rho_{\varepsilon^{AM}} & 1 & \cdot & \cdot & \cdot \\ 0 & 0 & \sigma_{\eta^M}^2 & \cdot & \cdot \\ 0 & 0 & \rho_{\eta^{AM}}\sigma_{\eta^M}\sigma_{\eta^A} & \sigma_{\eta^A}^2 & \cdot \\ 0 & 0 & \rho_{\eta^{OM}}\sigma_{\eta^M} & \rho_{\eta^{OA}}\sigma_{\eta^A} & 1 \end{pmatrix} \tag{5.6}$$

The important point, as in all random effect models, is that the permanent effects are not correlated with the transitory, and furthermore are assumed uncorrelated with the explanatory variables. We do, however, allow correlation among the transitory effects and among the permanent effects themselves, in order to capture potential endogeneity (of Origin) and selectivity (of non-attrition) in both the short run and the long run.

The Short-Run Horizon

The likelihood function for an individual is presented below

$$
L_i = \int_{-\infty}^{+\infty} \int_{-\infty}^{+\infty} \prod_{t_i=1}^{T_i} \int_{O^{*-}}^{O^{*+}} \left[\int_{A^{*-}}^{A^{*+}} \int_{M^{*-}}^{M^{*+}} \phi_2 \, (\varepsilon^A, \varepsilon^M) \, d\varepsilon^M d\varepsilon^A \right] \tag{5.7}
$$

$$
\bullet \frac{1}{\sigma_{\eta^A} \sigma_{\eta^M}} \phi_3 \left(\frac{\eta^A}{\sigma_{\eta^A}}, \frac{\eta^M}{\sigma_{\eta^M}}, \eta^o \right) d\eta^o d\eta^M d\eta^A
$$

where ϕ_2 and ϕ_3 represent respectively bi- and trivariate normal probability density functions. Essentially this is a trivariate ordered probit model for panel data. This is simplified (though more made messy than the standard case) by partial observability since mobility is not observed for those who disappear from the sample. Furthermore, since individuals are only observed for the first time once, the origin error term is only conditioned once per individual, so we do not have a transitory component in that error term.

The model is implemented in Gauss exploiting canned multivariate normal cdfs and numerically integrating out the random effects.

6. An Econometric Analysis of Low Pay and Earnings Mobility in Britain [1]

P.J. Sloane and I. Theodossiou

1 INTRODUCTION

The question of low pay has become a policy issue in a number of countries, especially those in which there has been a widening in the earnings distribution. This is the case in Britain where the Labour Party is committed to the introduction of a national minimum wage, though it has so far refused to commit itself to a particular figure on the grounds that this will be influenced by the prevailing economic circumstances. A number of trade unions have, however, argued for the minimum to be set at £4.10 per hour. This appears to be a relatively high figure. In the USA, for example, the minimum wage has recently been raised from $4.25 to $5.15 per hour, which would equate to £3.30. Indeed if one adjusted for the fact that earnings in the USA are higher than in Britain the comparable figure would be only £2.30 an hour, but the number of full-time workers earning below this figure in Britain is less than one per cent. There seems little purpose in setting a minimum wage so low that very few workers are affected. There is also the question of targeting those workers who are most in need of help. In this chapter we focus on earnings mobility, on the grounds that some workers may experience low pay only as a temporary phenomenon and, therefore, not be prime candidates for the support offered by a national minimum wage.

In an earlier study Sloane and Theodossiou (1996) utilized a multinomial logistic (MNL) regression to identify those individuals who fall into the low-pay category and who are unable to escape from it, using the first (1991) and third (1993) waves of the British Household Panel Study. However, the restrictions imposed by the so-called Independence of Irrelevant Alternatives (IIA) property required by the multinomial logit model are unappealing. In this chapter we extend our earlier analysis by utilizing a bivariate nested probit model, which unlike the MNL model does require the IIA property and in addition takes into account sequentially the likelihood of one staying in the employed labour force and the likelihood of whether or not one is located below the low-pay threshold. This method is also utilized by Theodossiou (1997).

There are both supply and demand considerations which determine the decision-making process. Thus an unemployed worker has to decide whether to take up a low-paid job or wait on the grounds that a high-paid job may become available in the future. On the other side employers may reserve recruitment to high-wage jobs for high-quality labour, thereby limiting opportunities for certain workers to low-paid jobs. As we estimate a reduced form equation we cannot identify whether the cause of current low pay represents employee or employer preferences. Assuming, however, that the former plays a significant role our approach is consistent with that of Mackay (1972) who distinguished two groups of workers whom he labelled 'stickers' and 'snatchers'. The former attempt to obtain a new job with attributes comparable to those of their last job and if their last job was high paid they may prefer to wait rather than accept a low-paid job although this exposes them to longer periods of unemployment. Snatchers, on the other hand, will be prepared to take the first job that comes along, even if it is low paid and use this as a base from which to search for higher-paying jobs. In our case the initial observations are limited to those who are in low-paid jobs. Thus it is appropriate to regard as the equivalent of stickers those who remain in low-paid jobs in the expectation that higher-paid job opportunities will emerge. Correspondingly, we may regard the equivalent of snatchers as those who vacate low-paid jobs for unemployment in the hope that additional job search will reveal high-paid job opportunities.

2 THE MEASUREMENT OF LOW PAY

Economic theory does not provide us with any clear evidence on how low pay should be defined. The choice is more likely to be influenced by the issue being addressed or the availability of data. Generally speaking reasons for studying low pay fall into equity or efficiency arguments. The former holds that there should be a fair reward for labour as embodied in the general principle of equal pay for work of equal value. Under this approach some individuals who earn more than the mean may be regarded as low paid. On the other hand some low-paid workers who have low levels of productivity or who prefer low-paid work because it is less exacting or more suited to their abilities may not be low paid in the equity sense.[2] The efficiency argument may arise when pay is too low to maintain a reasonable standard of living, so that the state has to intervene to eliminate family poverty. Alternatively, it may be argued that firms who pay below the norm for their industry are engaging in unfair competition. Some forms of efficiency wage arguments also suggest that raising the pay of low-paid workers may raise productivity.

Low pay may be defined in absolute or relative terms, the former being more appropriate if the major concern is with poverty and the latter if it is with equity. Using a measure such as the lowest decile, quintile or third decile[3] has the effect of accounting for a fixed percentage of all workers. The alternative of defining low pay as a percentage of median earnings allows for variations in the proportion defined as low paid over time and therefore is more suitable for answering the question of whether the problem of low paid is becoming less or more widespread. Here we adopt a relative measure of low pay which is expressed in terms of those earning less than 66 per cent of the median. We also use hourly earnings in order to make comparisons with the figure suggested for the introduction of a minimum wage in Britain. In fact using 66 per cent of the median produces figures of £3.35 in 1991 and £3.61 in 1993.

3 THE DATA AND DESCRIPTIVE STATISTICS

The analysis is based on the 1991 and 1993 waves of the British Household Panel Study (BHPS) which embraces some 10 000 individuals representative of the British population. The labour market component is designed to facilitate research on patterns of individual mobility, either by comparing jobs or labour market situations at successive waves, or by analysing the detailed work histories collected over the course of the panel such as education, income, household activities and health. The panel also incorporates a very detailed analysis of job characteristics. As expected it suffers somewhat from attrition so that we exclude all observations that appear only in the first wave. The period over which earnings mobility is observed is short, just two years, but this has the advantage of allowing us to identify transient low-paid workers for whom the problem of low pay may be less severe.

Defining the low paid as those earning less than the 66 per cent definition 19.5 per cent were low paid in 1991 and 13.5 per cent in 1993. A degree of caution is required because we are analysing only those who appear in both 1991 and 1993 samples, which is not the same as the total BHPS sample in 1993. Women are disproportionately represented among the low paid, comprising 73.6 per cent in 1991 and 72.3 per cent in 1993. Therefore, it appears that women would be the main beneficiaries of the introduction of a national minimum wage. Since well over half of low-paid women are married (and many of them in multiple earner households) a minimum wage appears to be a poorly targeted device for dealing with the problem of poverty.

Roughly three-quarters of the sample is employed on a full-time basis. Part-timers are, however, over-represented among the low paid, comprising 43.6 per cent in 1991 and 45.1 per cent in 1993. The majority of part-timers are females. Contrasts between low-paid and high-paid men and women are illustrated by differences in the sample means in Table 6.1. The low paid tend to be younger than the high paid, though no less than 48 per cent of low-paid women are in the 34–50 age group. The higher paid are more likely to undergo training, to be employed full-time in jobs with promotion prospects, and to be found in larger establishments. We are also able with panel data to examine the impact of change variables. No less than 40 per cent of the unmarried

Table 6.1   *Sample means – low pay defined as 66 % of the median 1993*

Variable	Men		Women	
	Low paid	High paid	Low paid	High paid
Age 19–24	0.29	0.07	0.11	0.06
Age 25–34	0.22	0.28	0.16	0.29
Age 35–50	0.25	0.45	0.48	0.46
Married	0.57	0.76	0.71	0.73
Got married	0.40	0.21	0.18	0.18
Training in 1991	0.12	0.31	0.12	0.27
Employed full-time (1991)	0.91	0.97	0.43	0.70
Promotion prospects	0.35	0.63	0.29	0.49
Additional qualifications	0.08	0.05	0.06	0.05
Degree or equivalent qualifications	0.11	0.42	0.13	0.32
A Level Qualifications	0.19	0.14	0.08	0.15
Low qualifications/ apprenticeships	0.32	0.25	0.41	0.36
Tenure (<2 years)	0.30	0.28	0.34	0.33
Energy and manufacturing	0.32	0.37	0.14	0.16
Construction/distribution	0.39	0.18	0.35	0.15
Banking and finance	0.04	0.12	0.07	0.15
Firm size 25–99	0.33	0.26	0.24	0.28
Firm size 100–499	0.19	0.27	0.15	0.22
Firm size 500 and over	0.06	0.21	0.03	0.14
Moved region	0.03	0.02	0.01	0.03
South	0.77	0.69	0.75	0.67
North	0.03	0.07	0.07	0.06
Wales	0.11	0.04	0.05	0.04
Scotland	0.07	0.09	0.08	0.11
Number of observations	143	1 585	405	1 359

low-paid males got married during the two-year period compared to 18 per cent of the female low paid. This raises the possibility that marriage may have an economic rationale since a low-paid male may find it easier to supplement earnings by having a working spouse (only 8 per cent being without a job in this category) than following other routes.

Transitions from low-paid to high-paid work or to other alternatives are shown in Table 6.2. Nearly 44 per cent of the low paid remained in low-paid jobs two years later. Some low-paid workers move into self-employment and in every case the self-employed earnings are above the low-pay–high-pay division. Clearly, therefore, a number of the low paid in the sample are transitory low paid. However, there is another substantial group which moves from low-paid employment into unemployment or non-labour market activities of which the most important are family care, retirement and full-time studies or government training.[4] The probability of moving out of low-paid employment is greater for men than for women; 46.7 per cent of women who were low paid in 1991 remained in this state in 1993, compared to 35.2 per cent of men. The probability of moving from low-paid employment into high-paid employment is also greater for men than for women; 39 per cent of low-paid men in 1991 moved into high-paid employment by 1993 compared to 31.5 per cent of the low-paid women.

Table 6.2   Transitions from low-paid work 1991–3, all workers

66% of median	
Number of low paid 1991	794
1993 Status	
Employed	347 (Low-paid) => 266 (High-paid)
Self-employed	18
Unemployed	36
Retired	30
Maternity leave	3
Family care	48
Full-time studies/government trainee	26
Long-term sick/disabled	13
Other	7

Note: All the self-employed in the table were in the high-pay category and therefore should be added to the high-pay employees to obtain a true figure of upward pay mobility for the low paid in 1991.

4 MODELLING EARNINGS MOBILITY

Modelling earnings transitions can be problematical. Panel studies suffer from attrition bias and our analysis is limited to observations that appear in both the first and third waves of the panel.[5] There is an initial condition problem in that we select those who happened to be low paid in 1991, giving rise to a potential sample selection problem. Under the assumption that the initial conditions are exogenous our initial approach is to use multinomial logistic regression to model the probability of an individual being in the low or high-pay category in 1993 given that he or she was in the low-pay category in 1991. This technique seems appropriate since we have three states – low pay, high pay or not in employment. It does, however, require the 'independence of irrelevant alternatives' (IIA) property, that is, the ratio of probability between any two choices should be unaffected by the availability of a third choice.[6]

The multinomial logistic regression procedure is as follows: assume that the categories of individuals in the survey sample are $j = 0,1,2$ recorded in Y_i, and the independent variables are denoted by x. The values of Y are unordered in the sense that 1<2<3 does not imply that outcome 1 is less than outcome 2, which in turn is less than outcome 3 (i.e. there is intransitivity). A set of coefficients β_1, β_2 and β_3 corresponding to each outcome category are then estimated as

$$P(Y = 1|X) = \frac{e^{x\beta_1}}{e^{x\beta_1} + e^{x\beta_2} + e^{x\beta_3}} \tag{6.1}$$

$$P(Y = 2|X) = \frac{e^{x\beta_2}}{e^{x\beta_1} + e^{x\beta_2} + e^{x\beta_3}} \tag{6.2}$$

$$P(Y = 3|X) = \frac{e^{x\beta_3}}{e^{x\beta_1} + e^{x\beta_2} + e^{x\beta_3}} \tag{6.3}$$

Since there is more than one possible solution to β_1, β_2 and β_3 which leads to the same probabilities for $Y=1$, $Y=2$ and $Y=3$, the above model is unidentified. Thus, we must arbitrarily set one of the β_1, β_2 and β_3 to zero. If β_3 is set to zero then the coefficients β_1 and β_2 measure a relative change with respect to β_3, so that the above model becomes

$$P(Y = 1|X) = \frac{e^{x\beta_1}}{e^{x\beta_1} + e^{x\beta_2} + 1} \tag{6.4}$$

$$P(Y = 2|X) = \frac{e^{x\beta_2}}{e^{x\beta_1} + e^{x\beta_2} + 1} \tag{6.5}$$

$$P(Y = 3|X) = \frac{1}{e^{x\beta_1} + e^{x\beta_2} + 1} \tag{6.6}$$

and the relative probability of, for example, *Y=2* to the category *Y=3* is then

$$\frac{P(Y = 2)}{P(Y = 3)} = e^{x\beta_2}, \tag{6.7}$$

which is the relative risk ratio.

Non-zero coefficients imply that the corresponding variable influences an individual's position in the distribution of earnings even when differences in the other independent variables are taken into account. The exponential value of the coefficient is the relative risk ratio per one unit change in the corresponding variable, this risk being measured as the risk of the category relative to the base category.

However the restrictions imposed by the IIA property are unappealing. One alternative is to formulate the model as a nested bivariate probit, following Theodossiou (1997). According to this model a low-paid individual confronts first the likelihood of being in employment or not in employment and then whether or not to remain under the low-pay threshold. The basic assumption in this model is that not all low-paid workers who wish to work in a high-paid job are able to find one. Thus the following two equations can be formulated:

The probability of someone being below the low-pay threshold is

$$Prob\ (w_I > w_{LP}) = P_{i1} = X_{i1}\delta_1 + \varepsilon_{i1} \tag{6.8}$$

where $\varepsilon_{i1} \sim IN\ (0, \sigma^2_{i1})$, X are individual characteristics including the individual's human capital endowments.

The probability that worker *i* will participate in the employed labour force can be written as

$$Prob\ (E = 1) = P_{i2} = X_{i2}\delta_2 + \varepsilon_{i2} \tag{6.9}$$

where $\varepsilon_{i2} \sim IN\ (0, \sigma^2_{i2})$ and X are individual characteristics including the individual's human capital endowments and past labour market experience.

Thus the error term in the above two equations are not independent but

$$
\begin{vmatrix} \varepsilon_{i1} \\ \varepsilon_{i2} \end{vmatrix} \sim Biv.\ Normal \left(\begin{vmatrix} 0 \\ 0 \end{vmatrix}, \sigma^2 \begin{vmatrix} I & \gamma I \\ \gamma I & I \end{vmatrix} \right) \tag{6.10}
$$

In this setting the latter equation is nested within the former one and therefore outcome P_{i1} is only available when $P_{i2} \neq 0$. The four possible outcomes for a given observation are

$$
O_{i11} = P(P_{i2} = 1,\ P_{i1} = 1) = \Phi_2(\ X_{i2}\delta_2,\ X_{i1}\delta_1, \sigma) \tag{6.11}
$$

$$
O_{i01} = P(P_{i2} = 1,\ P_{i1} = 0) = \Phi_2(- X_{i2}\delta_2,\ X_{i1}\delta_1, -\sigma) \tag{6.12}
$$

$$
O_{i10} = P(P_{i2} = 0,\ P_{i1} = 1) = \Phi(-X_{i1}\delta_1) \tag{6.13}
$$

$$
O_{i00} = P(P_{i2} = 0,\ P_{i1} = 0) = \Phi(-X_{i1}\delta_1) \tag{6.14}
$$

where Φ is the standard normal cdf, and Φ_2 the standard bivariate normal cdf. In this model, the estimation sample is the sample defined by the containing equation – the contained equation is assumed to be missing for observations where the dependent variable of the containing equation is zero (Hardin 1996).

5 EMPIRICAL RESULTS

5.1 The Multinomial Logistic Regressions

As noted above the multinomial logit model allocates individuals' earnings mobility to three states – high pay, low pay and a catch-all other category of non-employment, thus exhausting all possible states. The results of the multi-nomial logistic regressions are detailed in Table 6.3. The comparison group is those who moved above the low-pay threshold. The lower part of the table concerns those who moved to the out-of-employment state. They are reported only for completeness and are not discussed here. The results are compatible with Sloane and Theodossiou (1994). Thus, being in the younger age groups (the over fifties being the omitted category) reduces the probability of re-maining in the low-paid category and so does being married or cohabiting. Both a degree and lower-level education qualifications improve the chances of moving into higher-paid work.

Table 6.3   *Results of multinomial logistic and nested probit regressions*

Variables	Multinomial logistic regression (1)		Nested probit regression (2)	
	Being in low-paid empl.		Being in low-paid empl.	
	Coef.	t-stat	Coef.	t-stat
Age 19–24	-0.98	-2.77	0.53	2.45
Age 25–34	-0.68	-2.29	0.37	2.00
Age 35–50	-0.10	-0.40	0.07	0.39
Gender	-0.25	-1.74	0.15	1.73
Couple	-0.49	-2.06	0.32	2.18
Training 1991	-0.28	-1.13	0.16	0.99
Full-time job ('91)	0.08	0.39	-0.12	-0.88
Promotion prospects ('91)	-0.32	-1.64	0.16	1.28
Degree or equivalent qualification	-0.68	-2.35	0.51	2.92
A level or equivalent qualification	-0.38	-1.19	0.24	1.11
Low qualification/ apprenticeship	-0.49	-2.15	0.40	2.84
Tenure(< 2 years)	0.58	2.98	-0.37	-1.97
Energy, manuf. industry ('91)	0.07	0.25	0.01	0.06
Construction, distribution ind. ('91)	0.08	0.41	-0.06	-0.44
Banking industry ('91)	-0.15	-0.41	0.11	0.47
Firm size 25–99 ('91)	-0.49	-2.35	0.27	2.14
Firm size 100–499 ('91)	-0.63	-2.38	0.33	1.92
Firm size 500 and over ('91)	-0.80	-1.94	0.52	2.07
South of England	0.59	1.35	-0.48	-1.85
North of England	0.58	1.04	-0.45	-1.34
Wales	1.33	2.27	-1.03	-2.92
Scotland	-0.18	-0.35	-0.07	-0.24
Constant	0.96	1.54	-0.42	-0.97
	not in paid empl.		in paid empl.	
Age 35–50	-0.73	-2.42	0.48	3.18
Training 1991	-0.74	-2.35	0.27	1.58
Tenure(< 2 years)	-0.76	-2.82	0.56	4.08
Firm size 25–99 ('91)	-0.57	-2.27	0.15	1.09
Firm size 100–499 ('91)	-0.35	-1.15	-0.05	-0.33
Moved region			-0.62	-2.18
Got married			-0.43	-1.54
Additional qualifications			-0.27	-1.22
Constant	0.39	0.55	1.03	2.34
σ			0.22	0.33
Chi-squared(44)	133.82			
Chi-squared(47)			149.20	
Log Likelihood	-778.839		-762.697	

Note: Also included but insignificant are: age 19–24, age 25–34, gender, couple, full-time job (1991), promotion prospects (1991), degree or equivalent qualification, A level or equivalent qualification, low qualification/apprenticeship, energy, manufacturing industry (1991), construction, distribution industry (1991), banking industry (1991), firm size (500 and over, 1991), South of England, North of England, Wales, Scotland.

An important question is to what extent does a change of job imply a change of pay status? Those with tenure of less than two years in our sample must have made a job change. However, short tenure reduces the probability of escaping from a low-pay situation, suggesting that movement from low-paid to high-paid employment tends to occur without a job change, consistent with current low-pay status reflecting an investment in specific human capital. Being employed in larger firms (firms with less than 25 employees being the omitted category) also increases the probability of moving into a higher-paying job. Finally, the probability of moving to a high-paying job is lower in Wales (London being the omitted category).

To test whether the IIA property holds the Hausman and McFadden (1984) test is used. An implication of this property is that the model structure and parameters are unchanged when choice is analysed conditional on a restricted subset, r, of the full choice set, f. Define β_r and β_f to be the ML estimates of the restricted and unrestricted sets and v_r, v_f the corresponding variances. Under the null hypothesis that the IIA property holds, $\beta_r - \beta_f$ is a consistent estimator of zero. The statistic

$$H = (\beta_r - \beta_f)' (v_r - v_f)^{-1} (\beta_r - \beta_f) \qquad (6.15)$$

is asymptotically chi-squared with degrees of freedom equal to the rank of $(v_r - v_f)$. The x^2-test showed that in this model the null hypothesis cannot be rejected.

5.2 The Nested Probit Model

The estimation results using the nested probit model are reported in Table 6.3, column 2. The individuals under the low-pay threshold take the value zero and those above the value one. The results of employed labour force participation decisions for the individual low-paid worker are given in the lower part of the table, and the results on whether or not he/she has remained in a low-paid job are reported in the upper part of the table. In this study the former regression includes three additional variables not included in the latter in order to identify the model. These variables concern changes in individuals' circumstances which could influence their motivation and likelihood of participating in the employed labour force. They are whether the individual between 1991 and 1993 moved region of residence, whether he or she got married and whether he or she acquired additional educational qualifications. It is assumed that these variables do not affect the individual's location in a high or low-paid job, but only affect the individual's job choice of whether to join or not to join the employed labour force. All these three variables turned out to be jointly statistically insignificant when they were included in the set of variables determining the individual's location in a high or low-paid job.

Examining first the age variables and noting that we are examining only those who started out as low paid in 1991, being in the younger age groups reduces the probability of remaining in the low-paid labour force by 1993, but has no significant effect on the probability of remaining in the employed labour force. However being in the 35 to 50 age group increases the probability of remaining in the employed labour force, probably due to a high likelihood of increased family commitments, but does not appear to significantly affect an individual's chance of getting a high-paid job. Being married or cohabiting significantly and positively affects the likelihood of someone escaping from low-paid employment, as family commitments may affect an individual's motivation and hence productivity, although it does not seem to affect an individual's chances of joining the employed labour force. The latter may reflect the decisions of some married women to engage in full-time domestic activities.

Surprisingly educational qualifications do not appear to affect individuals' chances of joining the employed labour force but having a degree or equivalent qualification and being employed in a low-paid job in 1991 decreases the probability of remaining in the low-pay segment and so does having lower-level or apprenticeship qualifications

Short tenure (of less than two years) decreases the probability of obtaining a higher-paid job but increases the likelihood of remaining in the employed labour force. The larger the firm's size, the higher is the probability of escaping from a low-paid job. Being employed in Wales increases the probability of remaining in a low-paid job.

In general, it appears that the MNL successfully captures the real effects of the explanatory variables.

6 CONCLUSIONS

Taking a period of only two years there is some degree of earnings mobility from low-paid to high-paid jobs[7] in the British Household Panel Study, though many of the low paid move into unemployment rather than a higher-paying job. There remains a substantial group which is confined to low-paid employment, at least over a two-year period. The multinomial logistic regression and the nested probit model results point to a number of variables, including human capital variables, that affect the probability of moving out of low-paid employment. Perhaps demand-side factors also play an important role relative to supply-side factors. The number of employer-side variables is restricted in the BHPS data set due to the fact that it is a household survey. The results also suggest that a simple MNL model highlights a number of interesting relationships, though it does not take account of the nested nature of an individual's behaviour.

Notwithstanding the above points the difficulty of identifying those who have a low-paid problem cannot be resolved by this study, since the outcome is determined by the elasticity of demand for such labour, an issue that needs to be investigated. Intervention in the low-paid labour market is likely, therefore, to have varying effects. In particular this study points to the importance of demand factors in influencing both the extent and the concentration of low-pay employment within segments of the labour force.

NOTES

1   The data (tabulations) used in this chapter were made available through the ESRC Data Archive. The data were originally collected by the ESRC Research Centre on Micro-social Change at the University of Essex. Neither the original collectors of the data nor the Archive bear any responsibility for the analyses or interpretations presented here. We thank the participants at the Bordeaux conference for their helpful comments.
2   In this respect, see National Board for Prices and Incomes (1971).
3   This is the approach used by Sloane and Theodossiou (1994, 1996).
4   Fernie and Metcalfe (1996) note 'it is very important to distinguish between individuals always in employment and those who move between work and unemployment or inactivity. Most of those who are always employees climb the ladder and escape the low pay rung. But before jumping to the conclusion that low pay is a transitory problem, spells of unemployment or inactivity must also be considered. Such evidence suggests a much more cautious, even pessimistic, interpretation of the dynamics of low pay' (p. 22).
5   Taking a period of only two years does, however, have the advantage of reducing the degree of attrition.
6   Although in principle, the violation of the independence of irrelevant alternatives property causes inconsistent parameter and choice probability estimates, Horowitz (1980a, 1980b) has demonstrated that in practice the basic logit model appears to be reasonably robust against moderate violations of the property's assumptions.
7   There is also considerable mobility from high-paid to low-paid jobs, an issue which is not addressed here. See Sloane and Theodossiou (1996).

REFERENCES

Fernie, S. and D. Metcalf (1996), *Low Pay and Minimum Wages: The British Evidence, Special Report*, London: London School of Economics, Centre for Economic Performance, September.
Hardin, J.W. (1996), 'Bivariate Probit Models', *Stata Technical Bulletin*, September, pp. 15–20.
Hausman, J. and D. McFadden (1984), 'Specification Tests for Multinomial Logit Model', *Econometrica*, September, pp. 1219–40.
Horowitz, J. (1980a), 'Sources of Error and Uncertainty in Behavioral Travel Models' in W. Broy, P.R. Stopler and A.H. Meyburg (eds), *New Horizons in Behavioral Travel Research*, Lexington, US: Lexington Books.
Horowitz, J. (1980b), *Testing the Multinomial Logit Regression Model against the Multinomial Probit Model Without Estimating the Probit Parameters*, Washington DC: US Environmental Protection Agency.
Mackay, D.I. (1972), 'After the Shake-Out', *Oxford Economic Papers*, March.

National Board for Prices and Incomes (1971), *General Problems of Low Pay*, Report No. 169, Cmnd. 4648, HMSO.

Sloane, P.J. and I. Theodossiou (1994), 'The Economics of Low Pay in Britain: A Logistic Regression Approach', *International Journal of Manpower*, **15**, pp. 130–49.

Sloane, P.J. and I. Theodossiou (1996), 'Earnings Mobility, Family Income and Low Pay', *The Economic Journal*, **106**, pp. 657–66.

Theodossiou, I. (1997), *The Employer Capital Investment–Wage Effect: A Demand Side Explanation of Low Pay*, unpublished mimeo.

7. The Earnings Mobility of Low-Paid Workers in Britain [1]

M.B. Stewart and J.K. Swaffield

1 INTRODUCTION

The last two decades have seen a dramatic increase in earnings inequality in Britain and a marked deterioration in the relative earnings of those at the bottom end of the distribution.[2] While changes in earnings inequality can be examined by comparing cross-sectional snapshots at different points in time, such snapshots do not tell us about the earnings mobility of individuals or about inequality in the longer term. This chapter is concerned with earnings mobility at the bottom end of the earnings distribution: with transitions into and out of low pay.[3] The chapter investigates the extent to which the low paid are able to move out of low pay and up the earnings distribution.

In addition to movements up and down within the earnings distribution, individuals also make transitions between employment and non-employment, i.e. into and out of the earnings distribution. Exits from the earnings distribution are more likely to be made by those who are low paid. The chapter also investigates whether ignoring this distorts estimates of the earnings mobility of the low paid.

When modelling transition probabilities it is important that the initial conditions problem is addressed (Heckman 1981a). We can view this as an endogenous selection problem. Conditional on being initially low paid in modelling the probability of moving out of low pay in the next period, for example, will result in a selection bias in the estimates if being initially low paid is not exogenous. The chapter investigates the extent of the bias that is induced in the transition model estimates by assuming exogeneity.

The next section of the chapter discusses how to define low pay. Section 3 examines aggregate statistics on movements into and out of low pay and compares the probabilities when attention is restricted to transitions within the earnings distribution and when these transitions are analysed in conjunction with movements into and out of the earnings distribution. Section 4 then presents models of individual transition probabilities out of low pay and investigates the issue of endogenous selection into the initial, conditioned upon, low-paid state. Section 5 presents conclusions.

2 HOW SHOULD WE DEFINE THE LOW-PAY THRESHOLD?

A range of different low-pay thresholds have been suggested. They are usually expressed relative to mean or median earnings and differ according to whether they are defined relative to the earnings distribution for men and women or that for men alone, whether the distribution is restricted to manual workers or not, whether the cut-off is taken as a fraction of the mean or the median, whether the distribution of hourly earnings is used or the distribution of weekly earnings (with adjustment to an hourly basis afterwards) and whether overtime pay and hours are included or excluded.

The threshold is usually calculated using the New Earnings Survey (NES), considered the most appropriate since the NES is the largest survey of earnings available in Britain and is conducted every year on a consistent basis. However the NES is not an ideal source to use for the study of low pay, since for a number of reasons it undersamples those on low pay.[4] The NES is therefore not used for the analysis of low-pay transitions in this chapter. The main vehicle for this analysis is the British Household Panel Survey (BHPS).

However since the NES is almost always used in the calculation of the low-pay cut-offs used in the public debate, that is where any discussion of alternative definitions should start. Table 7.1 presents figures for various low-pay thresholds that have been suggested, calculated from the April 1991 NES. The first column gives calculations based on the overall (men and women) earnings distribution, the second column gives the corresponding calculations based on the distribution for males only and the third column those based on the manual male distribution. All three distributions are for full-time employees on adult rates whose pay for the survey pay-period was not affected by absence.

Proposed low-pay thresholds are typically expressed as some fraction of either the mean or the median. These differ quite considerably because of the skewness of the distribution. One disadvantage of defining a low-pay threshold relative to the mean is that the introduction of a statutory minimum wage would result in an increased value of the threshold. The first two thresholds given in the table are half the median and half the mean. For the combined male and female distribution, in terms of which they are commonly expressed, these give figures of £3.01 and £3.50 respectively for April 1991.

Table 7.1   Alternative low-pay cut-offs (£)

	Earnings Distribution		
	Males & females	Males only	Manual males only
1/2 Median gross hourly earnings (incl. overtime)	3.01	3.27	2.70
1/2 Mean gross hourly earnings (incl. overtime)	3.05	3.78	2.85
2/3 Median gross hourly earnings (incl. overtime)	4.02	4.35	3.60
Lowest decile gross hourly earnings (incl. overtime)	3.56	3.87	3.60
68% Mean gross hourly weekly earnings (incl. overtime) (Council of Europe's 'decency threshold')	193.60	216.85	172.11
+avg. hrs excl. overtime	5.15	5.68	4.40
+avg. hrs incl. overtime	4.84	5.23	3.88
1/2 Median gross weekly earnings (incl. overtime)	123.45	138.75	117.70
+avg. hrs excl. overtime	3.28	3.63	3.01
+avg. hrs incl. overtime	3.09	3.34	2.65
2/3 Median gross weekly earnings (incl. overtime)	164.60	185.00	156.93
+avg. hrs excl. overtime	4.38	4.84	4.04
+avg. hrs incl. overtime	4.12	4.46	3.53
Lowest decile gross weekly earnings (incl. overtime)	139.20	160.70	149.30
+avg. hrs excl. overtime	3.70	4.21	3.82
+avg. hrs incl. overtime	3.48	3.87	3.36

Note: Figures presented rounded, but calculations done with unrounded figures.

Source: April 1991 NES data for full-time employees on adult rates, whose pay for the survey
            pay-period was not affected by absence.

Organizations concerned with monitoring the existence and persistence of
low pay have discussed a variety of low-pay thresholds. Not surprisingly the
discussion of low pay is closely linked with that of a possible national minimum wage and typically no clear distinction is made between the definition
of a low-pay threshold and the desired national minimum wage level proposed. However any specified national minimum wage might be argued to
cover only the lowest of the low paid and therefore represent a lower bound
on a broader definition of low pay.

The Trades Union Congress (TUC) supports a national minimum wage of
half male median earnings rising to two-thirds of the male median over time.
Using the NES April 1991 data, this would define a low-pay threshold at
£3.27 per hour in the first instance, which lies roughly half way between the
figures for half the median and half the mean of the overall distribution referred to above. Their longer-term objective gives a figure of £4.35 per hour
in 1991 terms. Although the Labour Party currently has no official definition
of low pay or of a desired level for a national minimum wage the 1992 elec-
tion manifesto contained a commitment to a national minimum wage set at
half male median earnings (the same as the TUC's initial point).

The Low Pay Unit (LPU) defines low pay as being below two thirds male median earnings (the same formula as the TUC's final point), but evaluates this using the distribution of weekly earnings and then converts it to an hourly rate (LPU 1996). This conversion is achieved by dividing the weekly earnings (including overtime earnings) by average weekly hours excluding overtime. The LPU also makes use of the Council of Europe's 'decency threshold', defined as 68 per cent of full-time average weekly earnings. As is clear from Table 7.1 the inclusion or exclusion of weekly overtime hours from the denominator when converting weekly earnings to hourly values makes a large difference to the low-pay threshold determined. Using average hours excluding overtime gives a figure of £4.84 per hour. However the exclusion of overtime hours from the denominator of the calculation would seem somewhat inconsistent with the inclusion of overtime earnings in the numerator. Including overtime hours in the denominator gives a figure of £4.46, 38 pence down on the LPU figure, but still 11 pence above the TUC long-term objective.

The Child Poverty Action Group (CPAG) consider the extent of low pay in the context of its impact on poverty (CPAG 1995). Its analysis focuses on half the mean and two-thirds of the median hourly earnings of all adult full-time employees. In relation to the NES 1991 data this would be equivalent to £3.50 and £4.02 respectively. CPAG argues that the benchmark figure for low pay should include male and female full-time employees. The inclusion of women's rates of pay in the calculation differs from that of the TUC, Labour Party and the LPU. Although CPAG notes the argument for excluding women, namely that their pay may partly reflect discrimination, they argue for inclusion on the grounds that the hourly wage of non-manual women is higher than that of manual men and the rate of increase in their earnings has been higher than that of men.

This consideration of alternative definitions of low pay that have been proposed does not lead to the adoption of a unique threshold that is preferable to all others. Rather it suggests that it is useful to adopt more than one cut-off for any analysis of low pay. In addition it highlights points in need of consideration in selecting these thresholds. Clearly an important first question is whether to consider hourly or weekly pay. CPAG argues that the rise in part-time working and the increased range of usual weekly hours worked in the labour market makes an analysis of low pay centred around an hourly level more meaningful. The measure of low pay adopted in the subsequent analysis in this chapter is defined in terms of hourly pay. Given this, it also seems preferable to specify the thresholds directly in terms of points in the distribution of gross hourly earnings, rather than in terms of weekly earnings and then converting to an hourly basis. In selecting thresholds it is also important to be mindful of the numbers that a particular threshold will define to be low paid.

On the basis of this combination of considerations the first three thresholds in Table 7.1 are adopted for the analysis of low pay conducted in this chapter: half the median, half the mean and two-thirds the median, all in terms of the overall distribution of gross hourly earnings (including overtime) for full-time men and women on adult rates. The lowest threshold (half the median) is below the TUC's suggested initial minimum wage, but still defines 7.9 per cent of men and 24 per cent of women to be low paid on the basis of the 1991 wave of the BHPS. The highest threshold to be used in the analysis (two-thirds of the median) is below the TUC's long-term objective for a minimum wage (in 1991 terms), but defines 21.6 per cent of men and 48.7 per cent of women to be low paid on the basis of the 1991 wave of the BHPS. These seem reasonable highest and lowest thresholds for the analysis to be conducted in this chapter.

The distinction between low-pay definitions based on the mean rather than the median becomes more important as the two measures diverge. This is obviously an important consideration for the UK over the 1980s as wage dispersion has dramatically increased and the mean and median points have moved further apart. In April 1996 terms the thresholds adopted give NES values of £3.69, £4.36 and £4.91. The last of these, despite falling below the long-term objective for a minimum wage, is above any of the low-pay cutoffs considered by the TUC in their description of who is low paid (TUC 1995), adding further support to the choice of thresholds made.

The analysis of low-pay transitions in this chapter is based on the first four waves of the BHPS conducted in 1991, 1992, 1993 and 1994. As the BHPS interviews are conducted predominantly during September to November, with the median interview date for each wave being in October, we calculate October low-pay thresholds for each year by averaging those for the preceding and following Aprils.[5] These are given in Table 7.2. The calculations for October 1993, for example, give cut-offs of roughly £3.40, £4.00 and £4.50 an hour, all figures that have been extensively discussed in the public debate.

An investigation of the impact of individual and job characteristics on the incidence of low pay using these thresholds is reported in Stewart and Swaffield (1997a) in terms of *ceteris paribus* probability differences based on estimated probit models. The results are much as would be expected from the earnings function literature. For both men and women the probability of being low paid declines with age, full-time education leaving age and years of labour market experience. Women are more likely to be low paid than men. In addition characteristics such as being unionized, being employed in a firm with more than 25 workers and having had training within the last 12 months stand out as strongly reducing the probability of being low paid.

Table 7.2   *NES-based low-pay cut-offs for use with BHPS, October averages for each year (£)*

	Low Pay Definition		
	1/2 hourly median (I)	1/2 hourly mean (II)	2/3 hourly median (III)
1991	3.12	3.63	4.16
1992	3.29	3.84	4.38
1993	3.39	3.97	4.52
1994	3.49	4.09	4.65

Note: Each figure is the average of the corresponding figures for the previous and immediately following Aprils.

3 MOVEMENTS INTO AND OUT OF LOW PAY

There is mobility within the earnings distribution. Some people move out of low pay from one year to the next while others move into low pay. Table 7.3 gives the pattern of low pay over the three years 1991–3 for the three different low-pay thresholds, restricting attention for the moment to those who are employees in employment in all three years. Note first of all that the probability of being low paid in 1991 is lower for this group than for the totality of employees in the year (6.1 per cent vs. 7.9 per cent for men and 20.8 per cent vs. 24 per cent for women under the lowest threshold). This reflects the higher movement out of employment among the low-paid group. Table 7.4 gives the corresponding pattern of low pay over the four years 1991–4. A disadvantage to focusing on Table 7.4 alone is that the cell sizes get rather

Table 7.3   *Patterns of low pay over the three waves (%)*

	Male			Female		
Threshold	I	II	III	I	II	III
LLL	2.0	4.6	10.6	11.3	23.2	33.3
LLH	0.7	1.4	2.9	2.9	3.0	3.5
LHL	0.8	1.8	2.1	2.2	2.4	2.2
LHH	2.6	3.1	3.2	4.4	4.5	5.0
HLL	1.0	1.0	2.0	2.3	2.7	2.3
HLH	1.0	2.3	2.2	2.4	2.6	1.5
HHL	1.3	3.0	3.5	3.5	4.0	3.3
HHH	90.6	82.8	73.5	71.1	57.6	49.0

Note: L = Low paid (i.e. below the threshold for that column), H = High paid (i.e. above the threshold for that column). First letter gives pay state in year 1, second in year 2 and third in year 3.

small. In addition the overall sample size is further reduced by the require-
ment that individuals are employees in employment in 1994 as well as
1991–3. Note that the probability of being low paid in 1991 is further reduced for this sample (by removing those not employees in 1994): 5.3 per
cent vs. 6.1 per cent for men and 19.8 per cent vs. 20.8 per cent for women
under the lowest threshold.

Looking at the figures for men over the three years 1991–3 first, 2 per
cent are low paid (under the first threshold: half the median) in all three years
compared with 6.1 per cent in the first year, i.e. over two-thirds rise above the
threshold for at least one of the next two years, 43 per cent do for both.
Turning to Table 7.4, 1.2 per cent are below the first threshold in all four
years compared with 5.3 per cent in the first year, i.e. 77 per cent rise above
the threshold for at least one of the next three years; 42 per cent do for all
three years. For the second threshold (half the mean) 70 per cent move out of
low pay for at least one of the next three years and 27 per cent for all. For the
third threshold (two-thirds the median) the corresponding figures are 53 per
cent and 16 per cent. Mobility over the threshold is less the higher the threshold is set: 9 per cent, 18 per cent and 28 per cent of men experience low pay
in at least one of the four years under the three definitions of low pay (compared with 5 per cent, 10 per cent and 18 per cent in the first year).

Table 7.4   Patterns of low pay over the four waves 1991–4 (%)

Threshold	Male			Female		
	I	II	III	I	II	III
LLLL	1.2	3.1	8.4	9.1	19.7	29.4
LLLH	0.6	1.1	1.6	1.6	2.8	3.2
LLHL	0.1	0.2	0.9	0.8	1.0	1.5
LLHH	0.5	0.9	2.0	2.3	2.0	1.9
LHLL	0.6	0.5	0.9	1.0	1.1	1.1
LHLH	0.1	1.1	0.7	1.0	1.1	0.9
LHHL	0.1	0.6	0.4	0.4	0.7	1.2
LHHH	2.2	2.7	2.9	3.8	3.7	3.4
HLLL	0.3	0.4	0.5	1.3	1.8	1.8
HLLH	0.5	0.4	0.7	1.0	0.9	0.7
HLHL	0.1	0.4	0.5	0.8	1.0	0.4
HLHH	0.9	1.9	1.9	1.1	1.5	0.9
HHLL	0.2	1.0	0.7	1.3	2.0	1.2
HHLH	1.1	2.0	3.0	2.3	2.2	2.0
HHHL	0.7	2.1	2.7	2.1	1.8	1.8
HHHH	91.0	81.8	72.3	70.3	56.8	48.5

Note: L = Low paid (i.e. below the threshold for that column), H = High paid (i.e. above the
threshold for that column). First letter gives pay state in year 1, second in year 2, third in year 3
and fourth in year 4.

For women, 11.3 per cent are below the first threshold in all three years 1991–3 compared with 20.8 per cent in the first year, i.e. 46 per cent rise above the threshold for at least one of the next two years, only 21 per cent do so for both. From Table 7.4, 9.1 per cent are below the first threshold in all four years compared with 19.8 per cent in the first year, i.e. over a half rise above the threshold for at least one of the next three years. Only 19 per cent of the women who were low paid in the first year rise above the threshold for all the years. These probabilities are well below those for men. Similar results are found at the other higher two thresholds: only 11.4 per cent of low-paid women in the first year rise above the threshold for all the years, 38.7 per cent of those low paid in the first year rise above the threshold for at least one of the next years. For the third threshold the equivalent figures are 8.0 per cent and 31.2 per cent. 30 per cent, 43 per cent and 52 per cent of women experience low pay in at least one of the four years under the three definitions of low pay (compared with 20 per cent, 32 per cent and 43 per cent in the first year). The probability of moving out of low pay is considerably lower for women than for men.

The above discussion has been in terms of the conditional probabilities of subsequent patterns given that an individual is low paid in the first year. An alternative way of looking at the figures is also informative: conditional probabilities of being low paid at a point in time given various combinations of previous low-pay experience. These are presented in Table 7.5. The table shows the probabilities of an individual being low paid (under each of the three thresholds) in 1992 given that he or she was low paid in 1991 (first column), of being low paid in 1993 given low paid in *both* 1991 and 1992 (second column), and of being low paid in 1994 given low paid in *all* the previous 3 years (third column). The top half of the table estimates these probabilities on the maximum sample for each column. Thus column 1 restricts the sample to those who were employees in 1991 and 1992, column 2 further restricts it to those who were also employees in 1993 and column 3 restricts it to those who were employees in all four years (1991–4). In contrast the lower half of the table takes the restricted sample of those who were employees in all four years (column 3 of the top half of the table) for all three conditional probabilities.

The possibility of sample selection bias is increased in the lower half of the table, since, for example, the probability of being low paid in 1992 conditional upon 1991 low pay is also conditioned upon being an employee in future periods 1993 and 1994. If the probability of being an employee in employment is correlated with past low-pay experience, then a selection bias will result.

Comparing columns in Table 7.5 indicates that the probability of remaining low paid is much higher if both the previous two years have been low paid than just conditional on the most recent year. It is also interesting to note that the difference between them is greater for men than for women. Conditioning additionally on low-pay status three years previously makes much less difference to the probability. Indeed in four of the six cases considered it results in a lower probability. In only two (one for each gender) does the probability of remaining low paid rise further.

Table 7.5   Probabilities of low pay conditional upon previous low-pay experience

(a) Maximum sample each column				
	Threshold	P(lp92 l lp91)	P(lp93 l lp92 & lp91)	P(lp94 l lp93 & lp92 & lp91)
Men	1	0.42	0.74	0.68
	2	0.56	0.77	0.73
	3	0.71	0.79	0.84
Women	1	0.69	0.79	0.85
	2	0.79	0.89	0.88
	3	0.84	0.91	0.90
(b) Sample is the four wave panel of employees (column 3 above)				
	Threshold	P(lp92 l lp91)	P(lp93 l lp92 & lp91)	P(lp94 l lp93 & lp92 & lp91)
Men	1	0.44	0.76	0.68
	2	0.52	0.79	0.73
	3	0.73	0.77	0.84
Women	1	0.69	0.78	0.85
	2	0.79	0.88	0.88
	3	0.84	0.91	0.90

Note: Probabilities above based on unrounded figures.

The discussion thus far in this section has been based on statistics restricted to those who are employees in employment in each year. Transitions are also made into and out of this employees-in-employment group. The issue is further complicated by missing data and non-interview. If we want to distinguish self-employment from non-employment and between more than one non-employment state, the equivalent of Table 7.4 rapidly becomes unmanageable.

One simple approach is to extend Table 7.3 to just three categories. This is done in Table 7.6 where the transitions between low-paid employee, higher-paid employee and non-employee (covering all non-working and self-employed states) are shown for the three-year period 1991–3.[6]

Table 7.6   *Patterns of low pay and employee-employment over three waves*

	Male			Female		
Threshold	I	II	III	I	II	III
LLL	1.1	2.5	5.6	5.7	11.7	16.8
LLH	0.4	0.7	1.5	1.5	1.5	1.7
LLN	0.1	0.4	0.8	0.8	1.4	1.8
LHL	0.4	0.9	1.1	1.1	1.2	1.1
LHH	1.4	1.7	1.7	2.2	2.3	2.5
LHN	0.3	0.4	0.4	0.3	0.2	0.2
LNL	0.2	0.3	0.4	0.4	0.6	0.8
LNH	0.2	0.2	0.3	0.2	0.2	0.1
LNN	0.5	1.0	1.3	2.2	2.9	3.3
HLL	0.5	0.5	1.1	1.2	1.4	1.2
HLH	0.6	1.2	1.2	1.2	1.3	0.7
HLN	0.2	0.2	0.3	0.4	0.1	0.0
HHL	0.7	1.6	1.9	1.7	2.0	1.7
HHH	47.7	43.6	38.7	35.9	29.1	24.7
HHN	4.0	3.7	3.2	2.2	1.9	1.6
HNL	0.1	0.3	0.3	0.3	0.3	0.3
HNH	1.1	0.8	0.7	0.7	0.5	0.4
HNN	3.7	3.2	2.9	2.8	2.1	1.6
NLL	0.3	0.8	1.0	1.3	2.0	2.3
NLH	0.1	0.3	0.4	0.3	0.2	0.3
NLN	0.2	0.2	0.3	0.7	1.0	1.2
NHL	0.3	0.3	0.2	0.5	0.3	0.2
NHH	2.2	1.7	1.4	1.7	1.3	0.9
NHN	0.4	0.4	0.3	0.7	0.4	0.2
NNL	0.6	1.0	1.1	2.3	2.6	3.0
NNH	1.7	1.3	1.2	1.6	1.3	0.9
NNN	31.1	31.1	31.1	30.4	30.4	30.4

Note: L = Low paid (i.e. below the threshold for that column), H = High paid (i.e. above the threshold for that column), N = Not an employee in employment. First letter gives status in year 1, second in year 2 and third in year 3.

A second approach to incorporating non-employees is used in Table 7.7, which presents year *t* status by that in year *t*–1 (pooling *t* over 1992 to 1994) using six status categories (low paid, higher paid, employee but with missing earnings information, self-employed, unemployed, out of the labour force). Tabulations are given for each of the three low-pay thresholds and separately for men and women. The transitions are pooled so as to increase cell sizes for the analysis, but a comparison with the individual year transitions shows the results to be fairly stable over time. Those not interviewed or with unknown employment status are assumed to be missing at random and excluded.

Table 7.7   Mobility between labour market states t to t–1

Male: 1st low-paid threshold	Destination (*t*) State probabilities (%)					
Initial (*t*-1) state	Distr. *t*-1	1	2	3	4	5	6
1 low-paid	4.2	38.0	37.2	8.5	3.6	7.2	5.4
2 Higher Paid	51.9	2.0	84.2	6.6	2.2	2.7	2.3
3 Employee (missing earnings)	9.7	2.8	32.8	53.2	2.8	5.0	3.4
4 Self-employed	15.2	0.5	4.3	2.4	86.0	3.6	3.2
5 Unemployed	7.6	6.0	19.5	5.3	8.3	45.2	15.6
6 Out of the labour force	11.4	2.5	4.6	2.2	2.5	9.3	78.9
All	*100.0*	*3.7*	*51.1*	*10.0*	*15.6*	*7.3*	*12.4*
Male: 2nd low-paid threshold	Destination (*t*) State probabilities (%)					
Initial (*t*-1) state	Distr. *t*-1	1	2	3	4	5	6
1 low-paid	7.6	45.5	31.7	7.8	3.3	6.9	4.9
2 Higher Paid	48.5	4.0	82.6	6.6	2.1	2.5	2.2
3 Employee (missing earnings)	9.7	5.6	30.0	53.2	2.8	5.0	3.4
4 Self-employed	15.2	1.2	3.7	2.4	86.0	3.6	3.2
5 Unemployed	7.6	10.9	14.6	5.3	8.3	45.2	15.6
6 Out of the labour force	11.4	3.7	3.5	2.2	2.5	9.3	78.9
All	*100.0*	*7.4*	*47.5*	*10.0*	*15.6*	*7.3*	*12.4*
Male: 3rd low-paid threshold	Destination (*t*) State probabilities (%)					
Initial (*t*-1) state	Distr. *t*-1	1	2	3	4	5	6
1 low-paid	12.2	55.9	23.5	7.5	3.1	5.9	4.0
2 Higher Paid	43.9	5.6	81.4	6.6	2.0	2.3	2.1
3 Employee (missing earnings)	9.7	8.5	27.2	53.2	2.8	5.0	3.4
4 Self-employed	15.2	1.3	3.5	2.4	86.0	3.6	3.2
5 Unemployed	7.6	13.6	11.9	5.3	8.3	45.2	15.6
6 Out of the labour force	11.4	4.1	3.0	2.2	2.5	9.3	78.9
All	*100.0*	*11.8*	*43.0*	*10.0*	*15.6*	*7.3*	*12.4*
Female: 1st low-paid threshold	Destination (*t*) State probabilities (%)					
Initial (*t*-1) state	Distr. *t*-1	1	2	3	4	5	6
1 low-paid	13.2	54.7	23.0	5.6	2.1	3.5	11.2
2 Higher Paid	43.9	6.2	81.2	6.3	0.7	1.6	4.0
3 Employee (missing earnings)	6.9	10.5	41.4	34.8	2.5	2.5	8.5
4 Self-employed	5.0	3.8	7.8	3.6	72.6	2.5	9.7
5 Unemployed	4.9	16.2	18.1	4.7	2.2	26.5	32.3
6 Out of the labour force	26.0	5.1	5.1	1.9	2.0	6.7	79.2
All	*100.0*	*13.0*	*44.1*	*6.8*	*5.0*	*4.5*	*26.5*
Female: 2nd low-paid threshold	Destination (*t*) State probabilities (%)					
Initial (*t*-1) state	Distr. *t*-1	1	2	3	4	5	6
1 low-paid	20.7	64.3	16.0	5.9	1.6	2.9	9.2
2 Higher Paid	36.4	7.3	80.5	6.3	0.7	1.6	3.7
3 Employee (missing earnings)	6.9	17.2	34.6	34.8	2.5	2.5	8.5
4 Self-employed	5.0	5.3	6.3	3.6	72.6	2.5	9.7
5 Unemployed	4.9	23.3	11.0	4.7	2.2	26.5	32.3
6 Out of the labour force	26.0	6.6	3.6	1.9	2.0	6.7	79.2
All	*100.0*	*20.3*	*36.8*	*6.8*	*5.0*	*4.5*	*26.5*
Female: 3rd low-paid threshold	Destination (*t*) State probabilities (%)					
Initial (*t*-1) state	Distr. *t*-1	1	2	3	4	5	6
1 low-paid	26.4	68.9	12.2	6.1	1.4	2.9	8.6
2 Higher Paid	30.7	7.7	80.9	6.2	0.7	1.3	3.2
3 Employee (missing earnings)	6.9	23.7	28.2	34.8	2.5	2.5	8.5
4 Self-employed	5.0	6.3	5.3	3.6	72.6	2.5	9.7
5 Unemployed	4.9	26.5	7.8	4.7	2.2	26.5	32.3
6 Out of the labour force	26.0	7.5	2.7	1.9	2.0	6.7	79.2
All	*100.0*	*25.8*	*31.3*	*6.8*	*5.0*	*4.5*	*26.5*

A number of interesting features can be derived from Table 7.6. First, among men who are employees in the first two periods, the probability of no longer being an employee in the third period is greater if at least one of the periods was low paid (11–12 per cent according to threshold) than if both periods were higher paid (7–8 per cent). Second, men entering the distribution in period 2 from not being an employee in period 1 are roughly three times as likely to be low paid as those already employees in period 1 (0.17, 0.35, 0.47 for the three thresholds vs. 0.05, 0.10, 0.18). Third, men who move from not being an employee in 1992 to employment in 1993 are much more likely to be low paid in 1993 if they had been low paid in 1991 (0.55, 0.59, 0.63 for the 3 thresholds) than if they had been higher paid in 1991 (0.11, 0.23, 0.27). They are also more likely to be so than those who had been in other labour market states in 1991. The low paid are, therefore, both more likely to move out of employment and more likely to be low paid when they move back into employment (even relative to other entrants, who themselves have a higher probability of being low paid than those already in employment). There is thus evidence of a cycle of low pay and no pay.

Turning to Table 7.7 and looking first at the results for men and using the lowest threshold, almost a quarter of those low paid in year $t-1$ are excluded from the earnings distribution in year t. In some cases this is the result of missing earnings information (with employment status known). Assuming again that these are missing at random, the implied year t distribution can be calculated. Of those low paid in year $t-1$, 16.2 per cent are self-employed, unemployed or out of the labour force in year t, 42.3 per cent are still low paid in year t and the rest have moved up the distribution. Thus almost three-fifths do not move up the earnings distribution from low pay in year t, when those who are not employees in employment are also included in the transition analysis. Of higher-paid employees in year $t-1$, only 7.2 per cent are self-employed, unemployed or out of the labour force in year t, only 2.2 per cent have become low paid and over 90 per cent are still above the low-pay threshold.

Those unemployed or out of the labour force in year $t-1$ who enter at t are more likely to be low paid than average. Of those unemployed in year $t-1$ who become employees in year t, 23.5 per cent become low paid, compared with 5.7 per cent of those who were employees at $t-1$. Of those out of the labour force in year $t-1$, who become employees at t, 35.2 per cent become low paid. This reinforces the point made above based on Table 7.6.

Turning to the second threshold, 15.1 per cent of those low paid in year $t-1$ are self-employed, unemployed or out of the labour force in year t, 50.1 per cent are still low paid and 34.9 per cent have moved up the distribution. Thus almost two-thirds do not move up the earnings distribution from low pay. In the case of the third threshold, 13 per cent of those low paid at $t-1$ are self-employed, unemployed or out of the labour force at t, 61.2 per cent are still low paid and just over one-quarter have moved up the distribution. Thus nearly three-quarters of those below the third threshold at t–1 do not move up the earnings distribution from low pay at t.

For women and using the first low-pay threshold, of those low paid in year t–1, 16.8 per cent are self-employed, unemployed or out of the labour market at t and 58.6 per cent are still low paid, so that 75 per cent do not move up over the threshold. For the second threshold 83 per cent of low-paid workers at t–1 do not move up over the threshold in year t and for the third threshold 87 per cent do not move up from low pay at t–1 over the threshold at t.

Table 7.5 gives the probability of not moving up above the threshold in 1992 from low pay, which is 42 per cent, 56 per cent and 71 per cent for men in respect to each of the three thresholds, ignoring those no longer employees. The equivalent of Table 7.7 restricted to 1991–2 transitions gives corresponding figures of 54 per cent, 64 per cent and 75 per cent from the inclusion of the non-employees. Thus the exclusion of non-employees from the transition probabilities understates this probability by 12 percentage points in the case of the lowest threshold, 8 for the second threshold and 4 for the third threshold. In the case of women excluding those who become non-employees leads to underestimates of 7, 4 and 3 percentage points for the three thresholds respectively.

The above analysis suggests considerable *state dependence* in aggregate low-pay transition probabilities. However this does not necessarily imply that there is state dependence in individual transition probabilities (Heckman 1981b). The aggregate finding could be the result of *heterogeneity*, where certain individual characteristics increase the probability of an individual being low paid. This would create the appearance of state dependence in the aggregate transition probabilities (assuming some of the relevant characteristics exhibit persistence over time) even in its absence in individual transition probabilities. In addition there may be 'true' state dependence for individuals: low-paid status in one period may in itself increase the probability of being low paid in the next period relative to another individual with identical characteristics but not low paid in the first period. Distinguishing between state dependence and omitted heterogeneity is not straightforward. The next section presents models of low-pay transition probabilities allowing for both heterogeneity and true state dependence.

Prior to this modelling, Table 7.8 presents a simple investigation of the heterogeneity in these transition probabilities with respect to age and education. Estimates of three conditional probabilities are given based on the pooled sample. For men, the probability of an individual who is low paid in year t–1 not being low paid in year t is lower for those aged 18–20 than for those in the two older age groups, at the two higher thresholds and in both the employees only and employees and non-employees analysis. In the case of women the result holds only for the highest threshold. For women, those with a full-time education leaving age of 17 or more have a higher probability of moving up the distribution than those who left aged 16. For men this only holds for the lowest threshold.

Table 7.8   Transition probabilities

(a) Employees only: P(not low paid t I low paid t−1)						
	Men			Women		
Thresholds:	I	II	III	I	II	III
All	*0.49*	*0.41*	*0.30*	*0.30*	*0.20*	*0.15*
Age 18–20	0.47	0.30	0.17	0.34	0.20	0.08
21–40	0.54	0.44	0.32	0.32	0.22	0.18
Over 40	0.43	0.47	0.34	0.26	0.18	0.13
ELA under 16	0.46	0.41	0.30	0.27	0.16	0.11
ELA over 16	0.57	0.42	0.29	0.35	0.28	0.21

(b) Employees only: P(low paid t I not low paid t−1)						
	Men			Women		
Thresholds:	I	II	III	I	II	III
All	*0.02*	*0.05*	*0.06*	*0.07*	*0.08*	*0.09*
Age 18–20	0.14	0.18	0.24	0.16	0.20	0.14
21–40	0.02	0.04	0.06	0.06	0.07	0.08
Over 40	0.02	0.05	0.06	0.08	0.10	0.10
ELA under 16	0.03	0.07	0.10	0.11	0.13	0.15
ELA over 16	0.01	0.02	0.04	0.04	0.05	0.05

(c) All, include. non-employees: P(moved up t I low paid t−1)						
	Men			Women		
Thresholds:	I	II	III	I	II	III
All	*0.41*	*0.34*	*0.25*	*0.24*	*0.17*	*0.13*
Age 18–20	0.37	0.24	0.13	0.27	0.16	0.07
21–40	0.46	0.38	0.28	0.25	0.18	0.15
Over 40	0.35	0.39	0.31	0.23	0.16	0.12
ELA under 16	0.39	0.35	0.26	0.23	0.14	0.10
ELA over 16	0.43	0.34	0.24	0.27	0.23	0.18

Note: ELA denotes age when left full-time education.

Table 7.8 also shows that the probability of not being low paid in year *t* conditional upon being low paid in year *t−1* is higher for all groups (age and education) when attention is restricted to employees than when non-employees in year *t* are included. Restricting attention to employees only in all periods when analysing low-pay transitions results in overestimation of transition probabilities out of low pay. However since this is true for all age and education groups, the influence on estimated probability differentials between these groups will be lessened.

Finally the probability of those above the threshold in year $t-1$ being low paid in year t is higher for those aged 18–20 than for both the older age groups, for both men and women. It is also higher for those who left school at 16 or below than for those who left aged 17 or more, again for both men and women.

4 INDIVIDUAL LOW-PAY MOBILITY PROBABILITIES

This section focuses on transitions out of low pay and the factors that influence them. The model used is described more fully in Stewart and Swaffield (1997b). It restricts the autocorrelation in the disturbances (and hence unobservables) to be first order and approaches the initial conditions problem as one of endogenous sample selection. This is a more difficult problem to deal with in the discrete dependent variable case than in the linear regression case. The addition to the model of the usual selectivity correction term based on the Mills' ratio will not give consistent estimates in this case (O'Higgins 1994). Instead it must be addressed directly in terms of the joint distribution.

The model used here is a bivariate probit model with selectivity of the type used by Van de Ven and van Praag (1981) and described as case 3 in the Meng and Schmidt (1985) catalogue of bivariate models with partial observability. The *conditional probability* of being low paid in year 2 given low paid in year 1 in such a model is given by

$$P[y_{i2} = 1 \mid y_{i1} = 1] = \Phi_2(x_{i1}'\beta, z_{i2}'\gamma; \rho) / \Phi(x_{i1}'\beta) \qquad (7.1)$$

where y_{it} is an indicator variable taking the value one if individual i is low paid (i.e. has hourly earnings below the cut-off) in year t and the value zero if not, x_{i1} is a vector of earnings-determining characteristics in year 1, z_{i2} is a vector of factors that influence the probability that $y_{i2} = 1$ if $y_{i1} = 1$, Φ is the univariate standard normal cumulative distribution function and Φ_2 is the cumulative distribution function of the bivariate standard normal.[7]

In the special case where $\rho = 0$, this simplifies to

$$P[y_{i2} = 1 \mid y_{i1} = 1] = \Phi(z_{i2}'\gamma) \qquad (7.2)$$

In this case the conditional probability of remaining low paid can be modelled by a simple probit model, i.e. γ can be estimated using a probit for y_{i2} over the sample with $y_{i1} = 1$. An obvious problem with this restricted version of the model is that it takes the initial low-pay state (that in year 1) to be exogenous.[8] This requires the observed persistence in low pay to be entirely due to observed explanatory variables. Correlation across time between the unobservables $(\rho \neq 0)$ will generate a sample selection bias as a result of conditioning on being low paid in year 1.

If ρ is non-zero the more general bivariate probit with selectivity is required and identification restrictions are needed to make the model credible. The extra variables in x_1 not in z_2 can be viewed as instruments for the selection probability into the initial state. The main instruments used here for this endogenous selection are parental variables indicating the socio-economic group of the respondent's parents when the respondent was 14. These variables were found to have a significant effect on the probability of being low paid. The assumption being made here is that these variables do not, however, affect the probability of being low paid given the state in the previous period: they affect the level of the low-pay status variable, but not the change. These variables provide the primary *a priori* identification, but in addition some of the variables found to influence the probability of being low paid are found not to be significant influences on this probability given the state in the previous period and are excluded from z.

Table 7.9 reports the results from estimating the bivariate probit model with endogenous selection using the pooled BHPS sample ($t = 1992–4$). The univariate probit coefficients that result from imposing $\rho = 0$ are given for

Table 7.9   *Bivariate probit models with endogenous selection for the probability of being low paid in year t given low paid in t–1*

Threshold:	I	t-ratio	I	t-ratio	II	t-ratio	II	t-ratio	III	t-ratio	III	t-ratio
Age completed f-t education	-0.08	3.65	-0.01	0.47	-0.10	6.23	-0.05	2.06	-0.08	5.62	-0.01	0.66
Experience/10	0.06	1.53	0.11	2.67	-0.04	1.20	0.01	0.23	-0.05	1.58	0.01	0.33
Training in the last 12 months	-0.24	2.42	-0.10	0.92	-0.29	3.80	-0.16	1.89	-0.39	5.93	-0.22	2.89
Plant with 25+ employees	-0.21	2.42	-0.04	0.34	-0.32	4.59	-0.20	2.46	-0.31	4.86	-0.17	2.40
Union at workplace	-0.60	6.22	-0.33	2.53	-0.31	4.37	-0.16	1.92	-0.30	4.83	-0.15	2.24
Married	-0.13	1.38	-0.03	0.32	-0.05	0.67	0.02	0.27	-0.23	3.18	-0.12	1.60
Female	0.58	5.82	0.27	1.89	0.70	9.33	0.44	3.93	0.61	9.77	0.35	4.03
rho	0		-0.487		0		-0.417		0		-0.508	
s.e. (rho)	0.148				0.125				0.108			
Sample size	1 100		8 260		1 852		8 260		2 592		8 260	

Notes:
a. Sample restricted to employees in employment in both years.
b. ML coefficient estimates reported.
c. *t*-ratio = absolute asymptotic *t*-ratio.
d. Pooled BHPS data for t = 1992 to 1994.

comparative purposes. Comparison of the coefficients from the two models for a given threshold illustrates the bias from ignoring the endogenous selection.

For all thresholds, the restriction that $\rho = 0$ is strongly rejected. Comparison of the two columns for a given threshold shows that the magnitudes and significance of the explanatory variables are sensitive to the imposition of the restriction $\rho = 0$. Typically the estimated coefficients and their t-ratios are much reduced in the bivariate probit model with endogenous selection, i.e. imposition of $\rho = 0$ inflates the estimates (the experience coefficients are an exception to this). For example, age when left completed full-time education has a strong negative and highly significant effect in the $\rho = 0$ model. Its coefficient is −0.08 for thresholds 1 and 3 and −0.10 for threshold 2. In the model with endogenous selection, its coefficient is −0.01 (and insignificant) for thresholds 1 and 3 and −0.05 (and only marginally significant) for threshold 2. Imposing $\rho = 0$ (i.e. ignoring the endogenous selection) considerably distorts the estimated effects.

As seen above, the low paid were more likely to be out of employment in the next period than those higher up the earnings distribution. A simple examination of the sensitivity of the transition model results presented in Table 7.9 to this is provided by looking at the probability of being low paid or not an employee (i.e. of not moving up the earnings distribution and over the threshold) at t given low paid at $t-1$.[9] Results for these probabilities are presented in Table 7.10. For all the thresholds $\rho = 0$ is again strongly rejected.

Table 7.10   *Bivariate probit models with endogenous selection for the probability of being low paid or not an employee in year t given low paid in year t−1*

Threshold:	I	t-ratio	I	t-ratio	II	t-ratio	II	t-ratio	III	t-ratio	III	t-ratio
Age completed f-t education	-0.05	2.70	0.01	0.48	-0.09	5.79	-0.03	1.51	-0.07	5.47	-0.01	0.33
Experience/10	0.03	0.86	0.08	2.29	-0.05	1.60	0.01	0.16	-0.06	2.19	0.00	0.10
Training in the last 12 months	-0.28	3.04	-0.11	1.13	-0.32	4.42	-0.17	2.07	-0.42	6.52	-0.22	3.10
Plant with 25+ employees	-0.20	2.48	-0.01	0.08	-0.33	4.89	-0.18	2.46	-0.32	5.22	-0.17	2.63
Union at workplace	-0.54	6.06	-0.25	2.24	-0.32	4.73	-0.15	1.93	-0.31	5.23	-0.15	2.41
Married	-0.15	1.68	-0.03	0.31	-0.09	1.24	0.00	0.03	-0.25	3.61	-0.13	1.81
Female	0.50	5.58	0.18	1.44	0.63	8.94	0.35	3.48	0.58	9.67	0.31	3.85
rho	0		-0.537		0		-0.470		0		-0.537	
s.e. (rho)	0.126				0.112				0.100			
Sample size	1328		9038		2169		9038		2993		9038	

Note: See notes in Table 7.9.

5 CONCLUSIONS

This chapter provides an analysis of transitions into and out of low pay with particular focus on endogenous sample selection. The data used are from the first four waves of the British Household Panel Survey, 1991–4. The main findings of the chapter are as follows.

There is considerable persistence in low pay, particularly among those who have already been low paid for more than one period. Of those low paid in 1991, 1992 and 1993 over two-thirds are also low paid in 1994. However there is also much mobility out of low pay, particularly among those who have only recently moved from higher to low paid. Of those higher paid in 1991 and low paid in 1992, about half move back to being higher paid in 1993 (roughly double the chance of those also low paid in 1991). Roughly one and two-thirds times as many people experience low pay in at least one of the four years 1991–4 as are low paid in the first year.

It is important to note that those who are low paid are also more likely to make transitions into other non-employee states than those from higher up the earnings distribution and hence that restricting attention to those who are employees results in an overstatement of the probability of the low paid moving up the earnings distribution. However the impact of this on estimated effects of explanatory variables on this probability is found to be minor.

The low paid are more likely to move into non-employment; those entering employment from a spell outside are more likely to be low paid; and those who had prior to the spell outside been low paid are even more likely to be low paid again when they subsequently move back into employment than other entrants. There is thus evidence of a cycle of low pay and no pay.

The chance of moving back to low pay of those who were initially low paid, but moved up, declines with the length of time higher paid. Of those who move from low paid in 1991 to higher paid in 1992, about a third move back to low pay in 1993. Of those who moved from low pay to higher in 1992 and remained higher paid in 1993, only around one in six moved back to low pay in 1994.

This dependence of the probability of being low paid on past low pay experience may result either from heterogeneity among individuals or from the impact of the experience of low pay itself. It is therefore important to look at *ceteris paribus* effects. Other things equal, the probability of moving up the distribution and out of low pay is higher for those with more education, those with recent training, those in larger establishments and those covered by a union. It is considerably lower for women than for men.

Satisfactory modelling of the transition probabilities into and out of low pay is not straightforward. The question of endogenous sample selection is important and needs to be addressed in the modelling of transition probabilities. The empirical evidence in this chapter indicates that ignoring the endogenous selection of conditioning on the initial low-pay state distorts the estimated coefficients. Typically the estimated coefficients (and their asymptotic *t*-ratios) are much reduced (in absolute value) when allowance is made for endogenous selection. However certain factors such as training, plant size, union coverage and gender retain their significant influence on the probability of remaining low paid (particularly for higher thresholds).

NOTES

1   We thank the ESRC for financial support (under grant R000236125). The BHPS data used in this chapter were collected by the ESRC Research Centre on Micro-social Change at the University of Essex and made available through the ESRC Data Archive. Neither bear any responsibility for the analyses or interpretations presented here. We thank Wiji Arulampalam, Alison Booth and participants at the Bordeaux conference for their comments on the paper on which this chapter is based.
2   Gregg and Machin (1994) provide evidence for the UK and Levy and Murnane (1992) for the USA.
3   Evidence on earnings mobility is surveyed by Atkinson et al. (1992).
4   See Gregory and Elias (1994) and Stewart and Swaffield (1997b) for discussion of this undersampling of those on low pay.
5   Throughout this chapter, low pay in the BHPS is defined in terms of average hourly earnings, i.e. weekly earnings divided by total paid (including overtime) hours.
6   Those with missing earnings and/or hours data and those in non-interview groups are excluded.
7   This approach to handling the endogeneity of the initial state is similar to that of Bingley et al..(1995). The model here is simpler than theirs in that *y* is dichotomous and more general in that separate *γ*-vectors are allowed for those initially low and higher paid.
8   This is the assumption implicitly made, for example, by Sloane and Theodossiou (1996) in their model.
9   There are obviously some problems of interpretation with this approach. Proper treatment of the non-employees requires the use of a trivariate distribution. Sloane and Theodossiou's (1996) use of a multinomial logit model (as well as ignoring the initial endogenous selection problem) requires the 'independence of irrelevant alternatives' assumption to hold, which seems unlikely in the current context.

REFERENCES

Atkinson, A.B., F. Bourguignon and C. Morrisson (1992), *Empirical Studies of Earnings Mobility*, Reading: Harwood.
Bingley, P., N.H. Bjørn and N. Westergård-Nielsen (1995), 'Wage mobility in Denmark 1980–1990', Aarhus: CLS Working Paper 95–10.
Child Poverty Action Group (1995), 'Wages – Drawing the bottom line', *Poverty,* **90**, pp. 15–18.
Gregg, P. and S. Machin (1994), 'Is the UK rise in inequality different?' in R. Barrell (ed.) *The UK Labour Market*, London: NIESR.

Gregory, M. and P. Elias (1994), 'Earnings transitions of the low paid in Britain, 1976–91: A longitudinal study', *International Journal of Manpower*, **15**, pp. 170–88.

Heckman, J.J. (1981a), 'The incidental parameters problem and the problem of initial conditions in estimating a discrete time-discrete data stochastic process', in C.F. Manski and D. McFadden (eds), *Structural Analysis of Discrete Data with Econometric Applications*, Cambridge: MIT Press.

Heckman, J.J. (1981b), 'Heterogeneity and state dependence', in S. Rosen (ed.), *Studies in Labor Markets*, Chicago: Chicago University Press.

Levy, F. and R. Murnane (1992), 'US earnings levels and earnings inequalities: A review of recent trends and proposed explanations', *Journal of Economic Literature*, **30**, pp. 1338–81.

Low Pay Unit (1996), *The New Review*, **37**(5), January/February.

Meng, C-L. and P. Schmidt (1985), 'On the cost of partial observability in the bivariate probit model', *International Economic Review*, **26**, pp. 71–85.

O'Higgins, N. (1994), 'YTS, employment and sample selection bias', *Oxford Economic Papers*, **46**, pp. 605–28.

Sloane, P.J. and I. Theodossiou (1996), 'Earnings mobility, family income and low pay', *Economic Journal*, **106**, pp. 657–66.

Stewart, M. and J. Swaffield (1997a), 'The dynamics of low pay in Britain', in P. Gregg (ed.), *Jobs, Wages and Poverty: Patterns of Persistence and Mobility in the Flexible Labour Market*, London: CEP.

Stewart, M. and J. Swaffield (1997b), *Low pay dynamics and transition probabilities*, University of Warwick: mimeo, July.

Trades Union Congress (1995), *Arguments for a minimum wage*.

Van de Ven, P. and B. van Praag (1981), 'The demand for deductibles in private health insurance: A probit model with sample selection', *Journal of Econometrics*, **17**, pp. 229–52.

PART THREE

Low-Paid Employment: Some Further
Perspectives

8. Low Pay, A Matter of Occupation [1]

M. Arai, R. Asplund and E. Barth

1 INTRODUCTION

Low-wage employment has received a lot of attention over the past few years. This can be seen as the outcome of two interrelated trends. One is the increase in wage dispersion in a majority of OECD countries in the late 1980s (OECD 1993). As a consequence, the focus has increasingly turned to the labour market situation of people in low-paid jobs. The other is the gain in employment in the USA relative to most European countries, which has spurred discussions about the need for downward flexibility in wages to create employment opportunities at the lowest end of the wage scale.

In a recent *Employment Outlook* (OECD 1996) providing an international comparison of earnings inequality, low-paid employment and earnings mobility, it is concluded that low-paid jobs tend to be concentrated among the same kind of workers virtually everywhere, albeit different institutional settings do seem to account for some of the variation across countries in the overall incidence of low pay. In particular, the low-wage earners are noted to be concentrated in certain occupational categories, within certain industries and to a higher degree among women and the young. Furthermore, little evidence is found in support of the hypothesis that countries where low pay is less prevalent have to pay a cost in the form of higher unemployment rates or lower employment rates among the more vulnerable groups. The Nordic countries are reported to have a low incidence of low-wage employment compared to other OECD countries.

In assessing these OECD findings it should, however, be kept in mind that the Nordic countries are characterized by a comparatively compressed wage structure (e.g. Asplund et al. 1996), especially when it comes to interindustry wage differentials (Albæk et al. 1996, Zweimüller and Barth 1994). Accordingly also the meaning of low pay varies substantially across OECD countries. This is also evident from Table 8.1 which reports for selected

OECD countries the ratio of, respectively, the upper limit of the lowest wage decile (D1) to the median wage (D5) and the upper limit of the second highest decile (D9) to D1.

Table 8.1   *Wage dispersion in selected OECD countries*

Country	D1/D5	D9/D1
Finland (1993)	0.69	2.49
Norway (1991)	0.70	2.13
Sweden (1991)	0.77	1.94
Australia (1990)	0.70	2.23
Austria (1990)	0.51	3.53
Belgium (1990)	0.70	2.30
Canada (1990)	0.42	4.40
Denmark (1990)	0.73	2.15
France (1990)	0.65	3.02
Germany (1990)	0.67	2.45
Portugal (1990)	0.71	2.63
UK (1990, males)	0.61	3.21
USA (1989)	0.40	5.55

Source: OECD Employment Outlook (1993, Table 5.2).
Own calculations for Finland, Norway and Sweden.

The present chapter explores in more detail the link between low-wage employment and occupational attainment in three Nordic countries, viz. Finland, Norway and Sweden. The analysis is throughout based on 25 occupational categories which have, in all three countries, been constructed by aggregating three-digit occupations. A brief descriptive analysis of the 25 occupational categories reveals a high degree of similarity across countries in the distribution of occupational categories into high-pay and low-pay occupations.

The next question to address is whether the observed wage differentials across occupations survive also after accounting for occupation-specific differences in human capital endowments and industry dominance. One reason for expecting occupational wage differentials to remain, even after controlling for human capital and industry, is the presence of compensating wage differentials. Several hypotheses can, however, be put forth as to why the wage gap between occupations may, in effect, turn out to be either larger or smaller than the required compensating wage differential. Mobility across occupations might be constrained by the existence of sunk costs associated with investment in human capital. Credit market imperfections as well as imperfect foresight about future demand shifts for various qualifications may affect the occupational choice of the young. These occupational decisions are likely to be further influenced by the fact that in most countries formal education is provided under various rationing schemes. Finally, labour market institutions are reflected also in cross-occupational wage differentials, indicating that in countries with a high degree of unionization and centralized wage bargaining, like in the Nordic countries, only part of the observed wage differentials across occupations can be expected to be explained by individual and job-related background characteristics.

The chapter thereafter proceeds to the main part of the analysis, i.e. the wage structure or, actually, the age-wage profile of the occupational categories identified as low-pay occupations. It is, by now, a stylized fact that secondary labour markets are characterized by low wages and low returns to investments in human capital, indicating that the low-pay occupation easily becomes a 'trap' for those being in the occupation. A steep age-wage profile, in contrast, would suggest that the low wage level is most probably a transitory phenomenon, i.e. the occupation offers possibilities for the individual's relative wage position to be improved also if staying in the occupation.

An individual's occupational attainment, however, is not necessarily determined exogenously. People make occupational choices, and schools and employers make decisions about admission. The last part of the chapter compares the wage structure of low-pay and high-pay occupations after allowing for potential selectivity effects. The concluding part of the chapter discusses potential implications of the reported results.

2 THE DATA

The data sets used in the analysis are representative samples of the underlying population. The data for Finland come from the Labour Force Survey conducted by Statistics Finland. Data from two survey years are used, viz. 1989 and 1993. The data for Norway cover the years 1987 and 1991 and come from the Level of Living Survey conducted by Statistics Norway. Level of Living Survey data are also used for Sweden. The data, which cover the years 1981 and 1991, are collected by the Institute for Social Research at Stockholm University.

Most information in the country-specific samples derives from interviews with a fairly large number of respondents. The estimating data for Finland contain about 4 200 individuals for 1989 and some 2 500 individuals for 1993. The number of observations used in the analysis for Norway amounts to almost 2 200 for 1987 and close to 2 000 for 1991. The Swedish data cover nearly 3 300 individuals in both years investigated.

3 ARE THERE TYPICAL LOW-PAY OCCUPATIONS?

The subsequent analysis of low pay and occupational attainment in Finland, Norway and Sweden is based on a total of 25 occupational categories constructed from the *Nordic Classification of Occupations* (NYK). Classifying, for each country, the large number of three-digit occupational codes according to NYK guarantees a high comparability of occupational categories across the three countries, while simultaneously keeping the occupational disaggregation at a reasonable level.

Table 8.2   *Occupational position relative to the median occupational category*

OCCUPATIONAL CATEGORY	FINLAND ('93)	NORWAY ('91)	SWEDEN ('91)
0. Technical engineers and other technical professionals	A	A	A
1. Other professionals including physicians	A	A	A
2. Qualified nursing work	M	A	A
3. Unskilled health and day care work	**B**	**B**	**B**
4. Pedagogical work	A	A	A
5. Recreational and social work	**A**	**B**	**B**
6. Managerial work	A	A	A
7. Administrative work	A	A	A
8. Secretarial and clerical work etc.	**B**	**B**	**B**
9. Commercial work excl. shop assistants	A	M	A
10. Shop assistants	**B**	**B**	**B**
11. Agricultural work (employees only)	**B**	**B**	**B**
12. Ship officers, pilots and traffic supervision etc. work	A	A	A
13. Operation work	**B**	**B**	**B**
14. Postal and other messenger work	**A**	**B**	**A**
15. Textile work	**B**	**A**	**B**
16. Metal work	A	A	A
17. Mechanical work	A	A	M
18. Electrical work	A	A	A
19. Building and construction work	**B**	**B**	**A**
20. Printing work	**B**	**A**	**A**
21. Food manufacturing work	**B**	**B**	**B**
22. Chemical processing work	A	A	A
23. Hotel and restaurant work, private service work	**B**	**B**	**B**
24. Cleaning work	**B**	**B**	**B**

Notes: M refers to the median occupational category. A indicates that the average wage level of the occupation lies above the median. Correspondingly B points to an average wage level below the median. Details of the composition of the 25 occupational categories are available from the authors upon request.

For Table 8.2, the 25 occupational categories under study were first ranked according to their average hourly wage level. The median occupational category (denoted by M) was then defined as the occupational category splitting the sample into two equally large employment shares, i.e. with 50 per cent of the employees being in occupations with an average hourly wage above the median (denoted by A) and 50 per cent being in occupations with an average hourly wage below the median (denoted by B). To ease comparison across countries, the occupations were, finally, re-ranked according to their occupational numbering.

The table shows that there is a high degree of similarity across countries when it comes to the distribution of occupational categories above and below the median occupational category. Specifically, in all three countries the average hourly wage level falls below that of the median occupational category for individuals engaged in unskilled health and day care work, secretarial and clerical work, sales work, agricultural work, operation work, food manufacturing work, hotel and restaurant work, private service work and cleaning work.

Recreational and social work shows up as a relatively low-paid occupation in Norway and Sweden but not in Finland, which is mainly to be explained by the relatively favourable labour market position of public-sector employees (see e.g. Asplund 1997). Textile work implies a weak earnings position in Finland and Sweden, but not in Norway. A wage level below the median is also prevalent among individuals engaged in building and construction work, but only in Finland and Norway. The relatively weak labour market position observed for Finland among those engaged in building and construction work as well as printing work is mainly a result of the deep recession that the Finnish economy suddenly plunged into in 1991 and that hit these sectors extremely hard (cf. e.g. Asplund and Vuori 1996).

All in all, then, most of the occupational categories with an average hourly wage level below the median are found to be the same in Finland, Norway and Sweden. Put differently, an occupation identified as a low-pay occupation in one of the countries, most probably shows up as a low-pay occupation also in the other two countries. However this does not necessarily mean that the factual ranking of low-pay occupations according to their average wage level is identical in the three countries (cf. Table 8.3). But it is of interest to note already in this context that the least-paid occupations appear, in the last resort, to be more or less the same in all three countries. We return to this later on.

The next point to establish is whether those occupations identified as low-pay occupations seem to offer job opportunities mainly to the less educated, to young people and/or to women. Table 8.3 lists the 25 occupational categories under study according to their average hourly wage level along with information on the average years of schooling completed by those belonging to each occupational category, the share of individuals younger than 26 years of age and the share of women.

Table 8.3   *Average schooling years and shares of young and female employees by occupation*

FINLAND (1993)					NORWAY (1991)					SWEDEN (1991)				
Occup. categ.	Average hourly wage	Avg. yrs of schooling	Share of age < 26 years	Share of women	Occup. categ.	Average hourly wage	Avg. yrs of schooling	Share of age < 26 years	Share of women	Occup. categ.	Average hourly wage	Avg. yrs of schooling	Share of age < 26 years	Share of women
6	99.2	14.1	3.8	31.4	0	115.6	13.8	0.0	14.4	6	119.2	14.0	0.0	37.9
1	87.9	14.0	6.5	54.5	1	111.0	14.7	14.3	42.9	9	104.3	11.7	12.9	25.8
4	80.8	14.5	4.4	69.2	6	110.0	13.1	1.2	28.7	1	100.8	15.6	2.2	40.4
0	79.6	12.4	1.5	11.0	7	105.6	12.4	4.7	45.9	7	99.3	13.0	13.4	50.0
12	73.2	10.4	15.8	10.5	4	99.3	15.4	6.5	53.2	0	96.1	12.4	4.7	11.7
7	70.2	12.0	5.1	73.4	20	98.5	11.1	6.7	26.7	12	89.4	11.5	8.0	24.0
9	68.8	11.5	2.9	44.6	16	98.0	10.9	17.9	3.6	4	88.2	15.2	6.6	64.9
22	66.6	9.7	7.3	31.7	12	95.7	12.2	0.0	0.0	19	86.1	10.3	25.5	4.3
5	64.3	12.0	4.9	77.5	18	95.5	11.4	13.0	6.5	2	81.6	13.6	8.3	90.0
18	61.9	10.4	9.8	21.3	2	92.7	13.9	2.4	92.9	16	80.4	10.4	18.9	5.6
16	61.6	10.6	6.7	5.3	17	88.5	11.0	13.0	8.7	18	79.4	10.9	16.9	15.5
14	61.3	10.5	12.8	38.3	22	87.5	10.6	17.9	32.1	14	77.9	11.3	18.5	50.4
17	60.8	10.5	14.0	1.1	15	84.9	10.1	7.7	46.2	20	75.8	9.9	7.4	33.3
2	60.5	12.5	4.6	96.9	9	84.2	11.5	12.2	60.6	22	74.3	9.8	14.7	25.0
8	59.2	11.1	5.9	86.3	19	84.0	10.6	24.4	2.6	17	73.5	10.4	22.1	6.4
21	55.5	10.5	9.1	59.1	13	81.9	10.3	26.4	8.3	8	73.3	11.1	12.3	80.8
13	55.0	10.1	13.4	16.3	8	80.4	11.3	10.3	89.7	11	71.9	10.1	21.3	8.5
19	55.0	10.4	15.5	6.4	14	80.2	10.7	11.0	42.5	13	71.8	9.9	20.8	17.5
20	55.0	10.1	9.1	50.0	5	80.1	12.5	18.2	72.7	21	71.4	11.1	18.2	36.4
3	53.8	10.7	10.5	92.4	3	76.2	10.5	18.6	89.5	3	71.2	11.1	19.1	86.6
23	52.5	10.6	12.3	63.1	21	73.7	10.7	21.4	28.6	5	70.3	12.5	10.5	79.5
11	50.9	10.4	23.5	21.6	23	72.0	10.5	26.8	68.2	23	66.6	10.0	22.7	73.7
24	50.7	9.9	9.2	94.7	10	69.4	10.4	37.3	72.2	10	64.4	10.7	35.3	76.5
10	50.5	10.5	14.7	70.7	24	69.3	10.0	21.8	94.9	15	61.6	9.4	19.0	71.4
15	45.3	10.1	10.7	67.9	11	68.4	10.7	27.3	30.3	24	60.2	9.1	18.3	76.1

A more detailed investigation of the average schooling years completed by the employees in each occupational category reveals that the average educational level is, as is also to be expected, fairly high in at least certain high-pay occupations. But the figures also show that the average schooling level in many higher-wage occupational categories falls, in effect, clearly below the highest average schooling levels found among the lower-wage occupational categories. In Finland this holds for nearly half of the higher-pay occupational categories. In Norway and Sweden the corresponding share is over 60 per cent, indicating that less educated individuals can be found in virtually all 25 occupational categories under study. We will explore this phenomenon in more detail in subsequent sections.

According to Table 8.3, the share of young people tends, with only a few exceptions, to be notably higher in lower-paid occupations. In Finland a share of young people exceeding 10 per cent is observed among almost two-thirds of the lower-pay occupations, while in Norway and Sweden all low-pay occupations have a share of young people well above 10 per cent. These differences in the age structure between the high-pay and low-pay occupations offer a potential explanation of the observed wage gap across occupations despite minor differences in average educational levels; the less educated in higher-wage occupations are older people with long work experience.

The average share of women in each occupational category, finally, suggests that women have a notably higher probability than men of being in a lower-paid occupation. For Finland only one out of three higher-pay occupations has a share of women exceeding 50 per cent, while the corresponding relation is two out of three among lower-pay occupations. The share of female-dominated low-pay occupations appears to be approximately the same in Norway and Sweden, whereas female dominance in high-pay occupations is even less frequent than in Finland.

4 OCCUPATIONAL VERSUS INDUSTRIAL WAGE EFFECTS

The preceding section has shown that the average wage level of an occupational category tends to be correlated with, *inter alia*, the average schooling and work experience years as well as the gender of those belonging to the category. Consequently there is the possibility that the observed occupational wage gaps can be explained primarily by these types of wage-inducing factor. Moreover, in view of the considerable attention that has been paid to the existence of inter-industry wage differentials even after having controlled for a broad set of individual and job-related characteristics (e.g. Albæk et al. 1996), it is of interest to compare the relative importance of wage differentials across industries and occupations when standardized in an identical way.

In order to explore whether the individuals' occupational attainment exerts an independent influence on wages, the logarithm of individual hourly wages was regressed on years of schooling, age (and its square), gender, a set of industry dummies and the 25 occupational categories listed in Table 8.2 above. The variable definitions used are identical for the three countries throughout.

Table 8.4 reports two commonly used measures of, respectively, industry and occupational wage dispersion calculated from regression results, i.e. the standard deviation of the parameter estimates of the industry/occupational dummies (SD) and the standard deviation weighted by employment shares (EWSD).[2] First it may be noted that the explanatory power of merely

Table 8.4   Industry and occupational wage dispersion

INDUSTRY WAGE DISPERSION			
SD: Est. with control for:	Industry	Ind., human cap.	Ind., human cap., occup.
Finland (1993)	0.150	0.133	0.109
Norway (1991)	0.142	0.091	0.091
Sweden (1991)	0.122	0.077	0.062
EWSD: Est. with contr. for:	Industry	Ind., human cap.	Ind., human cap., occup.
Finland (1993)	0.096	0.080	0.074
Norway (1991)	0.097	0.065	0.059
Sweden (1991)	0.087	0.064	0.065
adj. R^2: Est. with contr. for:	Industry	Ind., human cap.	Ind., human cap., occup.
Finland (1993)	0.055	0.308	0.340
Norway (1991)	0.054	0.390	0.421
Sweden (1991)	0.081	0.368	0.435
OCCUPATIONAL WAGE DISPERSION			
SD: Est. with control for:	Occupation	Occup., human cap.	Occup., human cap., ind.
Finland (1993)	0.184	0.112	0.103
Norway (1991)	0.154	0.083	0.086
Sweden (1991)	0.159	0.102	0.105
EWSD: Est. with contr. for:	Occupation	Occup., human cap.	Occup., human cap., ind.
Finland (1993)	0.177	0.101	0.095
Norway (1991)	0.159	0.075	0.074
Sweden (1991)	0.145	0.091	0.091
adj. R^2: Est. with contr. for:	Occupation	Occup., human cap.	Occup., human cap., ind.
Finland (1993)	0.211	0.324	0.340
Norway (1991)	0.229	0.410	0.421
Sweden (1991)	0.241	0.411	0.435
NUMBER OF OBSERVATIONS			
Finland (1993)	2 526		
Norway (1991)	1 884		
Sweden (1991)	3 287		

Notes:
Figures obtained from estimating wage equations with the dependent variable being log average hourly wages. The human capital control variables include completed years of schooling, age and its square, and gender. The number of industry dummies is 26 and the number of occupational dummies 25. SD is the standard deviation of the coefficients estimated for, respectively, the industry and occupational dummies, while EWSD gives the standard deviation weighted by employment shares. (See Krueger and Summers 1988.)

controlling for the individuals' occupational attainment is markedly higher than that of their industry affiliation, as indicated by the adjusted R squared given in the table. In other words, regressing average hourly wages on the 25 occupational categories identified picks up a much larger fraction of the total variation in wages than does the inclusion of two-digit industry dummy variables (for instance, 0.229 compared to 0.054 for Norway). This difference, however, seems to be due mainly to the fact that occupational attainment is much more strongly correlated with human capital than is industry affiliation; the wage model including human capital and occupational controls performs only slightly better than the wage model standardizing for individual differences in human capital and industry affiliation.

It may be further noted that supplementing the wage model already including human capital and occupational controls with a vector of industry dummies, or vice versa, adds little to the explanatory power of the model (cf. the reported R squared). Likewise, the two measures of industry and occupational wage dispersion are affected only marginally when also accounting for the other set of dummy variables. Accordingly, once having controlled for individual differences in human capital endowments, wages seem to spread out along both dimensions. Specifically, individuals in high-pay occupations stand out as high-pay employees irrespective of the industry in which they are working. Simultaneously people in the same occupation are likely to be differently remunerated depending on the industry in which they are engaged.

Several patterns concerning the dispersion of occupational wages in Finland, Norway and Sweden emerge from Table 8.4. In all three countries, the (uncontrolled) wage differentials are found to be substantially larger across occupations than across industries. Once controlling, however, for individual differences in human capital and industry affiliation, the dispersion of occupational wages is reduced.

Furthermore, weighing the standard deviation of, respectively, the occupational and industry coefficients by the corresponding employment shares causes a much smaller drop in occupational than in industry wage dispersion. This, in turn, suggests that the industries located at the tails of the wage distribution cover a relatively small share of total employment, while this is not the case for high-pay and low-pay occupations. The employment-weighted standard deviations point, as a consequence, to wage dispersion being in all three countries clearly larger across occupations than across industries.

Figure 8.1 and Figure 8.2, finally, display the occupational wage premia obtained for Finland, Norway and Sweden from estimating wage equations including, respectively, occupational dummy variables only (uncontrolled) and controls for occupational attainment, human capital as well as industry affiliation. The wage premia are calculated as percentage deviations from the average wage in the economy using the formula $(e^D - 1) \times 100$, where D is the difference between the coefficient estimated for an occupation and the employment-weighted mean of all occupational dummy coefficients. The numbers underlying Figure 8.1 and Figure 8.2 are listed in Table 8.A1 of the Appendix.

Figure 8.1   Uncontrolled occupational wage premia: deviation from mean hourly wage (per cent)

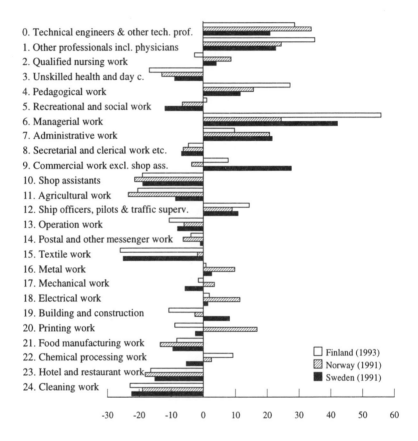

As is to be expected, Figure 8.1 shows much the same relative wage position of the 25 occupational categories as does Table 8.3. When, however, adding controls for individual human capital and industry affiliation the ranking of occupations changes, occasionally even to a notable extent. If focusing on the occupational categories with an average wage level below the median, the relative wage position of, for instance, individuals belonging to the category of unskilled health and day care work, improves remarkably in all three countries when controlling for cross-occupational differences in human capital and industry affiliation. This also holds for chemical processing work in Sweden, secretarial and clerical work in Norway and shop assistants in Finland (see Table 8.A2 of the Appendix).

Figure 8.2   *Occupational wage premia controlled for differences in human capital and industry affiliation: deviation from mean hourly wage (per cent)*

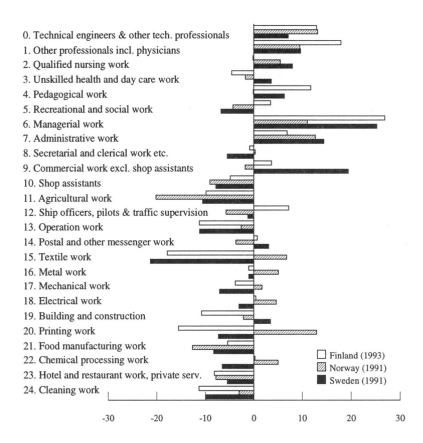

At the other extreme are lower-paid occupations with a marked worsening in their relative wage position when also adding controls for human capital and industry affiliation, moving them further down the occupational wage scale. Among these are operation and printing work in Finland, food manufacturing work in Norway and agricultural and operation work in Sweden. A third group that can be distinguished is made up of occupational categories characterized by no or minor change in the relative wage position, when account is taken of differences in human capital endowments and industry affiliation. It is noticeable that in all three countries, this group is dominated by the least-paid occupations.

5 LOW PAY WITHIN OCCUPATIONS

The analysis has so far focused entirely on wage differentials across occupational categories. Wages vary, however, also within occupations, implying that an average wage level falling below the median may mask very different wage dispersions; for instance, the average wage is the same irrespective of whether a majority of the wages of those classified into the occupation is concentrated around the average, or to the upper and lower ends of the wage scale. It is therefore of interest to look in more detail at the concentration of low-pay workers over the 25 occupational categories under study.

The low-pay workers are defined as those individuals situated in the lowest wage decile (D1), indicating that 10 per cent of the sample population are taken to be in low-wage employment. This measure is, of course, not suited to discuss the incidence of low pay across the three countries. But since our purpose is to study the relationship between occupational attainment and low pay, we have found it convenient to define a measure which abstracts from cross-national differences in the overall wage structure.[3]

Figure 8.3 displays the incidence of low pay in each of the 25 occupational categories investigated. To ease the identification of occupational categories with a high incidence of low-wage employment, the occupation-specific proportions of low-pay workers have been normalized at 10 per cent, which thereby marks a balanced share of low-pay workers in the occupation. If, in contrast, more than 10 per cent of those belonging to a given occupational category are found to be located in the lowest wage decile, then the low paid are said to be over-represented in that occupation. Likewise, if the proportion of low-wage employment falls below 10 per cent, then the occupation is defined to have a low concentration of low-pay workers.

The figure clearly shows that low-wage employment is much more prevalent in certain occupations, while in other occupations none or very few of the workers turn up in the lowest wage decile (e.g. technical engineers and electrical work). A very high incidence of low-wage employment is found among Finnish and Swedish textile and cleaning workers. The incidence of low-wage employment is slightly less among shop assistants, agricultural workers, hotel and restaurant workers, recreational and social workers and those engaged in unskilled health and day care work.

Figure 8.3   Incidence of low-wage employment by occupational category:
underrepresentation (−) and overrepresentation (+) in D1,
per cent

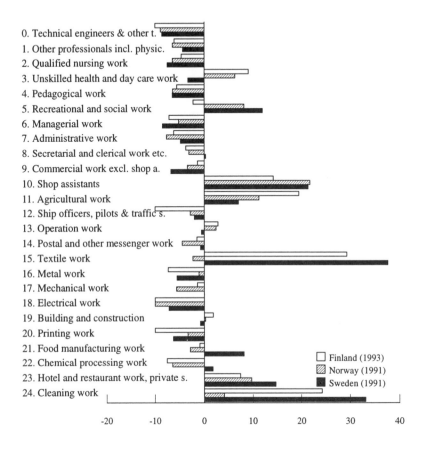

These particular occupational categories are thus characterized by a relatively high incidence of low-wage employment. Their importance as suppli-
ers of low-pay jobs varies considerably, however. This is highlighted in
Table 8.A3 of the Appendix which shows the occupational distribution of
employees located in the lowest wage decile. By comparing Figure 8.3 and
Appendix Table 8.A3 the following occupational categories stand out as the
most important low-pay occupations: recreational and social workers, shop
assistants, operation workers, textile workers, hotel and restaurant workers
and cleaning workers.[4]

Apart from a high incidence of low-wage employment, these six occupational categories employ more than 50 per cent of all low-pay workers in Finland, with the corresponding share being close to 60 per cent in Norway and Sweden. Based on Table 8.3 above it may further be stated that broadly speaking, these occupational categories are also characterized by comparatively high shares of young and female workers.

6 AGE-WAGE PROFILES OF LOW-PAY OCCUPATIONS

In all three countries a large majority of those in low-pay jobs are thus found to be concentrated into the same, relatively few occupational categories. The wage structure of these occupations is of great interest: if you start out as a low-pay worker in any of these occupations, are you then likely to remain at this low wage level over your whole working career, or is your relative wage position improved over your lifetime also if staying in the occupation? Theories of dual labour markets suggest that low-wage occupations easily become low-wage 'traps' in the sense that they are characterized by flat wage curves (e.g. Doeringer and Piore 1971).

To address this issue, we first estimate for each country a wage equation augmented with occupational dummy variables and interaction terms between occupation and age. Based on these estimation results, age-specific wage levels are calculated for all 25 occupational categories. Figure 8.4 graphs the estimated age-wage profiles of the six low-pay occupational categories identified in the previous section relative to the age-wage profile of all employees.

The overall pattern is fairly similar in Finland, Norway and Sweden. In particular, in all three countries the estimated occupation-specific wage levels turn out to fall well below the median wage at all age levels in the following low-pay occupations: shop assistants, hotel and service work and cleaning work. These three occupational categories are, moreover, characterized by relatively flat and, occasionally, even declining age-wage profiles. This pattern is most pronounced in Finland.

Next these three occupational categories, which seem to be worst off both in terms of wage levels and wage development, are scrutinized further, one reason being that the estimated age-wage profiles may be distorted by cohort effects. To check for this, identically specified wage models were estimated from a four (in Sweden ten) year earlier sample for each of the three countries: 1989 for Finland, 1987 for Norway and 1981 for Sweden. From these estimation results, age-specific wage premia were calculated for the same cohorts.

Figure 8.4   *Age-wage profiles of six low-pay occupations relative to the overall median: age effect (per cent)*

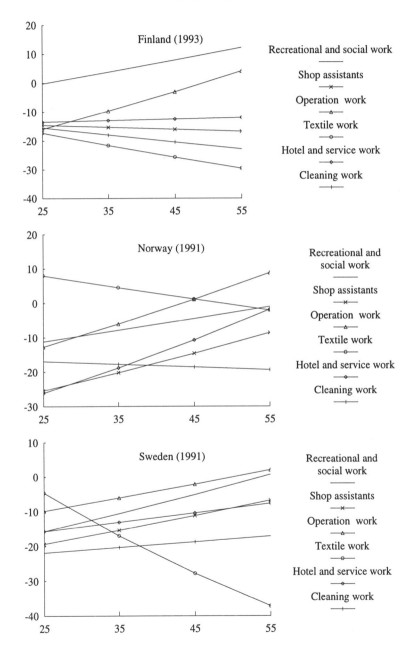

Figures 8.5, 8.6 and 8.7 thus provide, for each country, a 'quasi-panel' view of the wage profiles in the three low-pay occupations of shop assistants, hotel and restaurant work and cleaning work. The figures contain two types of information. First, the dotted lines reflect the cross-section age-wage profile relative to the median employee for the two years observed for each country (1989 and 1993 for Finland, 1987 and 1991 for Norway and 1981 and 1991 for Sweden). The age-wage profiles of the two years reveal much the same overall trend. Second, the solid lines (from age 21 to 25, 31 to 35, 41 to 45 and 51 to 55 for Finland and Norway, and from age 25 to 35, 35 to 45 and 45 to 55 for Sweden) may be interpreted as a quasi-panel estimation of the wage profile of each age group over the next four years (in Sweden the next ten years) relative to the median employee.

Figure 8.5   *Age-wage profiles relative to the median wage for cross-*
              sections (dotted lines) and quasi-panel estimations
              (solid lines) – Finland 1989 and 1993 (per cent)

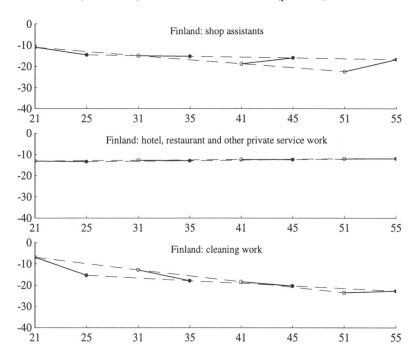

The figures suggest that in all three countries, the improvement with age in the relative wage position of shop assistants has been stronger than indicated by the cross-section estimates obtained for this particular occupation.

In Norway and Sweden this trend is evident in all age cohorts but in Finland among older shop assistants only. Much the same pattern emerges for hotel and restaurant workers, except in Finland where the age-wage profiles of this particular low-pay occupation are found to be rather flat.

Figure 8.6   *Age-wage profiles relative to the median wage for cross-sections (dotted lines) and quasi-panel estimations (solid lines) – Norway 1987 and 1991(per cent)*

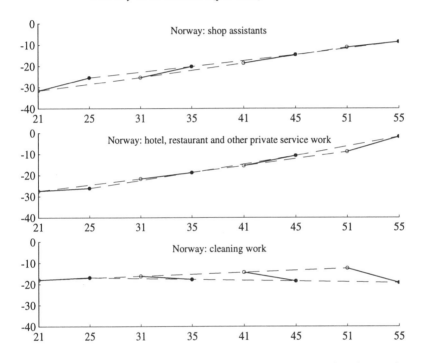

For those in cleaning work, in contrast, the quasi-panel estimations point to an even worse wage development than do the cross-section estimates. The wage development is exactly the opposite in Finland and Norway in the sense that the largest drop in relative wages over the investigated four-year period was experienced by the younger cleaners in Finland but among the older cleaners in Norway. In Sweden, the positively sloped cross-section age-wage profiles turn negative in the quasi-panel estimations for all age cohorts.

*Figure 8.7   Age-wage profiles relative to the median wage for cross-
sections (dotted lines) and quasi-panel estimations
(solid lines) – Sweden 1981 and 1991(per cent)*

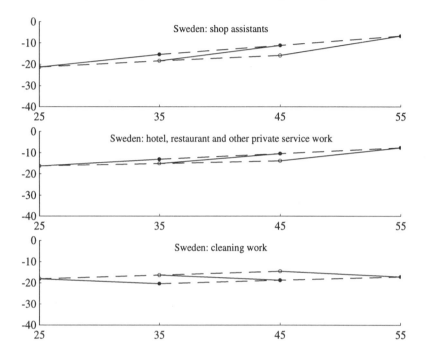

7   ARE THE WAGE STRUCTURES REALLY DIFFERENT?

We have established that the four least-paid occupations in Finland, Norway
and Sweden are characterized by a rather flat age-wage profile. These occupations stand out as 'traps' in the sense that they do not reward investment in
human capital, nor do they lead to higher pay over time. This pattern is more
distinct in Finland and Sweden than in Norway.

In this section, we utilize for each country the more recent cross-section
data set to investigate in more detail the wage profile of these low-wage
occupations. For this purpose, the low-wage occupations (LOW-OCC) are
defined by a dummy variable taking the value of one if the individual belongs
to one of the four low-wage occupations, i.e. is a shop worker, a textile
worker, a hotel/restaurant worker or a cleaner.

Model 1 of Table 8.5 represents a simple wage model augmented with the low-wage occupation dummy variable and regressed on the whole sample. We observe that women are paid lower wages, that age and education have a significant positive effect on wages, and that the low-wage occupations are characterized by significantly lower wage levels in all three countries (a negative wage premium ranging from 8 to 12 per cent). Since age is defined as age above 25 and education as years beyond compulsory schooling, the dummy for low-wage occupations measures the occupational wage gap between the four low-wage occupations and the rest of the occupational categories investigated for men at age 25 with a basic education only.

Table 8.5   *Estimation results for the wage structure of four low-wage occupations*

Variables	Model 1 Standard wage regression			Model 2 With dummy interactions			Model 3 Switching regression		
	Finland	Norway	Sweden	Finland	Norway	Sweden	Finland	Norway	Sweden
	(1993)	(1991)	(1991)	(1993)	(1991)	(1991)	(1993)	(1991)	(1991)
Constant	3.861**	4.249**	4.226**	3.832**	4.238**	4.221**	4.151**	4.358**	4.445**
Woman	-0.157**	-0.159**	-0.171**	-0.164**	-0.152**	-0.182**	-0.134**	-0.205**	-0.210**
Education	0.073**	0.042**	0.030**	0.075**	0.043**	0.031**	0.035*	0.038**	0.020**
Age	0.012**	0.022**	0.016**	0.014**	0.023**	0.017**	0.015**	0.016**	0.008**
Age squared/10	-0.001	-0.005**	-0.003**	-0.001*	-0.005**	-0.003**	-0.001	-0.003**	-0.001
LOW-OCC	-0.119**	-0.079**	-0.099**	0.060	0.004	-0.099**			
Woman·LOW-OCC				0.061	-0.051	0.098**			
Education·LOW-OCC				-0.052**	-0.015	-0.012*			
Age·LOW-OCC				-0.010**	-0.002	-0.004**			
Φ							1.389	-0.872*	-1.925*
Φ·Woman							0.350	0.673**	1.372**
Φ·Education							-0.044	-0.080*	-0.124
Φ·Age/10							-0.296**	-0.003	-0.067
ϕ							-2.090*	0.181	0.197
R squared	0.288	0.381	0.343	0.300	0.382	0.349	0.310	0.375	0.339
No of observations	2 526	1 884	3 287	2 526	1 884	3 287	2 526	1 884	3 287

Notes: Woman is a dummy variable taking the value of one if the individual is a female employee. Education refers to years in post-compulsory schooling. Age stands for older than 25 years. LOW-OCC is a dummy variable taking the value of one if the individual is employed in one of the four occupations identified as low wage occupations. The term Φ gives the probability of being in a low wage occupation, while ϕ is the density function. See further the text. ** and * denote significant estimates at, respectively, the 1 per cent and the 5 per cent level.

In model 2 an interaction term is introduced between the low-wage occupation dummy variable and each of the other covariates. The estimate for the low-wage occupation dummy variable remains significantly negative in Sweden only. The estimates for Sweden further indicate that females fare on average better than men in the low wage occupations, while no such gender difference is observable in the other two countries. Both in Finland and

Sweden, the return to education tends to be significantly lower and the age-wage profile significantly flatter in low-wage occupations. In Norway, in contrast, the differences in human capital rewards between the low-wage occupations and all other occupations investigated are minor or non-existent. At least for Finland and Sweden the results thus seem to support the notion that the low-wage occupations do have a distinct wage structure.

Occupational choice may, however, not be independent of the wage structure, implying that what we observe is the result of occupational choice rather than of wage differentials across occupations. We have, therefore, made a modest attempt to control for the potential presence of this kind of self-selectivity by interacting the wage regression covariates with the probability of being in a low-wage occupation (estimated from a probit equation including gender, education, age and its square as well as all interaction terms), and by further adding the predicted density function from the probit equation. This is a standard switching regression (see e.g. Maddala 1983). Since the covariates of the two wage structures – the low wage occupations versus all other occupations – are taken to be the same, the wage model may be written as

$$
\begin{aligned}
E(W) &= E(W|LOW\text{-}OCC = 1)\, P(LOW\text{-}OCC = 1) \\
&\quad + E(W|LOW\text{-}OCC = 0)(1 - P(LOW\text{-}OCC = 1) \\
&= \beta_{low} X\, \Phi + \beta_{rest} X\, (1 - \Phi) + \phi(\sigma_{rest}\, \mu - \sigma_{low}\, \mu) \\
&= \beta_{low} X + (\beta_{rest} - \beta_{low})X\, \Phi + \phi(\sigma_{rest}\, \mu - \sigma_{low}\, \mu)
\end{aligned} \tag{8.1}
$$

where β_{low} is the coefficient of the wage structure of the low-wage occupations, X is a vector of covariates, Φ is the probability of being in a low-wage occupation and ϕ is the density function. The term $\sigma_{low}\mu$ gives the correlation between the wage level of the low-wage occupations and the unobservable part of occupational choice, while $\sigma_{rest}\mu$ reports the corresponding correlation for the rest of the occupations investigated. If occupational choice is based on comparative advantage, the coefficient for ϕ should be positive.

In the Finnish case, correcting for self-selectivity produces much the same overall pattern as model 2. In particular, the results obtained from estimating a switching regression model indicate that the age-wage profile is significantly flatter in the low-wage occupations. The Finnish results also lend support to the hypothesis of occupational choice being guided by comparative advantage (significant estimate for ϕ). The results for Norway and Sweden, in contrast, provide no evidence of a clear correlation between wages and occupational choice. A significantly lower return to education in the low-wage occupations is obtained only in the Norwegian case, while women seem to have a relative advantage in the low-wage occupations in both Norway and Sweden.

All in all, albeit providing varying support for the notion that the wage structure of the low-wage occupations differs notably from that of the other occupations investigated, the estimation results reported in Table 8.5 seem to point in the following direction: the low-wage occupations tend to be characterized by a smaller male–female wage differential, lower returns to education and a flatter age-wage profile. Several caveats apply, however. First, the definition of low-wage occupations is open to debate, since several lower-wage occupations show up among the rest of the occupational categories investigated. A more satisfactory modelling should obviously involve multinomial response models rather than the simple bivariate approach used here. Secondly, our switching regression model is more or less based on identification by functional form, since compared to the wage equation the probit equation only includes additional interaction terms. A better modelling of occupational choice would include also other variables, like the parents' occupational status and/or education. Thirdly, panel data are required to be able to identify true cohort effects.

8 CONCLUDING REMARKS

Our findings from studying the incidence of low pay in Finland, Norway and Sweden can be summarized as follows. The low-pay workers are concentrated in certain occupational categories which, moreover, turn out to be largely the same in all three countries. Young and female workers are clearly over represented in these occupations. The results further indicate that the wage differentials observed across occupations cannot be explained entirely by occupation-specific differentials in individuals' human capital, working conditions and industry affiliation. Furthermore, pseudo-panel (as well as cross-section) estimations suggest that the age-wage profiles in these low-pay occupations are generally flatter than in higher-wage occupations.

Finally, selectivity effects cannot offer an explanation of the estimated cross-occupational differences in age-wage profiles. A worker in a low-wage occupation is thus likely to experience a steeper age-wage profile in a better-paid occupation. Likewise, a worker in a high-pay occupation would experience a flatter age-wage profile if shifting into a low-paid occupation.

In sum, these results indicate that the incidence of low pay is to a notable degree concentrated in a limited number of occupations characterized by comparatively flat age-wage profiles. This implies that in order to leave low-paid employment, one would have to move into a better-paid occupation, a mobility which, however, most likely requires acquisition of occupation-specific human capital. Given that more employment-related skills facilitate entry into higher-pay occupations, educational policies with the aim of improving the skill level of the least educated workforce could therefore be successful in raising the earnings of low-paid workers.

It may, though, be questioned whether an economy can really educate itself out of low-pay jobs. It seems more realistic to assume that low-pay employment will remain a fundamental element of economic reality. Securing the living standards of those in low-paid jobs then stands out as a crucial policy goal and especially so in countries where, to a higher degree than in the Nordic countries, low pay really refers to a low wage level.

Closely related to this issue is the question of whether attempts to increase the supply of low-pay jobs can contribute substantially to improving the current employment situation. The low-wage occupations identified in the three Nordic countries are in the most part jobs in the service sector, mostly protected from international competition. Whether reductions in the wages of service sector jobs could create a considerable demand for low-wage labour depends, in the last resort, on the demand elasticities for these categories of workers. Existing empirical evidence does not provide many guidelines with respect to these elasticities, since studies of labour demand usually analyse the whole economy or certain industries instead of occupational categories. Moreover, the limited information available on demand elasticities for low-paid labour indicates that the employment effects of cuts in the wages of low-pay service jobs would be marginal. Hence, alternative measures need to be worked out.

NOTES

1   Financial support from the Nordic Economic Research Council is gratefully acknowledged.
2   Experiments with the Swedish data indicate that adjustment of the standard deviations for sampling errors is not needed.
3   A discussion of internationally comparative measures of low-pay workers can be found in e.g. OECD (1996).
4   The occupational category of agricultural work is overlooked because of its relatively small employment share, while the category of unskilled health and day care work is left out because of the remarkable improvement in its relative wage position once controlling for cross-occupational differences in human capital and industry affiliation.

REFERENCES

Albæk, K., M. Arai, R. Asplund, E. Barth and E. Strøyer Madsen (1996), 'Inter-Industry Wage Differentials in the Nordic Countries' in E. Wadensjö (ed.), *The Nordic Labour Markets in the 1990's*, vol. I, part 2, Amsterdam: North-Holland.

Asplund, R. (1997), *Private vs. Public Sector Returns to Human Capital in Finland*, Helsinki: The Research Institute of the Finnish Economy (ETLA), Discussion paper no. 607.

Asplund, R. and S. Vuori (1996), *Labour Force Response to Technological Change*, Helsinki: The Research Institute of the Finnish Economy (ETLA), Series B118.

Asplund, R., E. Barth, C. le Grand and N. Westergård-Nielsen (1996), 'Wage Distribution Across Individuals' in E. Wadensjö (ed.), *The Nordic Labour Markets in the 1990's*, vol. I, part 2, Amsterdam: North-Holland.

Doeringer, P. and M. Piore (1971), *Internal Labor Markets and Manpower Analysis*, Lexington, MA.: Lexington Books.

Krueger, A. and L.H. Summers (1988), 'Efficiency Wages and the Inter-Industry Wage Structure', *Econometrica*, **56**, pp. 259–93.

Maddala, G.S. (1983), *Limited-dependent and Qualitative Variables in Econometrics*, Cambridge, MA.: Cambridge University Press.

OECD (1993), *Employment Outlook*, Paris.

OECD (1996), *Employment Outlook*, Paris.

Zweimüller, J. and E. Barth (1994), 'Bargaining Structures, Wage Determination, and Wage Dispersion in 6 OECD Countries', *Kyklos*, **47**, pp. 81–93.

APPENDIX

Table 8.A1   Calculated occupational wage premia and employment shares

	Uncontrolled wage premia				Controlled wage premia				Employment shares, %		
Occ. cat.	Finland	Norway	Sweden	Occ. cat.	Finland	Norway	Sweden	Occ. cat.	Finland	Norway	Sweden
0	28.70	33.86	20.93	0	12.94	13.17	7.10	0	5.40	4.70	6.50
1	34.95	24.39	22.67	1	17.96	9.53	9.68	1	3.00	1.50	2.70
2	-2.69	8.66	4.09	2	-0.16	5.47	7.99	2	5.20	4.40	3.60
3	-16.67	-12.80	-8.87	3	-4.55	-1.73	3.59	3	4.20	4.50	5.90
4	27.17	15.72	11.56	4	11.74	-0.11	6.30	4	7.20	7.30	6.90
5	1.14	-6.51	-11.86	5	3.44	-4.29	-6.75	5	5.60	2.90	6.40
6	55.69	24.37	42.09	6	26.85	11.05	25.24	6	4.20	8.70	2.00
7	9.71	20.70	21.49	7	6.87	12.68	14.43	7	3.10	4.40	7.00
8	-4.65	-6.29	-6.81	8	-0.85	0.28	-5.47	8	10.10	1.50	10.90
9	7.74	-3.64	27.54	9	3.64	-1.78	19.42	9	5.50	11.10	3.80
10	-18.97	-21.41	-18.85	10	-4.85	-9.05	-7.81	10	4.60	6.60	3.10
11	-20.44	-23.39	-8.69	11	-9.82	-20.13	-10.50	11	2.00	1.70	1.40
12	14.30	8.94	10.79	12	7.20	-5.73	-1.21	12	0.80	0.70	0.80
13	-10.61	-6.04	-8.07	13	-11.22	-2.60	-11.14	13	6.80	6.30	6.40
14	-3.88	-6.31	-0.88	14	0.69	-3.70	3.03	14	3.70	3.80	3.60
15	-25.89	-1.78	-24.92	15	-17.80	6.78	-21.28	15	1.10	0.70	0.60
16	0.81	9.78	2.60	16	-1.07	5.04	-1.01	16	3.00	2.90	2.70
17	-1.53	3.50	-5.70	17	-3.83	1.66	-7.05	17	3.70	3.60	4.30
18	1.88	11.40	1.42	18	0.40	4.59	-3.07	18	2.40	2.40	2.20
19	-10.72	-2.62	8.13	19	-10.76	-2.14	3.41	19	4.40	4.10	4.30
20	-8.93	16.75	-2.41	20	-15.51	12.93	-7.29	20	0.90	0.80	0.80
21	-8.30	-13.37	-9.51	21	-5.42	-12.62	-8.29	21	0.90	0.70	1.00
22	9.19	2.58	-5.28	22	0.23	4.97	-6.51	22	1.60	1.50	2.10
23	-16.35	-18.11	-15.05	23	-8.13	-7.84	-5.47	23	7.70	8.20	7.50
24	-22.87	-19.00	-22.33	24	-11.30	-3.07	-9.93	24	3.00	4.10	3.30

Table 8.A2   Ranking of occupations according to calculated wage premia

	FINLAND				NORWAY				SWEDEN		
Occ. cat.	Ranking acc. to uncontr. wage premia	Ranking acc. to contr. wage premia	Change in ranking order	Occ. cat.	Ranking acc. to uncontr. wage premia	Ranking acc. to contr. wage premia	Change in ranking order	Occ. cat.	Ranking acc. to uncontr. wage premia	Ranking acc. to contr. wage premia	Change in ranking order
0	3	3	0	0	1	1	0	0	5	6	-1
1	2	2	0	1	2	5	-3	1	3	4	-1
2	13	12	1	2	10	7	3	2	9	5	4
3	21	16	5	3	20	14	6	3	19	8	11
4	4	4	0	4	6	13	-7	4	6	7	-1
5	10	8	2	5	19	19	0	5	21	17	4
6	1	1	0	6	3	4	-1	6	1	1	0
7	6	6	0	7	4	3	1	7	4	3	1
8	15	13	2	8	17	12	5	8	16	14	2
9	8	7	1	9	15	15	0	9	2	2	0
10	22	17	5	10	24	23	1	10	23	20	3
11	23	20	3	11	25	25	0	11	18	22	-4
12	5	5	0	12	9	20	-11	12	7	12	-5
13	18	22	-4	13	16	17	-1	13	17	23	-6
14	14	9	5	14	18	18	0	14	12	10	2
15	25	25	0	15	13	6	7	15	25	25	0
16	11	14	-3	16	8	8	0	16	10	11	-1
17	12	15	-3	17	11	11	0	17	15	18	-3
18	9	10	-1	18	7	10	-3	18	11	13	-2
19	19	21	-2	19	14	16	-2	19	8	9	-1
20	17	24	-7	20	5	2	3	20	13	19	-6
21	16	18	-2	21	21	24	-3	21	20	21	-1
22	7	11	-4	22	12	9	3	22	14	16	-2
23	20	19	1	23	22	22	0	23	22	15	7
24	24	23	1	24	23	21	2	24	24	24	0

Table 8.A3   Distribution of employees in the lowest decile (D1), per cent

OCCUPATIONAL CATEGORY	FINLAND ('93)	NORWAY ('91)	SWEDEN ('91)
0. Technical engineers and other technical professionals	-	0.5	0.8
1. Other professionals including physicians	1.2	0.5	1.3
2. Qualified nursing work	2.8	1.6	0.8
3. Unskilled health and day care work	7.9	7.4	3.5
4. Pedagogical work	3.2	2.6	2.2
5. Recreational and social work	4.3	5.3	12.4
6. Managerial work	1.2	4.2	0.3
7. Administrative work	1.2	1.1	3.2
8. Secretarial and clerical work	6.3	1.1	10
9. Commercial work excl. shop assistants	4.7	7.4	1.1
10. Shop assistants	11.1	21.2	8.6
11. Agricultural work (employees only)	5.9	3.7	2.2
12. Ship officers, pilots and traffic supervision work	-	0.5	0.5
13. Operation work	8.7	7.9	5.4
14. Postal and other messenger work	3.2	2.1	3
15. Textile work	4.3	0.5	2.7
16. Metal work	0.8	2.6	1.1
17. Mechanical work	3.2	1.6	3.8
18. Electrical work	-	-	0.5
19. Building and construction work	5.1	4.2	3.5
20. Printing work	-	0.5	0.3
21. Food manufacturing work	0.8	0.5	1.6
22. Chemical processing work	0.4	0.5	2.2
23. Hotel and restaurant work, private service work	13.4	16.4	16.4
24. Cleaning work	10.3	5.8	12.7
Total	100	100	100

9. The Effects of Unemployment on Future Earnings: Low-Paid Men in Britain 1984–94

M. Gregory and R. Jukes

1 INTRODUCTION

The full implications of unemployment, both for the individual and for the economy as a whole, depend not only on how the experience of unemployment is spread across individuals, but also on its effects on the individual's subsequent experience in the labour market. If an unemployment spell makes the individual more prone to future unemployment, or if his subsequent earnings after re-employment are systematically lower, then the cumulative impact of unemployment may be much greater than the loss of earnings during the unemployment spell itself. To gain a full assessment of its effects, the experience of unemployment must be set in this dynamic perspective.

The issue is of particular relevance for the low paid. In all the industrialized countries the incidence of unemployment is substantially greater among low-skilled, low-paid workers than among those who are more educated, higher skilled and better paid. Not only do the low paid make up a disproportionate number of the unemployed, but they are also more prone to repeat spells. For them any longer-term effects of unemployment are of particular significance.

The current policy debates on the most effective approaches to tackling the high and persistent unemployment which has characterized the majority of European economies through the 1980s and 1990s, give enhanced significance to this issue. One approach which is being strongly urged is the need to improve the flexibility of labour markets. This approach has been most extensively developed in the *Jobs Study* (OECD 1994), the culmination of several years of research and analysis within the OECD. Among the policies urged on member countries is the removal of rigidities seen to restrict the adaptability of the labour market and to inhibit job creation. Policies being recommended include a reduction in employment protection and in minimum wage protection, in order to introduce greater flexibility in employment and wages. This type of flexibility in hiring and firing will involve greater labour turnover, and the increased exposure of individual workers to job termination and unemployment. The reduction in employment protection and the greater ease of firing are, of course, designed to encourage job creation by employers. This will bring increased hiring rates and therefore shorter durations for the unemployment spells. Proposals for greater hiring and firing flexibility imply a trade-off between the greater frequency of unemployment and the shorter duration of the unemployment spells. Similarly, the reduction in minimum wage protection is envisaged as removing an obstacle to the creation of lower-paid jobs. Not only can 'low pay' be argued as better than 'no pay', but low-paid jobs may serve as stepping stones, allowing the individual to acquire, or re-acquire, the skills and work experience which equip him to progress to better-paid jobs. This is the positive case for wage flexibility, particularly at lower levels of earnings. Against this optimistic scenario, however, it may be argued that depressed wages may become part of the problem rather than part of the cure. Greater flexibility may simply bring greater churning among low-wage, insecure jobs, and between 'low pay' and 'no pay'.

This chapter will present some estimates of the dynamic influences of unemployment. We will focus in particular on the effects of an unemployment spell on the workers' earnings and earnings progression in future employment. The specific questions to which we will offer some answers will be: does re-entry into employment involve a fall in wages, and if so by how much? Is any decline permanent, or if it is transient, how long does it last? Is it the incidence of unemployment, in one or more spells, which matters? Or is it the duration of the spells, and the overall time spent out of work which is relevant? Or are both important in affecting subsequent earnings?

We will examine these in the case of low-paid men in Britain between the mid-1980s and the mid-1990s. As the European economy which has proceeded furthest in the direction of labour market deregulation, the British case is a particularly suitable test-bed for this analysis. In its assessment of the progress made by individual member countries towards implementing the *Jobs Study* recommendations on labour market flexibility, the OECD notes that the most substantial progress towards implementing structural improvements in the labour market has been made in the UK. Minimum wage protection, previously provided through the sectoral Wages Councils, was brought to an end when the Councils were abolished. This left the UK as the only country in the EU with no formal mechanisms of minimum wage protection. The new government, elected in 1997, is pledged to introduce a legal national minimum, but this will not take place before 1999. Meantime, the experience of the 1980s and 1990s provides a context in which to examine the impact of this form of flexibility. Even under the Wages Councils, which had powers to set minimum wage rates within individual sectors, minimum wage protection was weak and patchy. Protection was patchy because the establishment of a sectoral Wages Council had been largely a matter of historical accident, and a number of industries, even where low pay was widespread, did not have one. It was weak because the inspectorate charged with enforcement had very limited resources, and the penalties for non-compliance, mainly fines, were so low that they did not constitute a serious deterrent. In spite of these weaknesses, however, Wages Councils did afford some degree of minimum wage protection within their sectors. When the Councils were abolished, wage rates offered in some of these sectors were documented as falling below the previous Wage Council minima.

The study will focus on the experience of men. In spite of the evidence of falling participation rates, lifetime attachment to the labour force, at least until the age of sixty, remains the norm for men. For many British women, on the other hand, one or more spells out of the labour force remains a common pattern during the child-rearing years; the analysis of labour market status is therefore much more complex in the case of women. In addition, the classification of unemployment which we will use is based on the receipt of unemployment benefit or unemployment-based income support. A woman's entitlement to these benefits may be affected by her husband's labour market status and her own choices on social security contributions. As a result of these features of the social insurance system unemployment, as we are measuring it, may not have the same meaning for women as for men. This is illustrated by the fact that registered unemployment among women in Britain is around half its rate among men, again a highly unusual feature within the European economies.

2 MEASURING THE IMPACT OF UNEMPLOYMENT ON EARNINGS

A natural first measure of the impact of unemployment on earnings is the comparison of the level of earnings for those who have been unemployed with earnings for those with continuous employment. This comparison, in terms of hourly earnings at constant prices, is shown in Figure 9.1. The raw earnings disadvantage for those who have experienced unemployment within the previous twelve months is clear and consistent; on average their earnings are only between 60 and 65 per cent of the earnings of those who have not recently been unemployed. This measure, however, risks exaggerating the impact of unemployment on earnings after re-employment. It is widely documented, for Britain as throughout the industrialized world, that the low paid are more likely to become unemployed than workers at higher earnings levels. This is due partly to their personal characteristics and partly to features of the jobs in which they are employed. The low paid have, on average, lower levels of educational attainment and tend to receive less training in their jobs; this leads to higher turnover rates, with intervening spells of unemployment. The observed wage differential between those who have been unemployed and those who have not conflates the effects of unemployment on earnings on the one hand with the greater incidence of unemployment among the low paid on the other.

Figure 9.1   Average earnings by unemployment in the previous 12 months

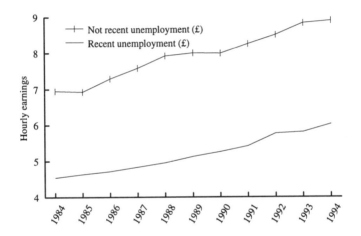

A more appropriate measure would be the difference, for a given individual, between his level of earnings before an unemployment spell compared with their level after re-engagement. This measure controls for the personal characteristics of the individual, observable and unobservable, which determine his general earnings potential. This measure, however, still omits two relevant aspects. The first is that, given the normal earnings growth associated with continuing employment, even re-engagement exactly at the pre-displacement wage implies an earnings penalty from the interruption to employment. The relevant basis for comparison is not actual earnings after re-engagement but the level which earnings would have reached, had employment been continuous. Similarly, the 'before' and 'after' comparison is an accurate measure only if earnings immediately prior to the unemployment spell were at their normal or trend level. There is substantial evidence from the USA and to some extent from the UK to indicate that this may not be the case. In establishments where redundancies are threatened or foreseen, due to loss of markets or deteriorating profits, earnings fail to keep up with their growth elsewhere, and may already be significantly depressed by the time disengagements take place (Jacobsen et al. 1993, Gregory et al. 1987, Blanchflower 1991).

Our estimates are therefore based on establishing the level of individual earnings, as derived from a range of personal and job characteristics, with the same determinants covering those with and those without unemployment experience. Including the individual's unemployment history, if any, among these determinants, allows us to identify its impact against the level which the individual's earnings would have been expected to attain had there been no period of unemployment.

Our basic framework is a standard human capital earnings function, following Becker (1975) and Mincer (1974). This relates the individual's earnings to the amount of human capital he possesses at that point in time. Human capital has three components. The number of years of formal education he has received gives rise to his general human capital, assumed to be equally valuable in any employment. Similarly, his cumulated work experience gives a measure of the human capital he has derived through the labour market, each year in employment being assumed to add to the stock of work skills which he can bring to any job. The third element is the length of his tenure in his current job, measuring the additional job-specific skills he has acquired, which enhance his productivity and therefore his earnings in that current job. This return to tenure accrues only in the current job, and, unlike work experience, is not cumulated across jobs (Addison and Portugal 1989). The level of individual earnings are also widely documented, from many countries, as varying systematically across industries, regions and occupations, between the public and private sector, and between full- and part-time workers. In part this reflects compensating advantages, for work in dirty or dangerous conditions, for jobs carrying a high level of responsibility, or located in areas where the living costs are expensive. In part these differentials reflect the rents to the market power of firms or workers. We will not explore these issues in detail, but will include all these factors in order to control for their potential influence on the individual's earnings. The final set of influences on the individual's earnings, which are the centre of our interest, are measures of his unemployment experience and their potential impact.

The general form of the earnings equation will therefore be

$$\ln w_t = f(human\ capital_{it},\ other\ influences_{it},\ unemployment_{it}) \qquad (9.1)$$

where *w* denotes the level of earnings, the subscript *i* denotes individual *i* in the sample, and subscript *t* the *t*-th year of the period 1984–94. For the many individuals in the sample who have not been unemployed the measures of unemployment experience will take zero values.

3 THE NESPD–JUVOS DATA SET

An analysis on this basis requires information on the individual's earnings and personal and job characteristics both before and after any spells of unemployment, combined with details of the timing and duration of each episode in his unemployment history. The data which we use are taken from the NESPD–JUVOS dataset. This is a large panel data set which has been constructed by combining the New Earnings Survey Panel Data (NESPD) with the Joint Unemployment and Vacancy Operating System (JUVOS). The NESPD contains longitudinal data on individual earnings and employment characteristics, while JUVOS gives comprehensive coverage of the individual's unemployment record, including the number, timing and duration of all unemployment spells.

The New Earnings Survey (NES) is the premier source of information on individual earnings in Great Britain. The survey has been conducted annually since 1970, and the NESPD contains the NES information in panel form from 1975. The survey consists of a 1 per cent sample of all employees in employment, based on a specified pair of terminating digits in the individual's National Insurance number. Since the National Insurance number allocated to each individual on attaining the minimum school-leaving age remains in force throughout his life and the same pair of terminating digits are used as the basis for each year's sample, a panel is automatically generated within the surveys. The sampling frame implies that, conditional on a balanced response rate, the survey represents a random sample of all employees in employment, irrespective of full- or part-time status, occupation, size or type of employer, or type of job. The NES questionnaire is sent to the employer, who returns the required information on the sampled employee from payroll and employment records. The earnings, hours of work, job description and other survey information relate to a specified week in April of each year. The employer is required by law to complete the survey questionnaire, thus ensuring a high response rate and avoiding the response biases which would otherwise be inevitable. Basing the survey on the employer's payroll records ensures that earnings and hours of work are reported with a high degree of accuracy. A further strength of the sampling frame is that it avoids cumulative attrition in the sample. Since the individual retains his National Insurance identifier for life, regardless of his employment status, his NI number on the employer's payroll ensures that he should be located for the survey in any future year when he is in employment, after any period when he has not been included in the NES due to unemployment, temporary withdrawal from the labour force, or a failure of sample location. While sample coverage cannot be perfect, and individuals may be missed from any year's sample, attrition is not cumulative.[1]

The JUVOS cohort is a 5 per cent sample of all computerized claims for unemployment-related benefits (Unemployment Benefit, Income Support and National Insurance credits) covering the period since the third quarter of 1983. The JUVOS records give the individual's complete unemployment history, including the number of spells of unemployment, with their timing and duration. The sample is again selected by reference to the claimant's National Insurance number. Since the terminating digits on NI numbers used to select the JUVOS 5 per cent sample include those used to select the NES 1 per cent sample it has been possible to match the individual's JUVOS records into the NESPD records, to give linked information on employment and unemployment histories.

The NESPD–JUVOS data set which we use contains full-linked records for the 11-year period 1984–94. In addition the NESPD component provides the individual's NES earnings and employment history, where appropriate, back to 1975. The JUVOS information contains his unemployment history, if any, from the third quarter of 1983, plus an indicator if he was recorded as unemployed in the preceding months during which the JUVOS system was being introduced. A full description of the compilation of the NESPD-JUVOS data set, along with the results of validation checks, are given in Jukes (1995).

The NESPD–JUVOS data file for the period 1984–94 contains information on over 150 000 men who are present in one or more years. In any single year over 90 000 are present. Since part-time employment is potentially significant among the low paid we include part-time as well as full-time employees. To retain part-time workers within our sample on a comparable basis to those in full-time work requires that we measure earnings on an hourly rather than a weekly basis. Arguably, this is the appropriate measure of low pay, capturing the wage return per unit of labour used. It does, however, preclude direct confrontation of the issue of low incomes, where low pay arises from the restricted availability of hours of work per week as much as from a low hourly rate of pay. Measuring earnings on an hourly basis requires us to exclude from the sample those employees who are reported to be in full-time employment but for whom normal weekly hours are not specified. As the men in this category are mostly professionals or in executive and managerial positions, their exclusion does not affect the group of low-paid men. Since the survey reports actual earnings in the specified pay-week, rather than 'normal' earnings, we have further restricted the sample to those whose earnings are not affected by absence. The total number of men in the panel which we use is shown for each year in Figure 9.2. The number varies from a low of 66 000 in 1994 to almost 77 000 in 1988. The reduction in the sample size in the 1990s reflects the falling male labour force participation characteristic of many European economies; in Britain this is partly offset by the growth in the number of self-employed who are not covered in the NES. The clear cyclical pattern in the sample numbers follows the macroeconomic cycle of upswing in the late 1980s followed by recession in the early 1990s.

Figure 9.2   Numbers of men in the survey 1984–94

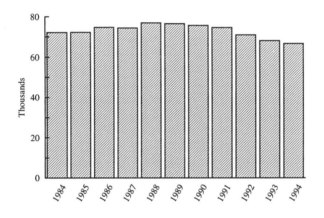

4 THE LOW PAID AND UNEMPLOYMENT

We define low pay in relative terms, identifying as the low paid those in the bottom quintile of the distribution of hourly earnings for men in each year. This gives a sample of around 14 000 low-paid men in any year, with the actual numbers varying to a limited degree from year to year with the changing size of the full sample.

Figure 9.3 shows the recent unemployment experience of low-paid men in comparison with those in the higher earnings quintiles. Those with a single spell of unemployment in the previous twelve months are shown separately from those with more than one spell. The proportion of the low paid (quintile 1) who have had recent experience of unemployment, either a single spell or multiple spells, is much higher than for those in the higher quintiles. Among low-paid workers between 10 and 14 per cent have experienced an unemployment spell within the preceding twelve months. Among those in quintiles 2–5 of the earnings distribution, on the other hand, just over 2 per cent have been unemployed within the previous year. Similarly, the low paid are around ten times more likely to have had recurrent unemployment; the proportions involved are, however, small: around 2 per cent of the low paid, and minimal numbers from the higher quintiles. Multiple spells of unemployment in the preceding year are almost as frequent among low-paid workers as a single spell among the higher paid. This confirms, from the perspective of those currently in employment, that recent experience of unemployment is rare among higher earners but relatively frequent among the low paid.

Figure 9.3   Unemployment in previous 12 months (%)

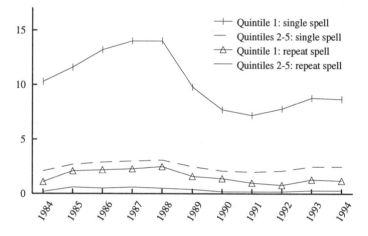

For both single and multiple spells these proportions are essentially un-trended over the decade. This evidence therefore does not give support to suggestions, from those concerned about a climate of growing job insecurity, that unemployment is becoming a more frequent experience among the male workforce. The overall patterns are, however, strongly pro-cyclical. The incidence of recent unemployment among employees in Britain rose not when unemployment was high in 1984–6 but when expansion was strongly under way in 1987–8. Similarly the number of workers who had recently been unemployed fell as the economy moved into recession in 1990–1, although the unemployment rate was still not particularly high at that point. This cyclical pattern reflects the return to work of the unemployed in periods of expansion and the reduced exits from unemployment in recession; it thus moves with unemployment outflows, and inversely to the unemployment rate measured in stock terms. The low paid are much the most cyclically sensitive group. A macroeconomic upswing is especially favourable in getting the unemployed back into work, even if it is in low-paid jobs, while the move into recession

Some Further Perspectives

curtails re-employment, including in low-paid jobs. This sensitivity to the cyclical developments in the macro-economy is particularly marked for those who have had recent multiple spells of joblessness.

Figure 9.4   *Duration of unemployment among low- and high-paid men (%)*

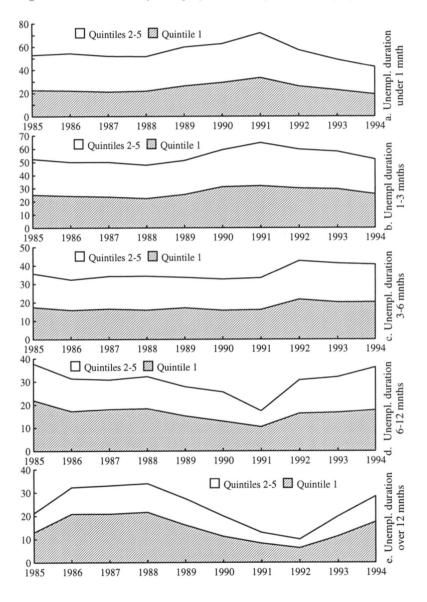

These sharp differences between low-paid workers and the higher paid in terms of unemployment incidence are more muted when we look at the duration of the unemployment spells which they experience. Differences persist, but on a much reduced scale. Figure 9.4 shows the different spell lengths experienced by low-paid men who have recently been unemployed as against those with higher earnings. For both groups short-term unemployment is more common than long-term unemployment, but this balance is less pronounced among those in low-paid jobs.

For men in the higher quintiles who have had an unemployment spell the most frequent duration is less than one month, the experience of 31 per cent of them. Among the low paid only 24 per cent of spells last less than one month, while the most frequent duration, affecting 27 per cent, is between one and three months. Very short-term unemployment, under three months, is thus the experience of 51 per cent of the low-paid against 59 per cent of those in higher earnings quintiles, and short-term unemployment, under six months, for 69 per cent of the low paid against 77 per cent among those in higher-paid jobs. Conversely, long-term unemployment is more prevalent among the low paid, with on average 15 per cent experiencing a spell of over twelve months, against 9 per cent among the higher paid. Thus, while the low paid tend to have experienced longer spells of unemployment than higher-paid men, the much bigger difference between them and workers in higher-paid jobs is that the low paid are much more likely to have experienced a recent spell of unemployment.

In the duration of unemployment the cyclical pattern is again prominent for all groups, but most strikingly for the low paid. A cyclical upswing keeps unemployment durations short, even more markedly for low paid than for higher-paid men. A cyclical downturn, on the other hand, limits re-engagement of the longer-term unemployed, among whom those who find low-paid jobs are concentrated.

5 RE-EMPLOYMENT OF THE UNEMPLOYED

It will be clear that we can estimate the impact of unemployment on future earnings only for those who re-enter employment after an unemployment spell. Our estimate must therefore be conditional on the individual subsequently being in employment. This is not equally likely for all unemployed men. As shown in Figure 9.5, 68 per cent of men from the bottom earnings quintile are present in the NES sample in the following year (i.e. in employment and located for the survey). This survivor rate is ten percentage points lower than for those in higher quintiles. The reasons for non-survival, in addition to unemployment, are retirement, pre-retirement withdrawal from the labour force and failures of sample location. The greater frequency of unemployment among those in the bottom earnings quintile has already been discussed. Non-survival for the two latter reasons is also more common among the low paid. Reduced participation rates for low-skilled men, as they withdraw from the labour force for reasons of ill-health or more general discouragement, have been noted widely across the OECD economies in the past decade. The principal reason for failures of sample location is that the individual is no longer with his recorded employer, because he has changed his job between the date at which the sample was located and the date of the Earnings Survey. Since it is widely documented that job turnover rates are higher among the low paid this again is likely to contribute to a lower success rate in sampling these workers.

Figure 9.5   Survivor rates in employment (%)

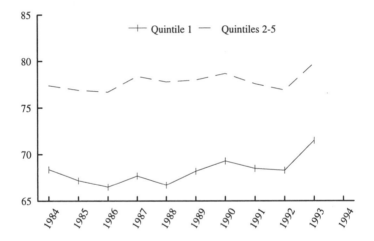

Before proceeding to estimate the impact of unemployment on subsequent earnings we must therefore first estimate the probability of a worker being in employment in the following year. Obvious influences to capture the individual's proneness to drop out of employment are his age, his average level of earnings and the earnings growth he experiences across the years when he is in the survey. More general influences conducive to non-employment are the aggregate macroeconomic and labour market conditions in each year. To allow for these influences on the probability that an individual remains in employment and in the NES Survey in any year we estimate a probit on presence/absence of the individual. The variables included in the probit are his age, his average earnings and his earnings growth across his years in the panel, combined with a dummy variable for each year to reflect general labour market conditions. These probit estimates, given in Table 9.1, confirm that the probability of year-on-year survival in the survey varies inversely with both the level of the individual's earnings, and the growth of his earnings. Both influences, but particularly the level of earnings, are strongly significant. As expected, survivor rates are substantially higher in all younger age categories than among the over-55s (the omitted group) and tend to fall as workers become older. The associated Heckman correction from the probit will be entered into the earnings equation as lambda.

Table 9.1   Probit estimates of the probability of presence in the sample

Variable	Coefficient dF/dX*	Standard error	z score
Average wage	-0.0091	0.0001	-123.4
Aver. wage squared	0.0001	9.97E-07	42.1
Wage growth	-0.0326	0.002	-16.4
Wage growth squared	-0.0043	0.0025	-1.7
Age to 18	0.3324	0.0018	180.5
Age 19-25	0.3487	0.001	332.2
Age 26-35	0.2078	0.0008	257.3
Age 36-45	0.1692	0.0008	210
Age 46-55	0.1625	0.0009	188.5
Plus time dummies			
Observed P	0.113		
Predicted P	0.081 (at means of indep. vars)		
Number of observations	2393706		
Chi-squared (19)	233028		
Log likelihood	-726177		
Pseudo R^2	0.138		

Note: dF/DX is for discrete change of dummy variable from 0 to 1.

6 ESTIMATING THE IMPACT OF UNEMPLOYMENT ON EARNINGS

As shown above, the unemployment experience of the typical low-paid worker differs from those with higher earnings in two dimensions: more frequent incidence and longer durations. Each of these may have an impact on his future earnings. The job separation which introduces an unemployment spell means the loss of the job-specific human capital acquired through training, work experience and the development of job-based skills. This loss of non-transferable skills is brought about by the termination of the job, and therefore the incidence of an unemployment spell, independently of its duration. It is often argued in addition, however, that general human capital and transferable skills also depreciate during unemployment, as the standard tasks of the working day no longer have to be carried out and its routine is lost. In its most pessimistic form this view suggests that this deterioration accelerates as the unemployment spell lengthens and demoralization sets in. The human capital approach therefore suggests that both the incidence of unemployment and the duration of the spell may, through separate channels, reduce human capital and therefore subsequent earnings. In both cases earnings recovery is to be expected, as new job-specific skills are developed and any depreciation of general skills is reversed once employment is resumed. An alternative hypothesis, which also suggests effects from both incidence and duration, is based on imperfections in information. In hiring a new employee the employer inevitably has only limited information about the worker's motivation, work attitudes and other factors contributing to his productivity. The employer will therefore look for indicators which can be taken as measures of his potential productivity. The new worker's unemployment history, both incidence and duration, provides a natural signal and an adverse one (Belzil 1995, Vishwanath 1989). This suggests that unemployment will imply a wage penalty on re-engagement, but that this should be short-lived as the employer acquires full information on the worker's productivity. Our objective is therefore to capture the effects of unemployment, if possible for incidence and spell duration separately, and to establish the detailed time-profile of these effects.

For each wage observation for the individual we identify the date of his most recent exit from unemployment. The time-span, in quarters, by which that date precedes the reported wage allows us to identify the time-profile of any impact of an unemployment spell on subsequent earnings. For any individual only one-quarter from this time-profile can take the marker for the most recent incidence of unemployment. For those who have been in continuous employment the entries are all zero, providing the base-line measure against which the impact of an unemployment spell can be measured. The duration of this most recent spell, and measures of the individual's earlier unemployment history are entered separately.

The wage equation which we estimate is

$$\ln w_i = f(Experience_{it}, Tenure_{it}, Age_{it}, UN\text{-}x_{it}, DAYUI_{it}, DAYUO_{it}, PU,$$
$$UN\text{+}x_{it}, Joc_{it}c, Occ_{it}, Ind_{it}, Region_{it}, PartTime_{it}, Public_{it}, Time_{it}) \quad (9.2)$$

The variables grouped in the first line of equation (9.2) measure the contribution of the individual's human capital to his earnings, those in the second line represent his unemployment experience, while the third set include controls for other systematic influences. The variables used are defined as follows:

Ln w − logarithm of hourly earnings, excluding overtime pay and overtime hours; deflated by the retail price index to 1994 prices.

Experience − the number of years of employment which the individual has accumulated, including in his present job, less total time spent unemployed. From 1975 the number of years in employment is taken as the number of years in which the individual is present in the NESPD. For those older workers who were in employment prior to 1975 the extra years of work experience are calculated as his age in 1975 less 17 years for time in education prior to work. From 1984 time spent unemployed is taken directly from JUVOS. Prior to that year it is estimated; those individuals with subsequent unemployment experience are attributed the average unemployment experience of their age-by-occupation group in each year between 1975 and 1982.

Tenure − the number of years the employee has been in his present job with his current employer. Each NES questionnaire reports whether the employee was in the same job with his employer twelve months previously. Tenure is cumulated as the number of consecutive affirmative responses to this question.

Age − this is included for two reasons. Both experience and tenure are measured with error, since they attribute one year's work experience to each year's presence in the survey (a point sample); age may partly offset this measurement error. In addition, by proxying personal maturity and the changes in productivity which it brings, age can be expected to be a separate determinant of earnings in addition to work experience.

UN–x − dummy variable taking a unit value when the individual's last completed spell of unemployment ended *x* quarters before the wage observation.

DAYUI − the duration, measured in days, of the individual's most recent unemployment spell. The square of this, *DAYUISQ*, is also included to allow the effect to accelerate or diminish as the spell lengthens.

DAYUO − the total duration, in days, of all prior unemployment spells. Its square, *DAYUOSQ*, again allows the effect to accentuate or diminish as the duration lengthens.

PU − dummy variable in force permanently after an unemployment spell, to capture any permanent effect outside the quarterly time-profile specified in *UN–x*.

UN+x − a dummy variable, indicating whether the individual was to become unemployed *x* quarters after the wage observation.

The set of further influences which are included in dummy variable form are the individual's industry of employment (the ten one-digit groupings (Divisions) of the Standard Industrial Classification), his occupation (the nine major groups of the Standard Occupational Classification), region of work (the eleven Standard Regions), full-time/part-time status, private/public sector (with central government, local government, and publicly-owned enterprises distinguished separately), and the individual years of the time period, proxying trend and cyclical influences on earnings.

Estimation is by fixed effects panel regression, to control for individual-specific, time-invariant influences which affect earnings in addition to those given above. There are two important categories of these. Educational attainment and training are in principle observable and highly relevant to earnings but we have no information on them in our data set. By assuming these to be time invariant we treat them as a fixed effect in our estimation. This allows us to control for their impact on earnings, subsuming it into an individual-specific intercept, but we are, of course, as a result unable to say anything about the impact of education and training on individual earnings. Other unobservable dimensions of individual heterogeneity affecting productivity and earnings, such as health status and work attitudes, are similarly controlled for as fixed effects.

7 ESTIMATION RESULTS

The equation is estimated separately for the low-paid (bottom quintile) and other workers (quintiles 2–5), with the impact of the various measures of unemployment on earnings shown in Table 9.2. The results are clear-cut, and show substantial differences between those in low-paid jobs and workers with higher earnings.

Looking first at the effect of the incidence of unemployment, this has no significant impact on the subsequent earnings of the low paid. An unemployment spell ending at any point in the preceding two years ($UN-1$ through to $UN-8$) has a tiny and statistically insignificant impact on current earnings for those in the bottom quintile. For those with higher earnings, by contrast, in the first quarter after exit from unemployment earnings are on average 15.4 per cent lower than they would otherwise have been, a figure which is both statistically and economically highly significant. Over the first year in continuous re-employment this earnings penalty declines to 10.4 per cent, and further to 6.9 per cent after two years. The permanent effect of an unemployment spell, captured by the dummy variable PU, shows a negligible impact for the low paid, while for the higher paid earnings remain 2.3 per cent below the trajectory they would otherwise have attained.

Table 9.2 *The impact of unemployment on earnings*

Dependent variable: ln hourly earnings		
Variable	Low-paid men (Quintile 1)	Other men (Quintiles 2 -5)
UN– 1	-0.017	-0.154
	(2.175)	(30.213)
UN– 2	-0.012	-0.120
	(2.128)	(27.697)
UN– 3	-0.010	-0.131
	(1.857)	(31.617)
UN– 4	-0.001	-0.104
	(0.257)	(24.272)
UN– 5	-0.001	-0.095
	(0.627)	(23.067)
UN– 6	-0.004	-0.090
	(0.482)	(20.845)
UN– 7	-0.003	-0.091
	(1.073)	(22.050)
UN– 8	-0.001	-0.069
	(0.244)	(16.487)
DAYUI /100	-0.036	-0.024
	(7.077)	(35.715)
DAYUISQ /10 000	0.002	0.001
	(2.467)	(24.422)
DAYUO /100	-0.059	-0.032
	(11.581)	(55.172)
DAYUOSQ /10 000	0.002	0.001
	(4.142)	(32.340)
PU	-0.002	-0.023
	(0.713)	(14.056)
UN +0	-0.027	-0.027
	(1.624)	(12.415)
UN +1	-0.037	-0.016
	(2.457)	(9.976)
UN +2	-0.014	-0.009
	(0.082)	(5.103)

Note: *t*-values in parentheses.

While becoming unemployed does not bring an earnings set-back for the low-paid, the duration of the unemployment spell within the preceding two years has an impact on future earnings *(DAYUI, DAYUISQ)*. A spell of 30 days unemployment reduces future earnings by 1.1 per cent, rising to 5.8 per cent for a six-month spell, and to 10.5 per cent for a one-year spell. While a short spell of unemployment does not bring loss of future earnings for the low paid, longer spells have an adverse effect. The effect is rather greater than for higher-paid men, for whom it is also significant, but for them as a further penalty in addition to the setback from the incidence of unemployment. Earlier prior spells of unemployment have a further depressive effect on earnings, whether measured by cumulated duration or by number of spells. Unlike the most recent spell, it is not possible to obtain separate contributions for cumulated duration as against cumulated number of spells. Cumulated duration appears to be the more direct influence, and is the measure which is included. Other estimates (not shown) indicate that the timing of earlier unemployment is not important; the effect does not decay over time.

The measure of future unemployment *(UN+x)* does not appear to be foreshadowed by lower prior earnings for the low paid; all the estimated coefficients are insignificant. For the higher paid, on the other hand, a small but significant effect can be seen, but only for unemployment to come within the next six months or so. In these groups the earnings of those who were to become unemployed later in the same quarter *(UN+0)* had slipped by 2.7 per cent, while where unemployment was still six months ahead the average earnings slippage was under 1 per cent. Unemployment in the more distant future (not shown) has no detectable effect.

For higher-paid workers these results show similar patterns to those found by other researchers, principally for the USA.[2] The overall time-profile for the impact on earnings shows the three phases of the impact of unemployment on the wage: the 'dip', prior to the disengagement, the 'drop' on re-engagement, and the extended but incomplete 'recovery' if employment is continuous (Jacobsen et al. 1993). The degree of wage variation shown for British men is, however, much lower. The 'dip' is modest and relatively short run, failing to confirm the evidence of three-year lead times and substantial pre-separation earnings losses, of 10–15 per cent, found for displaced workers in the USA (Jacobsen et al. 1993, de la Rica 1995). Similarly, the earnings penalty on re-engagement and the long-run effects are only around half of the magnitude estimated for US displaced workers (Jacobsen et al. 1993, Ruhm 1991). The most striking feature of our results, however, is that the low paid largely avoid these effects. In this respect our findings are closer to those of Ackum (1991) who finds that unemployment does not significantly reduce re-employment wages for young people in Sweden. In our results, however, although unemployment itself does not bring an earnings set-back, its sustained duration has an adverse effect on future earnings.

8 CONCLUSION

The labour market situation of the low paid is one of multiple disadvantages. Not only are their earnings low, but they are more frequently exposed to unemployment, and when this occurs they remain out of work on average for longer than their better-paid counterparts. The analysis above, however, offers one brighter feature to this bleak scenario. By contrast with the situation for higher earners, unemployment to come does not depress earnings for low-paid men, and experiencing an unemployment spell does not bring lower earnings on re-engagement. The low paid move through unemployment from one low-paid job to another; but the pay does not deteriorate further. The good news is, however, limited. Unemployment does have an adverse effect on future earnings for the low paid but through its duration. A lengthy spell begins to impact significantly on the level of subsequent earnings. To minimize the adverse effects of unemployment on the earnings position of the low paid the most important policy measures will be those targeted specifically at preventing the emergence of long-term unemployment among the low paid.

NOTES

1 A further description of the NES is given in Gregory et al. (1990) and of the NESPD in Elias and Gregory (1994).
2 See, among others, Hamermesh (1989), Podgursky and Swaim (1988), Swaim and Podgursky (1991), Kletzer (1989), Topel (1990), Farber (1993) and Hall (1995).

REFERENCES

Ackum, S. (1991), 'Youth unemployment, labor market programs and subsequent earnings', *Scandinavian Journal of Economics*, **93**(4), pp. 531–43.
Addison, J. and Portugal, P. (1989), 'Job displacement, relative wage changes and duration of unemployment', *Journal of Labor Economics*, **7**(31), pp. 281–302.
Becker, G.S. (1975), *Human Capital: A Theoretical and Empirical Analysis with Special Reference to Education*, New York: National Bureau of Economic Research with Columbia University Press, 2nd edition.
Belzil, C. (1995), 'Unemployment duration stigma and re-employment earnings', *Canadian Journal of Economics*, **XXVIII**(3), pp. 568–85.
Blanchflower, D.G. (1991), 'Fear, unemployment and pay flexibility', *Economic Journal*, **101**(406), pp. 483–96.
de la Rica, S. (1995), 'Evidence of pre-separation earnings losses in the Displaced Worker Survey', *Journal of Human Resources*, **XXX**(3), pp. 610–21.
Elias, P. and M. Gregory (1994), *The Changing Structure of Occupations and Earnings in Great Britain, 1975–90: An Analysis Based on the New Earnings Survey Panel Dataset,* London: Employment Department, Research Series no. 27.

Farber, H.S. (1993), 'The incidence and costs of job loss: 1982–91', *Brookings Papers on Economic Activity; Microeconomics*, pp. 73–119.

Gregory, M., S. Houston, C. Sanjines and A.Thomson (1990), 'The New Earnings Survey', in M. Gregory, and A. Thomson (eds), *A Portrait of Pay, 1970–82: An Analysis of the New Earnings Survey*, Oxford: Clarendon Press.

Gregory, M., P. Lobban and A. Thomson (1987), 'Pay settlements in manufacturing industry, 1979–84: A micro-data study of the impact of product and labour market pressures', *Oxford Bulletin of Economics and Statistics*, **49**(1), pp. 129–150.

Hall, R.E. (1995), 'Lost jobs', *Brookings Papers on Economic Activity*, pp. 221–73.

Hamermesh, D.S. (1989), 'What do we know about worker displacement in the US?', *Industrial Relations*, **28**, pp. 51–9.

Jacobson, L.S., R.J. LaLonde and D.G. Sullivan (1993), 'Earnings losses of displaced workers', *American Economic Review*, **83**(4), pp. 685–709.

Jukes, R. (1995), *NESPD–JUVOS Validation Paper*, London: EMRU, Employment Department.

Kletzer, L.G. (1989) 'Returns to seniority after a permanent job loss', *American Economic Review*, **79**, pp. 536–43.

Mincer, J. (1974), *Schooling, Experience and Earnings*, New York: National Bureau of Economic Research with Columbia University Press.

OECD (1994), *The Jobs Study*, Paris.

Podgursky, M. and P. Swaim (1988), 'Job displacement and earnings loss: evidence from the Displaced Worker Survey', *Industrial and Labor Relations Review*, **41**(1), pp. 17–29.

Ruhm, C.J. (1991), 'Are workers permanently scarred by job displacements?', *American Economic Review*, **81**(1), pp. 319–24.

Swaim, P. and M. Podgursky (1991), 'The distribution of economic losses among displaced workers: a replication', *Journal of Human Resources*, **26**(4), pp. 742–55.

Topel, R. (1990), 'Specific capital and unemployment: measuring the costs and consequences of job loss', *Carnegie Rochester Conference Series on Public Policy*, **33**, pp. 181–214.

Vishwanath, T. (1989), 'Job search, stigma effect and the escape route out of unemployment', *Journal of Labor Economics*, **7**(4), pp. 487–502.

10. Working Poor? An Analysis of Low-Wage Employment in Italy [1]

C. Lucifora

1 INTRODUCTION

The last two decades have been periods of significant change in the functioning of the Italian labour market. A number of distinct features concerning both the structure of the labour force and the institutional setting governing pay determination, have at different stages characterized the economic scene. On the one hand, there has been an increasing participation of females in the labour market and a shift in sectoral composition with the service industry and public employment progressively gaining importance over manufacturing. On the other hand, the strong union pressure and the rigid labour market regulation of the 1970s and early 1980s reverted, in recent years, to a more flexible set of rules associated with a less conflictual industrial relations climate (Dell'Aringa 1993, Salvati and Raichlin 1990). This picture is also complicated by an increasing trend in the overall rate of unemployment, which has proved particularly severe among prime-age workers and in the southern regions of the country (Bodo and Sestito 1991).

Such patterns are expected to exert major influences over the distribution of wages both over time and among different groups of individuals in the labour market.[2] Indeed, this has been the case in a number of industrialized countries which, under the pressure of different economic and institutional changes, experienced over the last decade a significant increase in earnings inequality (OECD 1993, 1996).[3] This evidence has increased concern about the pay conditions of those individuals located at the bottom end of the wage distribution. In other words, it is questioned whether an increase in earnings inequality should result in a higher proportion of workers (predominantly employed in low-skilled jobs) receiving a 'low wage': the so-called working poor. An increase in the share of individuals earning a wage rate which is

185

substantially lower than the national average might be undesirable for a number of reasons: first, from an 'equity' point-of-view a too dispersed wage structure – if wage differences are perceived as unfair – may undermine cohesion and co-operation among workers; second, low pay may affect the ability of individuals and households to maintain decent living standards and thus further exacerbate the problem of poverty; finally, from the perspective of firms, a significant undercutting based on wage rates might well hinder fair competition. The incidence of low pay has also implications for public policy, as governments are likely to face rising costs in terms of welfare programmes targeted on the well-being of individuals.

Against the views discussed above, it is often argued that the 'low wage' issue is a false problem as wages simply reflect differences in marginal productivity and it is through the operation of the market mechanism that resources are efficiently allocated. According to standard economic theory any attempt to alter wage relativities, for example introducing a statutory minimum wage, will result in a loss of jobs as less-skilled workers will be priced out of the market. Also, there is a well established view suggesting that low wages and poverty are only loosely related and that any attempt to reduce the incidence of low pay will have almost no effect in alleviating poverty.[4]

Despite the lack of consensus among economists and policy makers over the issues discussed above, assessing the relevance of low-wage employment in the Italian labour market appears particularly relevant in the light of the major changes which have occurred in recent years.

There have been a number of studies concerning the evolution of income distribution in Italy, but only some have focused explicitly on the distribution of earnings using micro-data (e.g. Sestito 1992, Contini and Revelli 1992, Erickson and Ichino 1995, Lucifora and Rappelli 1995, Manacorda 1997).[5] Although these studies differ, according to the main focus of interest, either in the methodology or with respect to the data source used (or both), nevertheless a general finding, common to most of them, can be identified. In particular, it is shown that Italy – over the 1970s and most of the 1980s – did not experience an increase in earnings dispersion such as the USA, the UK and, to a minor extent, other OECD countries.[6] Conversely, earnings inequality in Italy has been declining over most of the 1980s, with some indications of a more dispersed distribution emerging only in the late 1980s. The relative stability of the structure of wages might appear rather surprising when compared both with the experience of other countries and the significant changes occurring in Italy itself over the same period. All authors support the view that various institutional factors (such as national collective bargaining, strong unions and labour market legislation) had a considerable influence on the observed trends. In recent years, however, the role of these factors in shaping the wage distribution has become progressively less important, so that a growing dispersion in earnings and an increasing number of low-wage workers might reasonably have been expected to emerge.

As far as the present study is concerned, the focus will be placed on two main features of low-wage employment. First, we shall investigate which groups in the labour force are more likely to suffer from low-wage episodes and, *ceteris paribus*, which are the characteristics of either individuals or employers that are associated with low wage rates. In particular, we want to explore how these have evolved over time and whether the incidence of low pay has shifted from some groups to others. Second, and more importantly, we wish to analyse the dynamics of low wages, that is how individuals move within the earnings distribution and whether low wages are a transitory or a permanent feature of the individual's wage profile. In other words, it is important to ascertain if 'lifetime' earnings inequality – as compared to 'static' inequality – is significantly reduced by individuals' upward mobility in the earnings distribution.

In order to do this, we shall make use of different data sets with information at the micro level and follow individuals over a significant portion of their working life (longitudinal data). The structure of the chapter is as follows. In section 2 we discuss a number of problems concerned with the definition and the measurement of low wages and we describe the data sets used in the empirical analysis. Section 3 looks at some of the institutional features of the Italian labour market and presents some of the aspects governing pay determination. A descriptive analysis of the main features of low-pay employment in Italy is also offered. The probability of experiencing low wages, conditioned on a set of job and personal characteristics, is estimated and results reported in section 4. Finally in section 5, the mobility patterns of individuals 'into' and 'out' of low pay and over deciles of the wage distribution are investigated. The final section contains some concluding remarks.

2 LOW-WAGE EMPLOYMENT: DEFINITION AND MEASUREMENT

Economic theory provides different explanations for the existence of low wages. Among these some emphasize the role played by market forces in wage determination, while others stress the existence of non-competitive factors which might push wage levels below the perfect competition equilibrium. In the recent debate over the causes of the increased earnings inequality observed in most OECD countries both approaches have been suggested. On the one side, shifts in the supply and demand for labour market skills may influence the structure of wages, at both ends of the earnings distribution, by altering the distribution as well as the returns to individual characteristics

(Bound and Johnson 1992, Katz and Murphy 1992, Murphy and Welch 1992). Alternatively, other factors arising in non-competitive settings, where employers may have some power in setting wages, may be relevant to explain the occurrence of a significantly low level of pay. For example, the simple recognition that employers may not be able to hire all the workers they wish at the going rate is sufficient to allow firms some discretion in setting wage levels (Card and Krueger 1995, Rebitzer and Taylor 1991, Dickens et al. 1996). Clearly, policy implications aimed at alleviating the low-pay problem are radically different in each of the above cases and the ongoing controversy, on both sides of the Atlantic, on the economic effects of a statutory minimum wage is an example of the divergent views that exist on the desirability of such measures.

As far as the present study is concerned, however, no attempt will be made to discriminate among competing theories of wage determination. On the contrary, the focus will be placed on those factors affecting the probability of a low-wage employer-employee match. Hence, we shall first investigate the relevance and the composition of low-wage employment for different groups of workers and firms, and next try to assess the likelihood of low-wage episodes for given (observed) characteristics.

2.1 Definitions of Low-Wage Employment

The identification of the low-wage population among those individuals who contribute to the formation of the National Product is not an easy task. A number of clarifying remarks may help. First, despite the probability of low incomes being higher in the informal sector of the economy (excluding illegal activities), policy measures have traditionally been targeted towards the formal sector and, within the latter, towards employees, i.e. as opposed to the self-employed. Second, we shall be concerned with individual wages and not incomes, as the latter are also influenced by the existence of transfer payments. Furthermore, different definitions of earnings, which may differ substantially across individuals, can be used, such as hourly, weekly, monthly or yearly measures as well as gross as opposed to post-tax earnings. In principle, hourly earnings should be preferred (as significant differences might exist among individuals in the number of hours worked), though in practice data on the number of hours worked are very seldom available and are often measured with error. When net (post-tax) earnings are considered instead, the existence of a progressive income tax regime might alter the shape of the earnings distribution. In the present study equalized annual earnings (that is, corrected for the number of weeks/days effectively worked) will be used, both in gross and net terms.

The final crucial point concerns the choice of the earnings cut-off to determine low pay. Several different definitions have been suggested in the literature depending on whether an absolute or a relative measure is preferable. Whilst 'absolute' measures are usually defined with reference to a given level of income (in real terms), i.e. the official poverty line, 'relative' measures are taken either as a fraction of mean or median wages, or with respect to some specific quantiles of the earnings distribution. Although a number of problems arise with any of the above definitions, for the purposes of the present chapter a relative measure, closer to the idea of social distance and exclusion, seems preferable.[7] In practice, low-paid workers have been defined as the proportion of those falling below two-thirds of the overall earnings distribution. Despite its apparent arbitrariness, the measure chosen is in line with the Council of Europe's suggested 'decency threshold' (i.e. defined as 68 per cent of full-time average weekly earnings), as well as with most of the legal minimum wage levels enforced in several European countries.[8] In Figure 10.1, according to the definition of low pay given above, we report for a number of industrialized countries the proportion of workers falling below the threshold in a given year (1994).[9]

Figure 10.1   Proportion of low-wage workers in OECD countries (%)

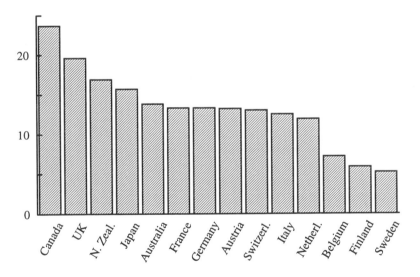

Source: OECD (1996)

Quite interestingly, significant differences in the relevance of low-wage employment across countries emerge. Italy, in particular, is located among those countries characterized by a relatively modest incidence of low wages. Some care, however, should be used in drawing conclusions from direct comparisons across countries since, as one might expect, the observed pattern is strictly related to the country's overall earnings inequality (OECD 1996). As previously discussed, the volume of low-wage workers measured at a given point in time indicates only one (rather partial) dimension of the phenomenon, and a great deal of heterogeneity is likely to exist both across different workers-employer matches as well as over time. For some groups of individuals or employers the risk of falling into low pay, as compared to the average, might be significantly higher. Also, low pay might be disproportionately concentrated among certain groups of workers or firms. In the following sections – using different micro data sets – various indicators of low-pay incidence and concentration will be compared across individual characteristics and employer attributes.

2.2 The Data

The empirical analysis will be based on the two main sources of micro-data which are currently available in Italy for the study of earnings. Both of them provide detailed information, at the individual level, on earnings and a number of characteristics related to the worker and the firm. The first data set is drawn from the Bank of Italy *Survey on Income and Wealth of Italian Households* (SHIW), which is a cross-section of approximately 8 000 households (with some specific questions referred to individuals within the household) distributed over all sectors of the economy. The survey covers individuals who are resident in Italy and is available on a yearly basis from 1978 and biannually from 1987 onwards (with the exception only of 1985).[10] In the following analysis, only income recipients within the household will be considered. A full set of standard human capital variables is available (i.e. schooling, experience, gender, etc.) as well as a number of additional controls for broad occupational groups and sectors of activity. Earnings figures are recorded net of direct taxation and corrected for the number of months effectively worked in the year.

The second data set is drawn from the INPS *Social Security Archives* (Istituto Nazionale di Previdenza Sociale) and is based on the earnings declarations of employers to the National Social Security Office. Since the data are collected mainly for administrative purposes and not originally intended for statistical use, the set of information on individuals' characteristics is not very rich (i.e. the major drawback is due to the lack of information on educational attainments); conversely, a clear advantage is that earnings figures are very accurate. In particular, earnings are defined as gross yearly wages, adjusted for the number of weeks effectively worked, inclusive of premia and other periodical payments, but excluding overtime payments and social charges. Moreover, the INPS data set has a longitudinal design, thus allowing individuals to be followed over their working life. Our sample covers approximately 10000 individuals employed in the private non-agricultural sector of the economy for the period 1975–88.

A number of caveats need some discussion. First, since the two data sets differ in several respects, particular care should be adopted when making comparisons. The presence of net earnings, in one data set (SHIW), and gross earnings in the other (INPS) – given the progressive taxation regime – could produce a different picture of low-wage employment. Also, while the SHIW sample is restricted to full-time workers employed continuously throughout the year, INPS data, though referring to full-time equivalent positions, include both part-time workers and those employed for only part of the year.[11] Second, if we are interested in the work histories of individuals, the presence of attrition in the panel, as individuals can leave the data set for several reasons, can be a problem.[12] In particular, if the source of 'attrition' is non-random (i.e. individuals with selected characteristics have a higher probability of dropping out of the sample) there might be selectivity effects. For the purposes of the present study, particular care should be adopted in the case of women leaving employment temporarily and re-entering afterwards, and individuals experiencing frequent spells of unemployment could be over-represented in the low-pay population.[13] These caveats should be borne in mind when interpreting the results.

3 INSTITUTIONAL FEATURES AND STYLIZED FACTS

The set of rules governing pay determination is of paramount importance when studying the structure and the evolution of low pay. The existence of any kind of 'safety net' designed to prevent (real) wages, in the lower portion of the earnings distribution, from falling too much is likely to influence significantly the relevance of low-pay employment. Moreover, it has been argued that the existence of mechanisms which introduce some form of downward rigidity to the relative wages of the least-skilled workers might adversely affect their employment rates. In particular, a trade-off between equity considerations (such as lower inequality) and economic efficiency (such as lower unemployment) might exist. This argument is often used to contrast the recent experience of both the USA (where a statutory minimum wage exists, but is set at a very low level) and the UK (where wage councils, responsible for setting minimum wages in selected industries, were abolished in 1993) with that of continental Europe, in which unemployment has been rising over most of the last decade. If this is the case, the analysis of low-wage employment cannot ignore the links that might exist with unemployment (Brown et al. 1982, OECD 1993). This view has obviously not gone unchallenged as new research has found little support for the hypothesis that the existence of minimum wages bears any systematic and significant relation with the level of (un)employment (Card and Krueger 1995, Dickens et al. 1996, OECD 1996). The following section is devoted to the analysis of the legislative and institutional setting in which pay determination occurs.

3.1 The Institutional Setting

In most European countries different forms of 'minimum wage', either set by the law or determined through collective bargaining (with provisions for the extension to non-covered workers), act so as to provide a threshold for the downward pressure on wages. Beside 'minimum wage' arrangements a number of other labour market institutions, such as union strength, collective bargaining coverage, unemployment benefits, etc. can significantly influence the incidence of low pay (Dolado et al. 1996). Italy, in this respect, even without a statutory minimum wage, has often been referred to as an example of a particularly rigid labour market with strict rules governing firms' hiring and firing behaviour, as well as a pervasive system of collective bargaining. It is, however, difficult to regard the effects of such rigidities as a constant factor either over time or across different segments of the labour market. On the one side, a significant change in overall flexibility emerged in the second half of the 1980s, as the levelling of differentials that had marked the wage structure in the previous decade was reversed and the extent of both external and internal flexibility in employment adjustment increased, with a generalized re-structuring of the economy (Dell'Aringa and Lucifora 1990, 1994). On the other side, a number of segments of the labour market have always escaped the effects of the above-mentioned rigidities, namely: small firms, several non-manufacturing industries and workers on temporary/fixed term employment contracts (i.e. leaving aside the quite large informal economy). Thus, even if the coverage of collective bargaining is very high and in general there is a *de facto* extension of the national wage minima, there might still be a conspicuous proportion of workers earning a wage rate which is substantially below the average (or median).

Yet evidence on low-pay employment in Italy, mainly due to the lack of adequate data, is rather scarce. Only recently have a number of studies attempted to shed light on the different dimensions of the phenomenon. Lucifora (1993), using SHIW data for 1987, suggests an overall figure of 14.5 per cent for full-time workers (on a regular contract) who fall below two-thirds of the median wage. Also, substantial heterogeneity is found across personal characteristics (such as gender, age, schooling, etc.) and occupation/industry attributes, both in terms of incidence as well as concentration of low pay. Not surprisingly, women, younger workers and the least educated, *ceteris paribus,* are more likely to be found amongst the low paid. An international comparison study produced by OECD (1996) indicates for Italy – using the same source of data – a figure of 12.5 per cent of full-time workers in a low-earnings job in 1993. The composition of low-pay employment in Italy is also found to be quite similar to that observed in other industrialized countries. Contini et al. (1997) using INPS data for 1986 and 1991, find that 23.1 per cent of men and 50.3 per cent of women within a five years' span fall below the third decile of the earnings distribution. Finally, Brandolini and Sestito (1996) investigate the evolution of earnings inequality and low pay using various years of SHIW data (from 1977–93). The incidence of low pay among full-time workers varies over the period, from over 16 per cent (in 1981) to a lower figure of 8 per cent (in 1989).[14]

From a purely descriptive perspective, what is missing from most of the above mentioned studies is a direct comparison – bearing in mind the caveats previously discussed – of the statistical sources available. This is what we do next.

3.2 Some Stylized Facts

For the purposes of analysing the distribution of low pay among different groups of individuals and in order to calculate the (unconditional) probability of experiencing a low-wage episode, in this section we investigate the incidence of low pay by looking at the proportion of workers who earn less than two-thirds of the median wage.[15] Since the likelihood of being low paid can vary substantially across personal characteristics and firm attributes, different breakdowns of the data are presented. We start by looking at the overall incidence of low pay over the years 1975–93. In Figure 10.2, the evolution of low-wage employment is assessed, comparing the incidence rate between the two sources of data.[16] Both data sources indicate a relative fall in the proportion of low-paid workers during the 1970s and most of the 1980s. As a matter of fact, the two sources track one another pretty closely over most of the time period; a notable exception is 1988 in which INPS data show a sharp increase in low-paid employment, while in SHIW data this is observed only later. In general, the incidence of low pay ranges from a peak of 17.5 per cent in 1975 (INPS) to a minimum of 7.9 per cent in 1989 (SHIW), reverting to an increasing trend thereafter (12.5 per cent in 1993, SHIW). Quite interestingly this pattern closely mirrors the evolution of earnings inequality observed in Italy over the last two decades (OECD 1996, Brandolini and Sestito 1996).

Figure 10.2   Incidence of low pay (%)

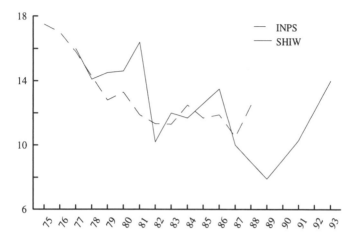

Given that significant differences exist in the participation patterns of males and females as well as in the distributions of low-paid jobs, in Figure 10.3 a disaggregation of the incidence rate by gender is provided. A finding common to most studies, which suggests that females are on average two times more likely to be affected by low-pay conditions than males, is supported by the evidence emerging from both data sets. Over the whole period approximately one female out of four is at risk of experiencing a low-paid spell; conversely, among males less than one in ten is at risk of low pay. Also, as earnings generally increase over the life cycle of individuals, a common finding is that younger cohorts are more likely to suffer from low pay than older ones. This is confirmed here as well. When comparing the evolution of low pay for two broad age groups – young (below 30) and mature workers (between 30 and 55) – younger workers exhibit higher incidence rates over the period (results are not reported).

A further important determinant of (low) pay is education. In Figure 10.4, using SHIW data (INPS data do not record educational attainments), we plot the incidence of low pay by educational qualifications. Years of schooling have a strong effect in reducing the likelihood of a low-pay spell; in particular, the recent trend toward higher earnings inequality appears to be matched by a proportionally increasing share of low-educated workers being low paid. Similar findings are obtained when the breakdown is done either by occupation or by skill groupings.[17]

The evolution of incidence rates for low-paid employment which has been presented in the above figures describes a world in which for a given set of characteristics (young, female, low educated, etc.) the risk of being employed in a low-paid job can be significantly higher than in the remainder of cases. However, further information that one would like to obtain a better understanding of the phenomenon of low pay is the distribution of the pool of low-paid workers across various personal and employer attributes. In other words, it might be instructive to look at the groups of individuals, firms and industries where low-pay jobs tend to be more concentrated. In order to do this, in Table 10.1 we report for selected years, different indicators of incidence and concentration.[18]

Figure 10.3   Incidence of low pay by gender (%)

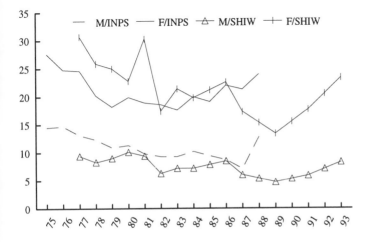

Figure 10.4   Low pay by educational levels (%)

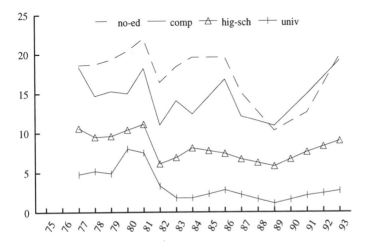

Some Further Perspectives

Table 10.1   Incidence and concentration of low pay by selected characteristics and gender

	(selected years: 1975, 1980, 1987)											
	incidence						concentration					
Characteristics	1975		1980		1987		1975		1980		1987	
	F	M	F	M	F	M	F	M	F	M	F	M
Total	17.5		13.3		10.5		–		–		–	
age: <30	36.2	24.4	31.8	20.6	30.0	20.1	41.4	24.1	37.6	25.0	36.1	25.8
age: 30-55	25.8	15.1	19.8	12.1	21.3	7.5	53.0	72.8	48.7	68.9	45.2	55.4
manual	34.8	18.3	22.4	14.0	21.4	8.7	68.4	89.4	60.7	86.0	51.0	86.2
non-manual	18.7	5.3	16.6	5.4	11.1	2.8	30.1	10.2	37.8	13.9	21.7	10.7
manager	0.0	0.0	0.9	0.0	0.0	0.6	0.0	0.0	0.1	0.0	0.0	0.4
size=1-20	48.8	33.7	45.4	25.1	36.6	14.2	50.1	70.5	67.6	68.7	65.5	78.2
size=21-50	27.1	10.9	16.6	6.3	15.6	3.0	15.5	11.1	13.9	8.4	12.5	7.0
size=51-100	28.6	6.2	10.6	5.3	13.5	6.5	13.9	4.8	7.3	5.3	7.4	11.1
size=101-250	16.7	2.2	6.4	0.6	7.3	0.9	14.1	2.8	7.2	1.0	7.7	2.3
size=251-500	10.5	10.1	6.4	13.9	14.7	0.8	4.3	8.9	3.3	16.4	5.8	1.0
size=+500	5.6	0.6	1.9	0.2	11.9	0.7	1.3	0.0	0.7	0.2	1.1	0.4
industry	19.7	6.6	6.9	4.2	12.2	3.8	29.3	23.8	12.8	21.2	18.0	28.1
craft-work	86.7	49.5	69.1	35.1	57.7	19.9	6.2	21.4	7.7	21.1	7.9	26.9
bank, insurance	7.3	1.0	6.4	0.9	3.3	0.4	3.3	0.6	3.7	0.6	1.1	0.3
retail t.-p. serv.	38.1	28.2	31.1	23.3	26.9	10.3	61.2	53.8	75.0	56.4	72.5	44.4
weeks: <52	41.8	22.6	37.8	20.1	43.8	13.4	40.0	38.2	27.2	24.5	30.1	39.0
weeks: 52	22.0	61.7	16.8	9.7	17.6	5.4	60.0	61.7	72.8	75.4	69.2	61.0
stayers	27.6	14.4	19.5	11.2	19.9	7.1	96.7	93.6	95.2	94.2	89.0	96.0
movers	25.8	16.6	35.4	15.1	55.7	9.0	3.2	6.3	4.8	5.8	11.0	4.0

Note: INPS data

In general, although women have a much higher probability of being in low-paid jobs, they appear to share equally the burden of low-pay employment with men. Low-paid employment on average tends to be highly concentrated among manual workers (over 60 per cent), those employed in small firms (65 per cent and more), and particularly in industries such as manufacturing-construction (20–25 per cent) and retail-trade (50–70 per cent). Finally, a large number of low-paid individuals appear to work regularly over the year (more than 60 per cent) and to stay with the same employer for most of their working life (90 per cent). Interestingly, the share of low-paid employment also appears to be roughly equally distributed between young (below 30) and mature (between 30 and 55) workers.[19]

As far as the evolution of low-pay employment is concerned, its incidence is found to be declining between the first (1975) and the last years (1987) considered here. However, as shown in the previous figures (between 1987 and 1989 incidence was at its minimum), this pattern reverted to its trend in more recent years. Conversely, the index measuring concentration in low pay appears rather stable over the years, suggesting a strong correlation between given characteristics and the bulk of low-paid jobs.

The simple descriptive evidence presented thus far suffers from a number of drawbacks. First incidence and concentration rates, indicating the probability of experiencing low pay and the distribution of the latter among a given set of characteristics, are not resulting from a *ceteris paribus* analysis. That is, some of the differences in observed probabilities might simply reflect compositional effects or differences in other (observed or unobserved) characteristics. Second, observing that a given percentage of workers is low paid (or at risk of being low paid) neglects the fact that it is not always the same individuals who are in low-paid jobs. Conversely, if there is considerable mobility across the earnings distribution, low pay might be a transitory condition as individuals will move up the earnings hierarchy. Finally, together with movements within the earnings distribution, also movements in and out of employment or the labour force can be relevant. In the following sections these issues will be addressed.

4 THE DETERMINANTS OF LOW PAY

In this section, we investigate the determinants of low pay using a binary probit model.[20] Setting the low-pay threshold, as we did before, at two-thirds of the median wage, the probability of being low paid can be specified as

$$P[w_i < \mu] = \Phi(X_i' \beta), \ i=1, \ ..., \ N \qquad (10.1)$$

where w_i is the wage of the *i-th* individual, μ is the low-pay threshold, Φ is the standard normal cumulative distribution function, X_i' is a vector of explanatory variables (for the individual and the firm) and β is a vector of parameters to be estimated. Since the interpretation of the coefficient estimates in a probit equations is difficult, the marginal effects of being low paid have been computed and are reported in Table 10.2.[21]

In order to compare the results and obviate the need to restrict the choice of explanatory variables, two cross-sections for 1987 have been drawn from each data set (i.e. SHIW and INPS). Separate estimates for males and females are reported when using INPS data, while controls for education are also included when SHIW data are used. Two different specifications for each data set are given in the table.

Both age and education have a negative, statistically significant effect on the probability of being low paid. Each additional year of age, using INPS data, reduces the likelihood of being low paid by 2.5 per cent for females and slightly more than 1 per cent for males. However, when controls for years of schooling are also added (using SHIW data) the impact is greatly reduced

Table 10.2   *ML estimates of the probability of low pay (1987): marginal effects (probit estimates)*

Characteristics	INPS data				SHIW data	
	(1)	(2)	(3)	(4)	(1)	(2)
	female	male	female	male		
age	-0.025	-0.013	-0.023	-0.011	-0.0023	-0.0022
	(2.38)	(4.51)	(2.56)	(4.92)	(13.3)	(13.3)
age (squared)	0.0002	0.0001	0.0002	0.0001	0.0001	0.0001
	(2.22)	(4.78)	(2.35)	(5.38)	(10.1)	(10.2)
education	–	–	–	–	-0.0010	-0.0011
					(8.10)	(8.12)
gender	–	–	–	–	-0.167	-0.161
					(12.6)	(13.4)
non-manual	-0.093	-0.062	-0.091	-0.064	-0.081	-0.082
	(10.7)	(5.1)	(11.1)	(6.0)	(5.28)	(5.27)
manager	-0.36	-0.081	-0.398	-0.078	-0.197	-0.198
	(0.09)	(1.79)	(0.07)	(1.77)	(5.38)	(5.43)
size=21-50	–	–	-0.071	-0.099	–	–
			(7.82)	(9.76)		
size=51-100	–	–	-0.157	-0.042	–	–
			(8.29)	(3.19)		
size=101-250	–	–	-0.146	-0.122	–	–
			(10.9)	(11.7)		
size=251-500	–	–	-0.025	-0.128	–	–
			(1.69)	(5.58)		
industry	–	–	0.016	0.105	–	-0.084
			(1.75)	(1.79)		(1.68)
bank, insurance	–	–	-0.398	-0.053	–	-0.026
			(0.09)	(0.68)		(0.52)
retail trade & pers. service	–	–	0.046	0.165	–	0.029
			(3.10)	(2.82)		(1.11)
continuous empl. (52 weeks work.)	–	–	-0.096	-0.078	–	–
			(8.57)	(7.53)		
north	–	–	–	–	-0.121	-0.122
					(12.2)	(12.3)
center	–	–	–	–	-0.074	-0.074
					(4.67)	(4.68)
constant	yes	yes	yes	yes	yes	yes
Log-likelihood	-1 681	-2 641	-1 494	-2 343	-1 398	-1 108
Pseudo R2	0.432	0.426	0.513	0.499	0.242	0.399
numb. observat.	3 539	11 008	3 539	11 008	4 658	4 658

Notes:
a.   Absolute asymptotic '*t*-ratios' in parentheses.
b.   Marginal effects computed from ML coefficient (see text).

(0.2 per cent). The effect of age is found to decrease over the life cycle for individuals in both data sets. The specifications in which males and females are grouped together (SHIW data), show that being a male, *ceteris paribus*, significantly reduces the probability of low pay (by 16 per cent). Higher qualifications reduce the probability of low pay; holding a non-manual job lowers it between 6 per cent (males) and 9 per cent (females), while being in a managerial job has a negative impact of nearly 40 per cent for women and 8 per cent for men (SHIW results, for both genders, are in between the above figures).

Workers employed in larger firms are – other things equal – less likely to be low-paid (though the effect of the largest sized firm category in the female equation is not statistically significant). The effect of industry dummies on the conditional probability of being low paid is jointly significant, though not always significant individually. The retail-trade and personal services industry shows a (statistically significant) positive impact. Also, having worked without any interruption in the year reduces the probability of being below the low-pay threshold (10 per cent for females, 8 per cent for males). Finally, the geographical location of the firm is also relevant for low pay. Working in the north of the country, as against the south, has *ceteris paribus* a negative impact equal to 12 per cent, while it is 7.5 per cent for the central regions.

Another useful way to interpret the results, instead of considering the marginal effect of each factor, is to select a number of stylized individuals who combine several characteristics and then look at their probability of being low paid. In Table 10.3, different estimates of these conditional probabilities are presented for each data set.[22]

Results concerning the so-called 'reference' individuals are shown in rows 1 of Table 10.3 (respectively for each data source). Individuals with 'base' attributes are defined as having average values for all continuous variables and all the dummy variables set to zero. To illustrate one specific case consider a male worker, aged 45, doing a manual job, in a firm with less than 20 employees, having worked only part of the year, in the other-services industry; according to the above characteristics he will have a probability of being low paid equal to 7.4 per cent. Conversely a female worker, with identical attributes (but aged 42), has a probability of falling below the threshold of 49 per cent (INPS data). Estimates for 'reference' individuals in SHIW data – though not comparable with those reported above, for they include average years of education and exclude firm size – are slightly lower: 2 per cent for males and 13 per cent for females. A more detailed description of the stylized individuals is reported in the table. Probabilities of being low paid range from 95 per cent (74 per cent), with INPS (SHIW) data, for a 'very young/low-skilled' female worker, to 0 per cent for an 'old/highly qualified' worker (irrespective of gender). Although conditional probabilities are substantially different from the unconditional ones, particularly for females (see Table 10.1); the picture that emerges from Table 10.3, indicates once more that being young/unskilled and female are the attributes that make a worker more likely to suffer from a depressed pay condition.

Table 10.3　*Conditional probability of being low paid: INPS and SHIW data, 1987*

INPS data (1987)			
Individual	description	female	male
1. Base	avg.age (42f, 45m), manual, small firm (1-20), incompl. particip (less 52 weeks), 'other service' ind.	0.4903	0.0741
2. Young	age=30, manual, small firm (1-20), incompl. particip (less 52 weeks), 'wholesale-retail trade' industry	0.7852	0.3351
3. Old	age=55, manager, big firm (+251), compl. particip (52 weeks), 'bank-insurance' industry	0.0000	0.0001
4.Very young, low-skilled	age=20, manual, small firm (1-20), incompl. particip (less 52 weeks), 'craft-work' industry	0.9511	0.6107
SHIW data (1987)			
1. Base	avg.age (40.3), avg. educat. (9.8 years), manual, 'other service' industry, south	0.1323	0.0220
2. Young	age=30, educat.=8 years, manual, 'wholesale-retail trade' industry, south	0.4614	0.1596
3. Old	age=55, educat.=18 years, manager, bank-insurance industry, north	0.0000	0.0000
4.Very young, low-skilled	age=20, educat.=8 years, manual, 'other service' industry, south	0.7492	0.4102

Note:　Conditional probabilities computed from ML coefficient estimates.

5　PATTERNS OF EARNINGS MOBILITY

Analyses based on cross-section data only offer a picture of low-paid employment at a given point in time. Since individuals can change their relative position within the earnings distribution over time, restricting attention to the pool of low-paid individuals at a point in time might tell us very little about how low pay is shared among the different groups of workers.

In this section we investigate the extent of earnings mobility which characterizes the lower end of the earnings distribution (OECD 1996, Bigard et al. 1996, Contini et al. 1997).[23] Individuals will be ranked according to their position in the earnings hierarchy, at two different points in time, and then arranged into deciles of the distribution.[24] For the purpose of this exercise, we selected approximately 3 000 workers present continuously from 1975 to

1988.[25] Mobility is analysed recording workers' transitions across deciles (transition matrix) and then comparing the relative position of each individual at the beginning and at the end of the period.[26] In Figure 10.5 we plot the frequency distribution of transitions occurring between the extreme years of the time period considered. The decile noted by D01 represents the lower end of the earnings distribution in the initial year of observation (D for departure), while the decile A10 represents the upper end of the earnings distribution in the final year of observation (A for arrival). In the case of 'perfect immobility' all transitions would lie along the main diagonal as individuals would end up exactly at the same (relative) position as they started. Conversely, in the case of 'perfect mobility' transitions would be uniformly distributed across deciles. In the figure, a substantial concentration along the main diagonal indicates the existence of a certain degree of earnings immobility.

Figure 10.5   Transition matrix (1975–88)

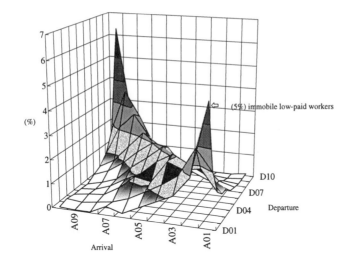

Focusing on low-paid workers, the spike observed at the lower extreme of the distribution (marked with the arrow in Figure 10.5) seems to suggest some persistence in the low-pay status. In particular, 50 per cent of the individuals who started at the beginning of the period in the lowest decile of the distribution (D01) can still be found in the same decile at the end of the period. If we consider the first two deciles this percentage rises to 60 per cent. On the whole, as shown in Table 10.4, the percentage of individuals who remain in the same relative earnings position is 30.5 per cent (compared with

10 per cent in perfect mobility) while 35.7 per cent are found to be worse off in terms of their relative earnings position. Hence, it is not always the same individuals who are low paid – although a significant proportion of them, as workers move within the earnings distribution, are changing their relative position over time.

Table 10.4   Indicators of mobility

| Description | Range | | Index |
	Perfect mobility	No-mobility	
Frequency of movements			
IMR - Immobility ratio (%)	10.00	100.00	30.53
ASR - Moving up (%)	0.00	45.00	33.74
DSR - Moving down (%)	0.00	45.00	35.72
Indicators of mobility			
AAJ - Absolute jump	0.00	3.33	1.42
ASJ - Ascending jump (N)	0.00	1.65	0.71
ADJ - Descending jump (N)	0.00	1.65	0.71

Besides the proportion of individuals moving up or down within the earnings hierarchy, it is interesting to investigate how many deciles on average individuals move; that is, the amplitude of the jumps. The indicator we use is the average absolute jump (AAJ).[27] The average magnitude of the jumps is 1.42 deciles (corresponding to a move of 15 per cent in the earnings distribution). The latter can be further decomposed into upward and downward movements. In the table we also report the average ascending/descending jumps (ASJ = 0.71, ADJ = 0.71), which show a fairly symmetric behaviour in the amplitude of the moves.

However, what might be more interesting for the purposes of the present work, is the possibility that the likelihood of moving (up or down) might be dependent on the starting position of the individual in the earnings hierarchy. That is, do individuals who start at the lower end of the earnings distribution (the low paid) stand the same chance of moving up as those higher up in the hierarchy? In Figure 10.6, we investigate this hypothesis, both conditioning the average jump on the decile of departure at the beginning of the period and normalizing with respect to perfect mobility (i.e. set equal to one).[28]

Looking at the individuals who start from the lowest deciles of the distribution, it can be noted that – with respect to perfect mobility – average ascending jumps are relatively small, while descending jumps are big. Hence, for those individuals characterized by a relatively weak starting position in the earnings hierarchy, the probability of remaining there or falling behind is quite high. In other words, some individuals might be stuck in a low-pay 'trap' for a significant portion of their working life.[29]

Figure 10.6   Ascending and descending jumps by deciles

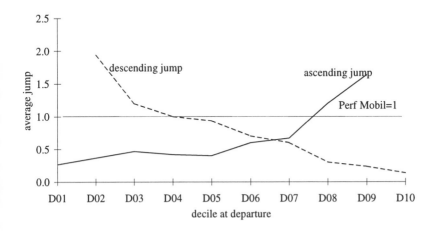

6 CONCLUDING REMARKS

In this chapter we have looked at the evolution of low-wage employment in Italy using micro data at the individual level for 1975–93. During this period significant changes occurred in the structure of the labour force as well as in the pay setting institutions, which exerted major influences over the distribution of wages. However, mainly due to distinct features, such as national collective bargaining, strong unions and labour market legislation, only moderate effects on the distribution of wages can be detected for most of the years considered. The role of these factors in shaping the distribution of wages, nevertheless, has become progressively less important in more recent years and increasing concern about rising earnings inequality and low pay has arisen. Indeed, the proportion of low-paid workers, after having been falling continuously over the 1970s and the beginning of the 1980s, has been rising over the late 1980s and early 1990s.

In the study, after describing the evolution of low-wage employment, we also investigate which groups in the labour force are more likely to suffer from low-wage episodes and, *ceteris paribus*, which characteristics of both individuals and employers are more frequently associated with low wage rates. In general the results show that males as opposed to females have a lower probability of earning a low wage, and that age and higher qualifications *ceteris paribus* reduce workers' likelihood of being low paid. Larger firms located in the northern regions are also less likely to pay low-wage levels. More specifically, comparing two stylized individuals with different characteristics; a 'very young/low-skilled' female worker and an 'old/highly qualified' worker (irrespective of gender), the likelihood of being low paid arises from 95 per cent in the former case to zero in the latter.

As discussed in the study, one major limitation of the analyses based on cross-section data is that they only offer a picture of low-paid employment at a given point in time. Since individuals can change their relative position within the earnings distribution over time, restricting attention to the pool of low-paid individuals might tell us very little about how low pay is shared among the different groups of workers or whether a low wage is a transitory or a permanent feature of the individual wage profile. The analysis of the dynamics of wages using longitudinal micro-data, shows that individuals who start from the lower end of the earnings distribution (i.e. the low paid) are less likely to move higher up in the hierarchy as opposed to those who start from higher positions.

These results offer a composite picture of low-wage employment in Italy with some implications for policy, as it appears not only that low-pay spells tend to be more frequent and concentrated among a given set of individuals, but also that individual earnings over the life cycle can be severely affected by long spells of low pay. Having said this the agenda of desirable policy measures is not an easy task as many of the options implemented elsewhere proved, at time, either ineffective or showed undesirable side effects. Clearly, more research is needed to identify and design the appropriate policy mix which will eventually reduce if not eliminate the low-pay 'trap'.

NOTES

1   I am grateful to R. Asplund, T. Atkinson, A. Bigard, F. Bourguignon, C. Dell'Aringa, Y. Guillotin, M. Keese, M. Manacorda, P. Sestito, P. Swaim, M. Stewart and participants to the TSER Conference on 'Low Wage Employment in Europe' (January 1997, Bordeaux-FR) and AFSE Conference on 'New Income Inequalities' (May 1997, Le Mans-FR) for comments and suggestions. The data used in the present study have been kindly supplied by INPS (Istituto Nazionale della Previdenza Sociale) and by the Bank of Italy. This research is also part of the activities of the LoWER Network under the CEE-TSER Programme. Financial support from CNR is also gratefully acknowledged. The usual disclaimers apply.

2   Evidence for Italy on the effects of technical progress on wage dispersion can be found in Casavola et al. (1996). Conversely, Erickson and Ichino (1995) and Dell'Aringa and Lucifora (1994) provide evidence on, respectively, the effects of institutional changes and unionization on wage dispersion.

3 Several complementary explanations for the changing structure of wages have been offered ranging from widespread (skilled-biased) technological change to growing trade with low-wage developing countries as well as to major labour market reforms aimed at increasing labour market flexibility (Katz and Murphy 1992, Wood 1994, Freeman 1993).

4 For an extensive survey of the different views on low-wage employment and the economic effects of minimum wages see the 'Policy Forum' section in the *Economic Journal* (1996).

5 Also the following studies provide evidence on income distribution patterns in Italy: Brandolini and Sestito (1994, 1997) and Rossi (1993).

6 OECD (1996) reports that only Canada, Finland and Germany have seen a decrease in the dispersion of earnings over the period.

7 See OECD (1996) for a discussion of the properties and limitations of the different measures for the low-pay cut-offs.

8 Other organizations have proposed different pay thresholds. The Trade Union Congress (TUC) suggests a measure for defining low pay, which ranges from half to two-thirds of median male earnings. Similar cut-offs are adopted by the British Low Pay Unit (BLPU).

9 The year chosen is not exactly the same for all countries. For some countries it refers to 1993 (Austria, Belgium, Italy, Sweden) while 1995 is available for others (Australia, France, Switzerland and the UK).

10 The original name of the survey is *Indagine sui Bilanci delle Famiglie*. See Banca d'Italia (Bank of Italy, 1993) for a more detailed description of the sample frame and for variable definitions.

11 It should be noted that the number of part-time workers is very low in the Italian economy.

12 Among the main reasons for dropping out of the panel we can list: retirement, self-employment, long-term unemployment, and if moving into the Public Administration. However, individuals who drop out of the panel and re-enter some years later can (in general) be tracked. Since attrition is likely to be more serious the longer the time period considered, there is a clear trade-off between long periods and sample representativeness.

13 In the Italian sample, if the individual becomes unemployed for less than a year he or she will appear in the data with a shorter number of weeks worked. Conversely, when the length of the unemployment spell is over 12 months there will be no individual record for that given year in the data. In a recent study using a different methodology, Bingley et al. (1995) try to correct for different sources of selectivity. Their main finding is that unemployment represents the most important source of selectivity.

14 An interesting result, which confirms previous findings in the literature (Sloane and Theodossiou 1996), is that in Italy also only a small proportion of the low paid are found in low-income households.

15 It should be stressed that the evolution of incidence rates (i.e. proportion of low-wage employment) for broad groups can be affected by variations in unemployment rates or by changes in (female) participation. If transitions to unemployment or to non-labour force activity are more likely to originate from low pay, then a large increase in the stock of the unemployed could induce an underestimation of the incidence of low pay. Experimentation using fixed employment proportions, however, showed little difference from the pattern reported in the figures, suggesting that the bias (if any) is very small.

16 Since SHIW data are not available for 1985, and from 1987 onwards they are only available every two years, in all subsequent figures – for graphical convenience – missing points have been interpolated.

17 Manual workers experience, in general, higher low-pay incidence rates as compared with non-manual workers. However, when differences across gender are considered, non-manual females appear to be worse off in terms of the risk of falling into low pay than manual males (results not reported).

18 In practice, in the empirical analysis the following indicators have been computed:

Total Incidence	*Incidence (Risk)*	*Concentration*
$TINC = (LW/E)$	$RINC = (Lw_i/E_i)$	$CON = (Lw_i/LW)$

where LW shows the total number of low-paid workers and E represents the total number of employees in employment, Lw_i indicates the number of individuals of the *i-th* group (age, industry, occupation, etc.) who fall below the low-pay threshold, while E_i reports the total number of employees belonging to the i-th group.

19 It should be noted that the very young are not included in our sample ('young' workers are aged 24 or less in 1975). This is partly intended to exclude from the sample full-time students doing small jobs and alternating education and work within the year. Furthermore, there is significant evidence suggesting that in Italy the age at which individuals start work-ing is on average much higher than in other countries (Casavola et al. 1995).

20 A previous study using a similar methodology to analyse low pay in Italy is Lucifora (1993).

21 Marginal effects can be computed, as follows: $\partial P[w_i < \mu]/\partial X_i = \phi[\ X_i'\ \beta]\beta$ where ϕ is the density function of the standard normal and the other symbols are as previously defined. As is common practice, continuous variables have been evaluated at their means; conversely, for dummy variables (D_i) the effect is computed – after partitioning the X vector – looking at the change from zero to one.

$$P[w_i < \mu|\ D_i{=}1] - P[w_i < \mu|\ D_i{=}0]$$

Statistical significance, however, refers to the original ML coefficients: absolute asymptotic t-ratios have been reported in Table 10.2.

22 For exposition purposes, stylized individuals have been chosen so as to represent rather extreme cases. Conditional probabilities have been computed from ML coefficient estimates (not reported).

23 Some of the evidence reported in this section is part of a joint research with A. Bigard, Y. Guillotin and F. Rappelli. I am grateful to them for numerous and useful discussions. Con-tini et al. (1997) also estimate a logit model for the probability of being low paid at two different dates.

24 Considering the shape of the earnings distribution (which in general is not uniform), it must be stressed that the distance in absolute terms between earnings ranks is not the same. In particular, a movement from position 3 to position 5 of the earnings hierarchy, in relative terms, is similar to a movement from position 8 to position 10; in absolute terms, however, the earnings difference is not the same. Also, due to the fact that there might be individuals earning an identical salary, the number of observations in each decile can be slightly differ-ent.

25 For a more detailed description of the data set used and the methodology, see Bigard et al. (1996).

26 Transition matrices indicate the proportion of individuals (n_{ij}), in the i-th decile of the earn-ings distribution at time t (D_i denotes departure), who are observed at time $t{+}k$ in the j-th decile (A_j denotes arrival).

27 The Average Absolute Jump (AAJ) is computed as follows: AAJ $= \Sigma_{ij}\ (n_{ij}/n)|j{-}i|$. Note that under 'perfect mobility', the AAJ index is equal to 3.3; conversely, the average 'signed' jump is equal to zero by construction.

28 Note that since average absolute jumps are different depending on the decile of departure, a normalization is necessary for comparison purposes. To see how this could be consider the case of 'perfect mobility': the average absolute jump for D01 and D10 is 4.5, however it is 2.5 for D05 and D06.

29 One limitation of the analysis which should be stressed is that we are treating the relative earnings position of the individual at departure as exogenous. Also, as attention has been restricted to a sample of individuals with continuous employment, this is likely to underes-timate the additional mobility which also occurs through movements into and out of em-ployment. For an interesting discussion and an application, see Stewart and Swaffield (1997).

REFERENCES

Bank of Italy (1993), 'I bilanci delle famiglie italiane nell'anno 1991', Supplemento al Bollettino Statistico, *Note metodologiche e informazioni statistiche*, Banca d'Italia, no. 44.

Bigard, A., Y. Guillotin, C. Lucifora and F. Rappelli (1996), *An International Comparison of Earnings Mobility: The Case of Italy and France*, Milano: Università Cattolica, Istituto di Economia dell'Impresa e del Lavoro, DP no. 13.

Bingley, P., N.H. Bjørn and N. Westergård-Nielsen (1995), *Wage Mobility in Denmark 1980–1990*, Aarhus: Centre for Labour Market and Social Research, Aarhus University.

Bodo, G. and P. Sestito (1991), *Le vie dello sviluppo*, Bologna: il Mulino.

Bound, J. and G. Johnson (1992), 'Changes in the Structure of Wages in the 1980's: An Evaluation of Alternative Explanations', *American Economic Review*, **82**, pp. 371–92.

Brandolini, A. and P. Sestito (1994), *Cyclical and Trend Changes in Inequality in Italy, 1977–1991*, Banca d'Italia, mimeo.

Brandolini, A. and P. Sestito (1996), *Low Paid Workers: some figures for Italy 1979–1995*, Banca d'Italia, mimeo.

Brown, C., C. Gilroy and A. Kohen (1982), 'The Effect of the Minimum Wage on Employment and Unemployment', *Journal of Economic Literature*, **20**, pp. 487–528.

Card, D. and A. Krueger (1995), *Myth and Measurement: The New Economics of the Minimum Wage*, Princeton University Press.

Casavola, P., A. Gavosto and P. Sestito (1996), 'Technical Progress and Wage Dispersion in Italy: Evidence from Firm's Data', *Annales d'Economie et de Statistique*, pp. 41–2.

Casavola, P., A. Gavosto and P. Sestito (1995), *Salari e mercato del lavoro locale*, Lavoro e Relazioni Industriali: Rivista di Economia Applicata 4/95.

Contini, B. and R. Revelli (1992), *Imprese, occupazione e retribuzioni*, Bologna: il Mulino.

Contini, B., M. Filippi and C. Villosio (1997), *Earnings Mobility in the Italian Economy*, University of Turin, mimeo.

Dell'Aringa, C. (1993), 'Il mercato del lavoro nel contesto internazionale', in Micossi, S. and I. Visco (eds), *Inflazione, concorrenza e sviluppo: l'economia italiana e la sfida dell'integrazione europea*, Bologna: il Mulino.

Dell'Aringa, C. and C. Lucifora (1990), 'Wage Determination and Union Behaviour in Italy: An Efficiency Wage Interpretation?', in R. Brunetta and C. Dell'Aringa (eds), *Markets, Institutions and Cooperation: Labour Relations and Economic Performance*, London: Macmillan.

Dell'Aringa, C. and C. Lucifora (1994), 'Wage Dispersion and Unionism: Do Unions Protect Low Pay?', *International Journal of Manpower*, **15**, pp. 150–69.

Dickens R., S. Machin and A. Manning (1996), *The Effects of Minimum Wages on Employment: Theory and Evidence from the U.K*, London: London School of Economics, Centre for Economic Performance, DP.

Dolado, J., F. Kramarz, S. Machin, A. Manning, A. Margolis and C. Teulings (1996), 'The Economic Impact of Minimum Wages in Europe', *Economic Policy*, **15**, pp. 317–57.

Erickson, C. and A. Ichino (1995), 'Wage Differentials in Italy: Market Forces, Institutions and Inflation', in R. Freeman and L. Katz (eds), *Working Under Different Rules*, New York: Russell Sage Foundation.

Freeman, R. (1993) 'How much has de-unionisation contributed to the rise in male earnings inequality', in Danziger, S. and P. Gottschalk (eds), *Uneven Tides: Rising Inequality in America*, New York: Russell Sage Foundation.

Katz, L. and K. Murphy (1992), 'Changes in relative wages 1963–1987: supply and demand factors', *Quarterly Journal of Economics*, **107**, pp. 35–78.

Lucifora, C. (1993), 'I salari minimi in Italia: un'analisi dei lavoratori a bassa remunerazione', in Dell'Aringa, C. (ed.), *Rapporto sui salari, 1992*, Milano: Franco Angeli.

Lucifora, C. and F. Rappelli (1995), 'Evoluzione delle retribuzioni nel ciclo di vita: un'analisi su dati longitudinali', *Lavoro e Relazioni Industriali: Rivista di Economia Applicata*, **1**, pp. 77–110.

Manacorda, M. (1997), *How Did the Distribution of Men's Wages Evolve in Italy over the Last Two Decades*, London: London School of Economics, Centre for Economic Performance, mimeo.

Murphy, K. and F. Welch (1992), 'The Structure of Wages', *Quarterly Journal of Economics*, **107**, pp. 285–326.

OECD (1993), *Employment Outlook*, Paris.

OECD (1996), *Employment Outlook*, Paris.

Rebitzer, J.B. and L.J. Taylor (1991), *The Consequences of Minimum Wage Laws: Some New Theoretical Ideas*, National Bureau of Economic Research, Working Paper no. 3877.

Rossi, N. (1993), *La Crescita Ineguale. 1981–1991. Primo Rapporto CNEL sulla distribuzione e la redistribuzione del reddito in Italia*, Bologna: il Mulino.

Salvati, M. and L. Raichlin (1990), 'Industrial Employment in Italy: The Consequences of Shifts in Union Power in the 1970s and 1980s', in Brunetta, R. and C. Dell'Aringa (eds), *Markets, Institutions and Cooperation: Labour Relations and Economic Performance*, London: Macmillan.

Sestito, P. (1992), *Empirical Earnings Functions in a Decade of Turbulence: the Italian Experience*, Banca d'Italia, mimeo.

Sloane, P. and I. Theodossiou (1996), 'Earnings Mobility, Family Income and Low Pay', *Economic Journal*, **106**, pp. 657–66.

Stewart, M. and J. Swaffield (1997), *Low Pay Dynamics and Transition Probabilities*, University of Warwick, mimeo.

Wood, A. (1994), *North–south trade, employment and inequality*, Oxford: Clarendon Press.

11. Wage Growth of Low- and High-Skilled Workers in the Netherlands

R. van Opstal, R. Waaijers and G. Wiggers

1 INTRODUCTION

The wage position and wage mobility of the lowest-paid workers is attracting considerable interest, both nationally and internationally (see e.g. OECD 1996, Chapter 3). Is low income a permanent state or do low-skilled workers receive higher wages over time? And to what extent does wage growth of the low-skilled deviate from wage growth of higher-skilled workers? This article explores these questions for the Netherlands.

The wage position of an individual worker can develop in different ways. Wages may increase over time at the same job, or they may increase when a worker moves to a better job. Hourly wages may vary also with the length of the working week. This article analyses wage growth resulting from age and job tenure, both for low-skilled and high-skilled workers. We explore the wage profile and the effects of age and tenure by using the theory of human capital and the related concepts of general experience and firm-specific experience (see Becker 1964).

According to human capital theory, workers invest in new skills during their working lives because skills enhance productivity and improved productivity gets rewarded with increased wages. Workers earn relatively little at the start of their career, both because they are still spending time on training on the job and because their productivity is low owing to a lack of human capital. As time spent on production increases, and as productivity rises with skill, workers find their wages increasing rapidly early on in their careers. Faced with a shorter horizon over which to reap the benefits, workers reduce their investment in skills as they get older and approach retirement. Coupled with increased obsolescence of skills, workers' productivity and wages flatten out and may even decline towards the end of their working life.

In order to explain age and tenure effects on wage growth, human capital theory distinguishes between general and firm-specific experience. General experience improves productivity (and wages) at any firm, while specific experience improves productivity only at the current firm. The difference between the two types of experience can be identified when a worker changes jobs. At that time only the higher earnings accumulated with specific human capital are lost, depressing wages. Whether such a decline in individual wages will be observed depends to a large extent on the cause of the observed job change; i.e. whether it is involuntary (layoff) or voluntary (quit). In our analysis general experience is approximated by the time since leaving formal full-time education and firm-specific experience by tenure.

The next section describes the econometric model we applied and the datasets used. Some summary statistics that characterize the data set are provided. Subsequently we present the estimation results of the econometric model. The article ends with conclusions and a short description of intended future research at CPB on individual wage growth.

2 ECONOMETRIC MODEL AND DATA

The starting point for the empirical analysis is a standard micro wage equation

$$\ln w_{ijt} = \alpha \; gexp_{it} + \beta \; ten_{ijt} + \gamma \; Z_{ij} + \varepsilon_{ijt} \quad with \quad \varepsilon_{ijt} = f_{ij} + e_{ijt} \qquad (11.1)$$

where w_{ijt} is the hourly wage rate of worker i in job j in year t, $gexp$ represents general labour market experience and ten stands for tenure. Higher order terms for both experience and tenure are included in the empirical analysis, but are left out in equation (11.1) for ease of notation. Z_{ij} is a vector of personal and job characteristics which are assumed to be constant over time. The error term ε is the sum of a match-specific component (J_{ij}) and a white noise error term (e_{ijt}).

Estimating equation (11.1) using cross-section data produces biased estimates for the true return to experience and tenure. The reason is that wage profiles are influenced not only by human capital accumulation, but also by the process of job search matching specific workers to specific jobs (represented by J_{ij} in the equation). For an extensive discussion of this problem, we refer to the literature, e.g. Abraham and Farber (1987) and Topel (1991).

The use of panel data circumvents most, although not all, estimation problems. We use a two-step estimation introduced by Topel (1991). In the first step, equation (11.1) is estimated in first differences for individual workers who work at the same firm in two consecutive years. This eliminates the match-specific component J_{ij}. Within a job, the increase in general experience coincides with the increase of tenure. Accordingly, the first step yields consistent estimates for the sum $(\alpha+\beta)$ of the effects of general and firm-specific experience and for the parameters for the higher order terms of experience and tenure.

To be able to separate the first-order effects of general experience (α) and tenure (β), we estimate a second equation as in Topel (1991):

$$\ln w_{ijt} - (\hat{\alpha} + \hat{\beta}) ten_{ijt} = \alpha\, gexp_{i0} + \gamma Z_{ij} + \varepsilon_{ijt} \qquad (11.2)$$

The expected wage of an individual at entry into a job is calculated as the difference between the actual wage and the estimated increases over time at that job (using the parameter $(\alpha+\beta)$ estimated in step (1)). The expected initial wage is then regressed on experience at entry and on the other factors (see equation (11.2)), resulting in an estimate of general experience on initial wages (α). By combining the results from both steps, we obtain an estimate for β.[1]

To execute this two-step estimation procedure, we use two different data sources. The first data set is the Social and Economic Panel (SEP) from Statistics Netherlands, which contains information on wage levels for a panel of households over a number of years (about 5 000 households per year). We use information on 2 778 workers in the market sector for the years 1985 to 1989 and on 2 419 workers for the years 1989 to 1992.[2] In addition we use data from annual Wage Surveys from the Ministry of Social Affairs and Employment for 1993, 1994 and 1995. Each Wage Survey is a cross section of individual workers taken from payroll records of a sample of firms, and contains, among other things, one-year wage changes. Each Wage Survey involves around 20 000 individuals working in the market sector.

Both data sets have advantages and disadvantages. The main advantage of the SEP, being a household survey, is that data on workers who change employers (movers) are recorded. The Wage Survey contains data only for workers who stay with the same employer in two consecutive years (stayers). However, wage data collected from household surveys are less accurate than those from payroll records, such as those contained in the Wage Survey.

Low-skilled and high-skilled workers are defined on the basis of formal educational attainment. Workers with qualifications no higher than lower vocational education (LBO) or lower general secondary education (MAVO) are classified as 'low-skilled', while the remainder is defined as 'high-skilled'. According to this definition, between 30–40 per cent of workers are low skilled, depending on the particular year and sample.

Table 11.1 presents summary statistics on annual wage growth of individual workers in both data sets. Wages are deflated by general contractual wage increases to make them comparable across years. Workers aged 22 years and younger are excluded from the table. Wage patterns of the young in the Netherlands are affected by special institutional factors. Although youngsters acquire a lot of work experience in their first years in the labour market, this can hardly be the full explanation for their rapid wage growth. The system of minimum youth wages in the Netherlands plays an important role as well (see the Appendix). Owing to this complication, youngsters are excluded from the analysis.

Table 11.1   Average annual wage growth (in per cent), deflated by contractual wage increases, by skill level, workers 23–64 years, market sector

	1985–1989		1989–1992		1992–1995
	Movers	Stayers	Movers	Stayers	Stayers
Low-skilled	4.3	3.0	2.8	2.3	1.4
High-skilled	5.7	3.3	4.9	3.1	2.8

For the wage changes taken from the SEP a distinction is made between earnings growth of movers and stayers. For both sub-samples wage growth of movers is well above that of stayers. This seems to indicate that most movers in our sample change jobs voluntarily. We return to this issue below.

3 ESTIMATION RESULTS

Table 11.2 and Table 11.3 summarize the results[3] from the estimated wage equations using the estimation method described above. Table 11.2 shows the partial effect on pay of accumulated general experience.

Table 11.2   Estimated annual earnings growth (in per cent) with accumulating general experience

Years of general experience	1985–1989		1989–1992		1994–1995	
	Low-skilled	High-skilled	Low-skilled	High-skilled	Low-skilled	High-skilled
0–5		5.2		5.6		5.2
5–10	2.3	3.1	1.7	3.5	1.7	3.2
10–20	0.9	1.2	0.5	1.2	0.8	1.7
20–30	–0.1	–0.2	0.1	–0.5	0.2	1.1
30–40	–0.1	0.6	–0.1	–0.3	0.1	0.4

Since the estimates are based on data from adult workers only, there is no figure for wage growth of the low skilled with only 0–5 years of general experience. By their 23rd birthday, these workers have typically been active in the labour market for at least five years. In order to illustrate the partial effect of general experience on wages, Figure 11.1 plots wage growth of a fictitious low-skilled worker and a fictitious high-skilled worker by making use of the estimated parameters from the wage equation and of the calculated wage growth for youngsters in the Appendix. In these plots we implicitly neglect the effect of tenure on wages. We assume that the low-skilled and high-skilled workers start their career in the labour market at the ages of 16 and 23 years, respectively. For both workers, we assume that the starting wage is 35 per cent above the relevant minimum wage.

Figure 11.1   Wage patterns for fictitious workers (at 1994 levels) as a result of accumulating general experience

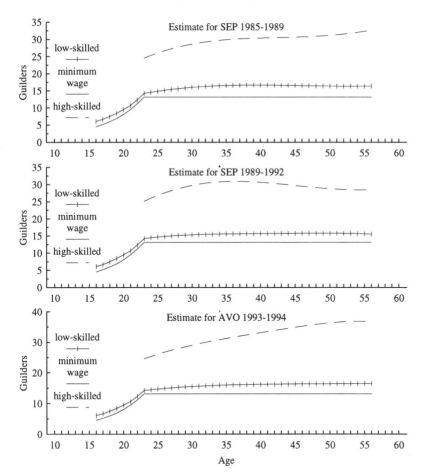

Human capital theory predicts that earnings rise most sharply in the early phase of a person's working life and then gradually flatten out. Pay of low-skilled workers barely increases after 20 years of general experience, while the high-skilled see their earnings rise up to 35–40 years' experience. The earnings growth of low-skilled workers lags well behind that of the high skilled. Experience that is accumulated after the first five years until retirement adds roughly 20 per cent to wages for low-skilled workers. The corresponding figure for the high-skilled earnings is 60 per cent based on the 1994 Wage Survey. For both sub-samples from the Social and Economic Panel the experience-profile of high-skilled resembles that from the Wage Survey up to about 20 years of experience. Due to fewer observations and more measurement errors the estimates of the higher order terms are less accurate in these data sets.

Human capital theory explains differences in wage growth between high-skilled and low-skilled workers by differential productivity developments. Low-skilled workers obviously reach their maximum productivity levels at a much earlier age than higher-skilled workers. Income tested benefits, resulting in a high marginal wedge, might also depress wage growth for low-paid workers. Due to a high marginal wedge, employers' wage costs have to rise disproportionately in order to give the employee a net earnings increase. Employers may increase gross labour cost outlays in line with productivity increases, but this would translate into a smaller increase in after-tax wages.

The accumulation of firm-specific experience, shown in Table 11.3, contributes far less to earnings growth than general experience does, especially in the case of high-skilled workers.

Table 11.3   Estimated annual earnings growth (in per cent) with accumulating firm-specific experience

Years of tenure	1985–1989		1989–1992		1994	
	Low-skilled	High-skilled	Low-skilled	High-skilled	Low-skilled	High-skilled
0–5	1.2	–0.2	1.7	0.8	0.7	0.8
5–10	1.1	0.8	0.8	0.4	0.6	0.4
10–15	1.1	1.4	0.5	0.6	0.4	0.1

In comparison with similar estimates for the United States, the contribution of tenure to earnings growth turns out to be much smaller in the Netherlands, especially during the first years of tenure. Firm-specific experience in the USA yields annual wage increases of 3.5 per cent during the first five years of tenure, flattening out to 1.3 per cent between 5 and 10 years of tenure and to 0.8 per cent between 10 and 15 years of tenure (Topel 1991). For France (Margolis 1996), tenure effects are roughly in between those for the

USA and the Netherlands (2.5 per cent between 0 to 5 years, 0.5 per cent between 5 to 10 years and 0.8 per cent between 10 to 15 years).

The reasons behind these international differences have not been analysed. Even so, some possible causes can be identified.[4] First, Dutch firms might invest relatively little in firm-specific training. However, this is not borne out by international comparisons of investment in company training (Ministry of Social Affairs and Employment 1996). Still, the firm-specific content of company training may vary internationally. Insofar as the acquired knowledge is applicable also in other jobs, the effect of firm-specific experience on pay will be reduced. This argument may be more relevant for non-manual than for manual workers, thereby explaining part of the difference in the estimated tenure profiles for high-skilled and low-skilled workers.

Another possible explanation for the limited seniority effect may originate in the relative importance of voluntary and involuntary job changes.[5] Although the existing data do not permit a 'clear-cut' comparison between the Netherlands and the USA, several studies suggest that in the United States relatively more job changes are involuntary (Altonji et al. 1993, Hassink 1996, OSA 1996). Since involuntary job change (or the threat of one) increases the chances that the worker has to accept a less well-paid new job, the seniority effect on pay is likely to be stronger in the United States.[6] Moreover, owing to the relatively low or even wholly absent unemployment benefits in the United States, unemployed American workers are under far greater pressure than their Dutch counterparts to accept a new job quickly, such a job does not pay well. An unemployed Dutch worker, in contrast, can afford to take more time to look for a job close to the previous wage level.

4 CONCLUSIONS AND FURTHER RESEARCH

We found that wage growth of low-skilled workers is much lower than that of high-skilled workers. Furthermore, wage growth of high-skilled workers depends above all on age (general experience) and not so much on tenure (firm-specific experience). For low-skilled workers, the relative contribution of tenure to total wage growth is somewhat larger than for high-skilled workers.

Although we cannot draw firm conclusions about the underlying reasons behind our empirical findings, we have suggested some relevant factors. In future research, we plan to explore the importance of these factors further. In particular, we intend to study the effects of high marginal wedges on hourly wage growth by making use of the SEP over a longer period (1985–96). This allows us to analyse the wage growth of persons receiving housing benefits, who sometimes face marginal wedges up to 100 per cent. This analysis should bring us a step further in understanding labour marker behaviour in general and wage growth differentials in particular.

NOTES

1   For details on the estimation procedure and potential remaining biases, see Topel (1991).
2   Owing to changes in the survey questions on earnings and hours worked, the panel data on hourly wages are not comparable between these two sub-periods. We have a double observation for 1989 because from the 1990 survey onwards, *previous* year's earnings are asked for.
3   For the Wage Survey we present only the results for the 1994 sample. The results for both other sample years as well as the three years pooled are very similar. Full estimation results are shown in the Appendix.
4   Also differences in data selection (age groups, no educational distinction) may contribute to the differences in results.
5   For yet another explanation, which has to do with the possibly of greater insider power of employees in the United States compared to the Netherlands, see Hartog et al. (1997).
6   Analyses of pay profiles following mass layoffs in the United States do indeed reveal major pay cuts; see Jacobson et al. (1993).

REFERENCES

Abraham, K. and H. Farber (1987), 'Job duration, seniority and earnings', *American Economic Review*, **77**, pp. 278–97.

Altonji, J.G. and N. Williams (1993), 'Using wage growth model to estimate the return to experience, seniority and job mobility', in J.C. van Ours, G.A. Pfann and G. Ridder (eds), *Labor demand and equilibrium wage formation*.

Becker, G. (1964), *Human capital*, New York: National Bureau for Economic Research.

Hartog, J., R. van Opstal and C.N. Teulings (1997), 'Inter-industry wage differentials and tenure effects in the Netherlands and the U.S. ', *De Economist*, **145**, pp. 91–9.

Hassink, W.J.H. (1996), *Worker flows and the employment adjustment of firms*, Amsterdam: Free University, PhD-thesis.

Jacobson, L.S., R.J. LaLonde and D.G. Sullivan (1993), 'Earnings losses of displaced workers', *American Economic Review*, **83**, pp. 685–709.

Johnson, R.W. and D. Neumark (1996), 'Wage declines among older men', *Review of Economics and Statistics*, **78**, pp. 740–48.

Margolis, D.N. (1996), 'Cohort effects and returns to seniority in France', *Annales d'Economie et de Statistique*, no. 41/42, pp.443–64.

Ministry of Social Affairs and Employment (1996), *The Dutch welfare state in an international and economic context* (in Dutch: De Nederlandse verzorgingsstaat in internationaal en economisch perspectief), Den Haag.

OECD (1996), *Employment outlook*, Paris.

OSA (1996), Demand for labor, trends report 1996 (in Dutch: Trendrapport vraag naar arbeid 1996), OSA report, no. 22.

Topel, R. (1991), 'Specific capital, mobility and wages: wages rise with seniority', *Journal of Political Economy*, **99**, pp. 145–76.

APPENDIX

Wage growth of youngsters
In the Netherlands wage growth of workers 22 years and younger is much higher than the average wage growth of adult workers. Although economic theory supports faster wage growth at younger ages, in this case the system of minimum youth wages plays an important role as well. Young workers are entitled to a minimum youth wage that approaches the statutory adult minimum wage in stages, rising from 30 per cent of the adult wage for 16 year olds to 85 per cent for 22 year olds.

With the minimum youth wage rising on average 16 per cent per year, a floor is set for wage raises for all workers earning up to around 16 per cent above the relevant minimum wage. The rising minimum wage is not binding for individuals whose wage is further removed from the minimum in a given year. The table below shows the effect: wage growth is much higher for individuals who are close to the relevant minimum wage in the initial year, and is lowest for those who are furthest removed. The link between skill, productivity, and wages is clearly not operative for those close to the minimum. Roughly half young workers earn less than 130 per cent of the minimum wage.

Table 11.A1   Wage growth of low-skilled workers aged 16–22, market sector 1994

Initial wage per worker in 1993 as a proportion of the statutory minimum wage appropriate to the worker's age.	Share (%)	Wage growth (%)
< 101%	6.0	19.2
101–105%	5.5	18.3
105–110%	6.8	16.1
110–120%	14.5	15.3
120–130%	16.7	12.5
130–140%	16.1	9.0
140–150%	12.9	7.2
> 150%	21.5	5.9
Total	100.0	11.2

Estimation results

Table 11.A2   *Estimation results for first step; dependent variable: first difference of hourly wage, workers 23 years and older, market sector*

	1985–1989		1989–1992		1993–1994	
	Low skilled	High skilled	Low skilled	High skilled	Low skilled	High skilled
delta (tenure/experience)	0.053	0.054	0.067	0.079	0.041	0.075
Standard errors	*0.011*	*0.011*	*0.040*	*0.011*	*0.003*	*0.003*
delta tenure2 (x 100)	–0.001	0.146	–0.184	–0.139	–0.022	–0.054
Standard errors	*0.044*	*0.085*	*0.167*	*0.099*	*0.013*	*0.026*
delta tenure3 (x 1000)	0.000	–0.036	0.074	0.076	0.003	0.005
Standard errors	*0.009*	*0.041*	*0.081*	*0.050*	*0.006*	*0.012*
delta tenure4 (x 10000)		0.004	–0.01	–0.011	0.000	–0.001
Standard errors	*0.000*	*0.006*	*0.012*	*0.008*	*0.001*	*0.002*
delta experience2 (x 100)	–0.145	–0.265	–0.242	–0.239	–0.13	–0.304
Standard errors	*0.058*	*0.125*	*0.320*	*0.124*	*0.027*	*0.038*
delta experience3 (x 1000)	0.016	0.046	0.062	0.024	0.023	0.079
Standard errors	*0.008*	*0.048*	*0.101*	*0.049*	*0.009*	*0.015*
delta experience4 (x 10000)		–0.002	–0.006	0.001	–0.002	–0.008
Standard errors	*0.000*	*0.006*	*–0.011*	*0.006*	*0.001*	*0.002*
R^2	0.006	0.010	0.004	0.029	0.021	0.060
S. E.	0.114	0.115	0.134	0.105	0.047	0.060
sample size	2 323	3 064	1 079	2 424	13 069	7 398

Note:
Nominal wages are deflated by general contractual wage increases to make them comparable over years.

Table 11.A3   Estimation results for second step; dependent variable: estimated hourly wage at the start of the present job, workers 23 years and older, market sector (standard errors in parentheses)

	1985–1989		1989–1992		1993–1994	
	Low skilled	High skilled	Low skilled	High skilled	Low skilled	High skilled
Experience	0.042	0.063	0.043	0.065	0.032	0.064
	(0.001)	(0.001)	(0.001)	(0.002)	(0.000)	(0.000)
University degree		0.353		0.337		0.352
		(0.021)		(0.019)		(0.006)
Mining and quarrying		0.195	0.444	0.260	−0.046	−0.05
		(0.192)	(0.126)	(0.121)	(0.046)	(0.082)
Manufacturing	0.163	0.146	0.103	0.043	−0.014	0.026
	(0.054)	(0.063)	(0.086)	(0.068)	(0.011)	(0.022)
Public utilities	0.064	0.079	0.119	0.085	0.028	0.033
	(0.090)	(0.084)	(0.122)	(0.088)	(0.028)	(0.034)
Construction industry	0.161	0.063	0.043	−0.068	0.096	0.042
	(0.057)	(0.067)	(0.089)	(0.072)	(0.011)	(0.024)
Trade, hotels etc.	0.152	0.143	0.033	−0.014	−0.065	−0.033
	(0.055)	(0.064)	(0.087)	(0.069)	(0.011)	(0.023)
Transport	0.166	0.182	0.132	0.040	−0.07	−0.064
	(0.057)	(0.067)	(0.089)	(0.071)	(0.012)	(0.024)
Banking, finance, insurance	0.289	0.218	0.180	0.108	−0.001	0.010
	(0.058)	(0.064)	(0.091)	(0.068)	(0.013)	(0.023)
Other commercial services	0.110	0.105	−0.092	0.042	−0.141	0.040
	(0.062)	(0.073)	(0.094)	(0.079)	(0.014)	(0.025)
Part–time (0< 30 hours)	−0.188	−0.238	−0.015	−0.146	−0.11	−0.175
	(0.027)	(0.073)	(0.037)	(0.029)	(0.006)	(0.011)
Female	−0.129	−0.139	−0.154	−0.197	−0.121	−0.137
	(0.023)	(0.023)	(0.032)	(0.021)	(0.005)	(0.007)
10–19 employees					0.024	0.048
					(0.007)	(0.013)
20–99 employees					0.028	0.072
					(0.006)	(0.011)
> 100 employees					0.068	0.113
					(0.006)	(0.011)
Constant term	2.292	2.405	2.597	2.676	2.706	2.643
	(0.054)	(0.062)	(0.086)	(0.067)	(0.012)	(0.024)
R^2	0.670	0.680	0.610	0.720	0.690	0.800
S. E.	0.26	0.33	0.30	0.31	0.20	0.25
sample size	1 160	1 528	840	1 579	14 415	8 412

PART FOUR

Low-Paid Employment in the OECD Countries:
An International Comparison

12. The Incidence and Dynamics of Low-Paid Employment in OECD Countries[1]

M. Keese, A. Puymoyen and P. Swaim

1 INTRODUCTION

The evidence that earnings inequality rose in several OECD countries during the 1980s has led to a revival of interest in issues concerning the distribution of income and the situation facing low-paid workers in particular. The pace and nature of technical change and growing trade with low-wage countries are often seen as key factors behind major shifts in the composition of labour demand in most industrialized countries over the last two decades. These developments may be putting downward pressure on wages of low-skilled workers. This has raised concerns about rising numbers of 'working poor'. However, falls in relative wages for low-skilled jobs may be required if these jobs are not to disappear altogether. In other words, there may be a trade-off between equity and efficiency, often characterized by the situation of low earnings inequality but rising unemployment in Europe versus rising earnings inequality but stable unemployment in the United States.

In order to develop appropriate policy responses to these issues, it is important to first understand the dimensions and dynamics of low pay in different countries and their relationship with employment and unemployment outcomes for different groups of workers. Apart from technical change and trade, institutional factors such as trade union coverage, wage bargaining arrangements and minimum wages also play an important role in the determination of wages for low-skilled workers. Examining cross-country differences in both the incidence and composition of low pay can help to disentangle universal pressures behind low wages from these institutional features. It is also important to take earnings dynamics into account: one country may have a higher incidence of low-paid employment at any point in time compared to another but it may also have higher earnings mobility and thus a more equal distribution of lifetime earnings.

Therefore, in this chapter we compare the incidence, distribution and dynamics of low-paid employment across several OECD countries. In section 2 we first discuss some methodological and data issues confronting international comparisons of low pay. For a sample of 19 countries, we then show that there are large differences in the overall incidence of low-paid employment, although low-paid jobs tend to be concentrated among the same types of workers in all countries. In section 3 we examine the role played by institutions in establishing wage floors which limit the incidence of low pay. The relationship between these wage floors and employment and unemployment outcomes for unskilled and inexperienced workers is also explored in this section. We then turn to our longitudinal analysis of a smaller number of countries in section 4, and examine the dynamics of shifts into and out of low-paid jobs. We conclude with a brief summary of our results and offer some reflections on where future work is warranted on low pay from an international perspective.

2 INTERNATIONAL DIFFERENCES IN THE INCIDENCE OF LOW PAY

2.1 Measurement and Data Issues

Measurement of the incidence of low pay will be sensitive to: i) the way low pay is defined; ii) the earnings concept used; iii) whether full-time and/or part-time workers are included; and iv) the choice of data source. The most important factor affecting international comparisons is probably the choice of either an absolute or relative measure of low pay. An absolute measure poses a number of difficult problems for making comparisons across countries, such as finding appropriate conversion factors for determining an equivalent benchmark for low pay in terms of each country's national currency. Moreover, what is considered a subsistence or low wage may change over time and may differ substantially across countries.

Therefore, for our comparison of OECD countries, we have chosen to use relative measures of low pay. In our cross-section analysis, low pay is defined as less than two-thirds of median earnings. The exact cut-off for defining low pay is somewhat arbitrary but, in fact, country rankings with respect to the incidence of low pay do not appear to be particularly sensitive to this choice (see OECD 1994, Table 1.11, for a comparison using a range of cut-offs). In section 4, on the dynamics of low pay, we take the bottom quintile of workers according to earnings as a supplementary measure of low-paid employment. This latter measure can still be classified as a relative measure because, even though the incidence of low pay is fixed, the earnings cut-off is effectively tied to the upper earnings limit of this group of low-paid workers and, thus, is not fixed in absolute terms.

The choice of a relative measure of low pay such as two-thirds of median earnings does mean, however, that some 'low-paid' workers in one country may actually earn more than some 'high-paid' workers in another country (in terms of a common currency). For example, as shown in Figure 12.1 (Panel A), median earnings for full-time workers and, hence, the relative cut-off for

Figure 12.1 Median and low earnings of full-time workers 1994: annual gross earnings, expressed in US$ using PPPs for private consumption

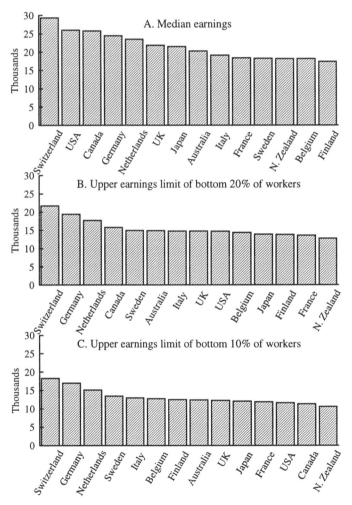

Source: The earnings data are from the OECD Database on Earnings Inequality; the purchasing power parities (PPPs) are from OECD, National Accounts.

determining low pay, are higher in the USA than in all other OECD countries with the notable exception of Switzerland.[2] At the same time we know that earnings inequality in the USA is much larger than in other countries so that even if median earnings are somewhat higher in the USA than elsewhere there may still be a substantial number of workers in the USA with low earnings even when compared to other countries in absolute terms. This is confirmed by the cross-country comparisons in Figure 12.1 of the upper earnings limit of the bottom quintile (Panel B) and bottom decile (Panel C) of all full-time workers. Whereas the USA ranks close to number one in terms of median gross earnings this ranking slips considerably for earnings of the bottom 20 per cent of workers. Nevertheless, the USA still ranks ahead of a number of other major industrialized countries such as Japan and France. However, the earnings of workers in the bottom decile in the USA, along with Canada, are lower than in all other countries except New Zealand.[3] At the opposite end of the scale is Sweden where median workers rank badly in terms of their earnings and yet, because of highly compressed earnings differentials, low-paid workers rank quite highly.

In terms of the universe of workers covered in our analysis, we have chosen to focus on full-time workers. Including part-time workers introduces the additional complication of disentangling differences in time worked from differences in wage rates. Hourly earnings could be compared for all workers but this type of data, as opposed to weekly or monthly earnings data, is not always available or subject to substantial measurement error. In fact, it turns out that for the United Kingdom the overall incidence of low pay is not substantially different whether measured with respect to hourly earnings for all workers or weekly earnings for full-time workers only.[4]

A final choice to be made concerns data sources. In general there are three types of data sources which can potentially provide earnings data at the individual level: i) establishment surveys; ii) household surveys; and iii) administrative data such as tax data or social security data. Each source has its advantages and disadvantages in terms of coverage and accuracy. From a review of a few countries for which it has been possible to confront the results of several sources, it would appear that: i) variation across countries in the measured incidence of low pay are more substantial than differences across data sources within countries; and ii) there is no systematic overstatement or understatement of the incidence of low pay by one type of source relative to another. Therefore, we decided to take a pragmatic approach. For each country we took the data source which could provide us with earnings distributions of full-time workers broken down by a number of characteristics such as age, sex, education, industry and occupation. Table 12.1 provides an overview of the principal data source used for each of the 19 countries we were able to include in our cross-section analysis (further details and additional data sources are provided in the Appendix and OECD 1996, Ch. 3).

Table 12.1   Overview of low-pay data sources

Country	Data source	Earnings definition	Comments
Australia	Household survey (labour force survey)	Gross weekly earnings	Similar data can also be obtained from an establishment survey.
Austria	Household survey (Mikrozensus)	Net monthly earnings	Social security data on gross earnings can also be obtained.
Belgium	Social security records	Annual average of daily earnings	
Canada	Household survey (Survey of Consumer Finances)	Gross annual earnings	Data refer to full-year, full-time workers.
Czech Republic	Establishment survey (Earnings Survey)	Gross annual earnings	Data refer to workers paid for annual hours of at least 1 700.
Finland	Household survey/administrative data (Income Distribution Survey)	Gross annual earnings	Data refer to full-year, full-time workers. Most data collected through tax records.
France	Household survey (labour force survey)	Net monthly earnings	Net of social security contributions only and including the monthly equivalent of annual bonuses. Similar annual data can also be obtained from administrative sources (DADS).
Germany	Household survey (German Socio-Economic Panel)	Gross monthly earnings	Annual bonuses are not incl. but are covered by the survey. Data on full-year, full-time workers can also be obtained from social security records.
Hungary	Enterprise survey (Survey of Individual Wages and Earnings)		Including 1/12th of non-regular payments from previous year.
Italy	Household survey (Bank of Italy's Survey of Household Income and Wealth)	Net monthly earnings	Net of social security contributions and income taxes. Social security data on gross earnings can also be obtained.
Japan	Enterprise survey (Basic Survey on Wage Structure)	Gross monthly scheduled earnings	Annual bonuses and overtime earnings are not included but are covered by the survey.
Korea	Enterprise survey (Basic Survey of Wage Structure)	Gross total monthly earnings	Including overtime earnings and 1/12th of annual bonuses.
Netherlands	Establishment survey	Gross annual earnings	Converted to a full-year equivalent basis.
New Zealand	Household Economic Survey	Gross annual earnings	
Poland	Enterprise survey (Earnings Distribution in the National Economy)	Gross monthly earnings	Including monthly equivalent of periodic bonuses.
Sweden	Household survey (Income Distribution Survey)	Gross annual earnings	Data refer to full-year, full-time workers.
Switzerland	Household survey (labour force survey)	Gross annual earnings	Annual earnings converted to a full-year equivalent basis.
United Kingdom	Employer survey (New Earnings Survey)	Gross weekly earnings	Workers on adult rates of pay whose pay was not affected by absence.
United States	Household survey (Current Pop. Survey)	Gross annual earnings	Data refer to full-year, full-time workers.

Note: In all cases, the data taken from these sources refer to full-time workers.

2.2 The Incidence and Distribution of Low Pay in OECD Countries

Having briefly discussed measurement issues, we can now turn to our findings based on our definition of low pay as less than two-thirds of median, full-time earnings. The overall incidence of low-paid employment in each of the 19 countries included in our cross-sectional study is shown in Figure 12.2. This refers to the proportion of full-time workers receiving less than two-thirds of median earnings. The variation across countries is striking: one-quarter of all full-time workers in the United States are in low-paid jobs compared with under 6 per cent in Finland and Sweden.

Figure 12.2   Incidence of low pay and earnings inequality, mid-1990s

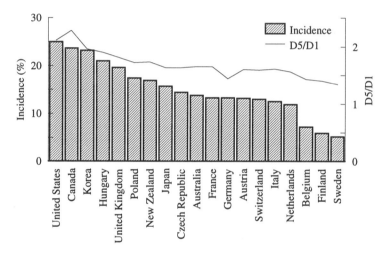

Notes:
The incidence of low pay and earnings inequality (D5/D1) refer to full-time employment only. Low pay is defined as less than two-thirds of median full-time earnings. See Table 12.2 for the reference year for each country.

Source: For the incidence of low pay, see Appendix; the D5/D1 ratio is taken from the OECD Database on Earnings Inequality.

The variation in the incidence of low pay across countries closely mirrors differences in a simple measure of earnings dispersion in the bottom half of the earnings distribution, namely the ratio of median earnings to earnings of the 10th percentile worker (D5/D1). In fact, the simple correlation between the two is very high at over 90 per cent (see Table 12.3). Thus, not surprisingly those countries with large earnings inequality are also the ones with a higher incidence of low-paid jobs.

For a smaller number of countries, changes in the incidence of low pay over the past 20 years are shown in Figure 12.3. The most dramatic rise in the incidence of low pay has occurred in Hungary and Poland since the late 1980s. Rutkowski (1996) presents data showing that this has also been the case in the other transition countries of Central and Eastern Europe. A smaller upward drift in the incidence of low pay has occurred over a longer period in Australia, the United Kingdom and the United States. In Italy, the rise has been more recent and from a lower base. Elsewhere there has been either stability or some declines.

Figure 12.3   Trends in the incidence of low pay, 1975–96 (%)

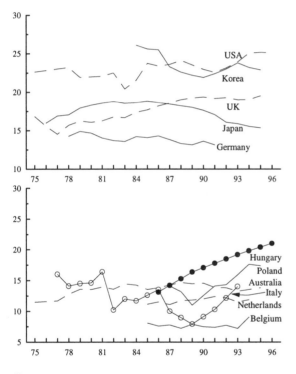

Notes:
a.   Percentage of full-time workers receiving less than two-thirds of median earnings.
b.   According to social security data whereas the data in Table 12.2 refer to the German Socio-
Economic Panel (GSOEP).
c.   Low paid in all primary jobs, whereas the data in Table 12.2 refer to full-time jobs only.

Sources: See Appendix.

In Table 12.2 the incidence, distribution and relative risk of low-paid employment are reported according to sex, age and education. In all countries

Table 12.2   *Incidence and distribution of low-paid employment by sex, age and education (percentages)*

A. Incidence[b]

	Australia	Austria	Belgium	Canada	Czech Rep.	Finland	France	Germany	Hungary	Italy	Japan	Korea	Netherlands	N. Zealand	Poland	Sweden	Switzerl.	UK	USA
	'95	'93	'93	'94	'95	'94	'95	'94	'96	'93	'95	'94	'94	'94/95	'95	'93	'95	'95	'94
Total	13.8	13.2	7.2	23.7	14.4	5.9	13.3	13.3	21.0	12.5	15.6	23.1	11.9	16.9	17.4	5.2	13.0	19.6	25.0
By sex: men	11.8	7.0	3.9	16.1	7.0	3.3	10.6	7.6	15.6	9.3	6.1	11.2	8.1	14.4	13.5	3.0	6.8	12.8	19.6
By sex: women	17.7	22.8	14.2	34.3	24.7	8.7	17.4	25.4	26.5	18.5	36.4	52.7	26.8	20.7	21.6	8.4	30.4	31.2	32.5
By age[c]: Under 25	34.5	19.5	22.2	57.1	n/a	27.1	49.5	50.4	37.8	27.0	36.8	n/a	58.1	41.3	n/a	18.7	44.0	45.8	63.0
By age[c]: 25-54	8.8	12.1	5.3	20.1	n/a	5.5	10.6	6.7	19.4	6.7	9.9	n/a	5.8	11.6	n/a	4.3	9.0	15.0	21.2
By age[c]: 55 and up	12.5	9.6	4.9	20.8	n/a	4.4	10.5	5.4	11.0	7.4	20.0	n/a	3.6	15.6	n/a	2.9	9.2	22.9	23.7
By educ.: basic	n/a	16.2	n/a	36.3	n/a	8.7	15.6	15.9	40.1	18.5	22.3	35.9	n/a	23.5	n/a	6.5	32.1	n/a	54.5
By educ.: upper sec.	n/a	9.4	n/a	28.5	n/a	5.2	9.5	26.3	18.1	6.7	19.1	24.5	n/a	10.7	n/a	4.8	11.1	n/a	32.4
By educ.: higher	n/a	4.3	n/a	17.6	n/a	0.7	4.2	4.2	3.2	1.6	7.3	8.3	n/a	14.2	n/a	2.8	3.4	n/a	15.5

B. Distribution[e]

	Australia	Austria	Belgium	Canada	Czech Rep.	Finland	France	Germany	Hungary	Italy	Japan	Korea	Netherlands	N. Zealand	Poland	Sweden	Switzerl.	UK	USA
	'95	'93	'93	'94	'95	'94	'95	'94	'96	'93	'95	'94	'94	'94/95	'95	'93	'95	'95	'94
Total	100	100	100	100	100	100	100	100	100	100	100	100	100	100	100	100	100	100	100
By sex: men	55.7	32.2	36.6	40.0	28.1	28.2	47.8	38.9	50.0	48.2	26.9	34.6	53.8	52.5	40.4	34.4	49.1	41.7	45.4
By sex: women	44.3	67.8	63.4	60.0	71.9	71.8	52.2	61.1	50.0	52.2	73.1	65.4	46.1	47.5	59.6	65.6	50.9	58.3	54.6
By age[c]: Under 25	46.6	24.3	34.7	22.9	n/a	11.5	26.1	58.6	10.8	60.9	38.8	n/a	58.1	41.0	n/a	25.9	38.8	28.5	21.6
By age[c]: 25-54	47.1	72.4	60.8	69.9	n/a	82.7	68.5	37.9	84.3	30.8	45.3	n/a	40.3	51.9	n/a	67.4	53.8	59.8	68.7
By age[c]: 55 and up	6.2	3.2	4.6	7.2	n/a	5.8	5.4	3.7	4.9	8.5	15.9	n/a	1.6	7.1	n/a	6.8	7.5	11.7	9.8
By educ.: basic	n/a	82.4	n/a	7.7	n/a	76.7	76.5	75.4	47.5	80.1	20.7	38.1	n/a	56.5	n/a	71.0	36.8	n/a	21.3
By educ.: upper sec.	n/a	12.7	n/a	56.5	n/a	20.3	8.6	11.1	49.8	19.2	63.8	52.7	n/a	21.9	n/a	12.6	59.0	n/a	43.7
By educ.: higher	n/a	4.9	n/a	35.8	n/a	3.0	6.7	6.8	2.7	1.3	15.1	9.2	n/a	20.8	n/a	16.1	4.1	n/a	34.9

Notes:
a. The data refer to full-time employees only. Low pay is defined as less than two-thirds of median earnings for all full-time workers.
b. Percentage of workers in each category who are low paid.
c. For Italy, the age groups refer to: under 31; 31 to 50; and 51 and over.
d. The sum across the three education levels may not equal 100 because, for some countries, a small number of workers could not be classified by education level.
e. Percentage share of all low-paid employment in each category.
f. n/a = not available.

Source: See Appendix.

younger, female and low-skilled workers are more likely to be employed in low-paid jobs than older, male and high-skilled workers. Given that wages tend to increase with experience, skill and tenure, it is not perhaps too surprising that younger workers are much more likely to be in low-paid jobs than older workers. In the case of women, their higher risk of being low paid relative to men can only partly be accounted for by gender differences in average job tenure and experience as well as in the composition of employment by industry and occupation. Blau and Kahn (1995), for example, find that a substantial part of the gap in earnings between men and women remains unexplained even after controlling for these and many other factors.

While the gap in the incidence of low pay between men and women remains large it has been narrowing over time in most countries for which comparisons over time can be made (Figure 12.4). In the United Kingdom, for example, whereas women were more than 8 times more likely than men to be low paid during most of the 1970s they were just over twice as likely to be low paid in 1995. Against the background of a small rise in the overall incidence of low pay in the United Kingdom this has implied a substantial rise in the incidence for men but a fall for women, although over 30 per cent of all full-time female workers are still in low-paid jobs.

Figure 12.4   Trends in the risk of low pay for women relative to men, 1975–96 (%)

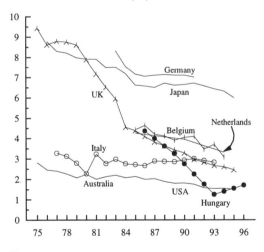

Notes:
a. Percentage of full-time workers receiving less than two-thirds of median earnings.
b. Germany: according to social security data whereas the data in Table 12.2 refer to the German Socio-Economic Panel (GSOEP).
c. Italy: low paid in all primary jobs, whereas the data in Table 12.2 refer to full-time jobs only.

Source: See Appendix.

By sector and occupation the pattern of low pay also tends to be similar across countries (see OECD 1996, Table 3.2). Typically, a high proportion of all jobs in the wholesale, retail and catering sector are low paid, whereas such jobs are scarce in transportation and communications and in public administration. Being in a non-manual occupation is not a guarantee of being in a relatively high-paid job. Sales workers and, in some countries, clerical workers face a higher risk of being employed in low-paid jobs than trades and craft workers. On the other hand, very few managerial, technical and professional workers are in low-paid jobs. Workers in smaller firms also face a higher risk of low pay than those in larger firms.

Despite these broad regularities across countries in the groups of workers most affected by low pay, there are still some important differences. Between 30 and 50 per cent of all women working full-time are low paid in Japan, Korea, Switzerland, the United Kingdom and North America, compared with less than 10 per cent in Finland and Sweden. Relative to male workers, female workers face a particularly high risk of low pay in Japan, Korea and Switzerland. In the United States, nearly two-thirds of full-time employed youths are low paid compared with about one in five in Sweden. However, relative to all workers the incidence of low pay for youths is highest in the European countries (excluding Italy and the United Kingdom). Japan and, to a lesser extent, the United Kingdom, are the only countries where the incidence of low-paid employment is significantly higher for older workers than for prime-age workers.

3 INSTITUTIONAL SETTINGS, LOW PAY AND LABOUR MARKET OUTCOMES

Part of the substantial variation across countries in the overall incidence of low pay may be the result of differences in institutional settings. Labour market institutions can affect the extent of low pay through a variety of channels, some of which are more direct than others. Indeed, one of the principal aims of statutory minimum wages is to limit the extent of low pay. Extensive collective bargaining coverage and trade union representation may also prevent wages from falling below a certain level. Wage floors may also be established indirectly by social security arrangements such as unemployment benefits which raise the reservation wages of some groups of workers. Therefore, in this section we examine the relationship between different institutional settings and the incidence of low pay.

We then look at the relationship across countries between the low pay and labour market outcomes in terms of employment and unemployment. If some institutional settings do effectively establish high wage floors which limit the incidence of low pay then this may price some less productive workers out of jobs altogether. This would show up as a positive relationship between the incidence of low pay and employment rates, particularly for low-skilled and inexperienced workers.

3.1 Institutional Settings and Low Pay

In Table 12.3 the incidence of low pay in 15 countries is correlated with a range of indicators concerning earnings inequality and institutional settings.[5] As mentioned already, given the way our measure is constructed, the incidence of low pay is closely related to the dispersion of earnings in the bottom half of the earnings distribution (see Figure 12.2). The correlation between the two is highest for all persons but remains significant whether each measure refers separately to men, women or youths. Therefore, the factors behind the different degrees of earnings inequality across countries largely overlap with those behind the differences in the incidence of low pay.

The correlations in Table 12.3 suggest that institutional settings with respect to wage setting and social security arrangements do play an important role in explaining country differences in the incidence of low pay. The simple correlations with the measures of collective bargaining coverage and trade union density are quite high and negative, i.e. lower coverage and density rates are associated with a higher incidence of low pay. These results hold irrespective of whether we measure the incidence of low pay separately by sex or age or for all persons.

In their international study, Blau and Kahn (1996) also find that institutional features, such as high rates of unionization and collective bargaining coverage, appear to create wage floors and reduce earnings dispersion, particularly in the bottom half of the distribution.

Other features of wage-setting practices may also affect the incidence of low pay. For example, a number of countries have mandatory minimum wages which may truncate the earnings distribution from below. Mishel and Bernstein (1994) and Dinardo et al. (1996) suggest that the decline in the value of the Federal minimum wage relative to average wages was an important factor behind the rise in earnings inequality in the United States during the 1980s. In the United Kingdom, minimum wages in a number of low-pay sectors prior to 1993 were established by Wages Councils which have subsequently been abolished. Machin and Manning (1994) have estimated that, in these sectors, the decline in the minimum relative to the average wage over the 1980s accounted for between 9 to 20 per cent of the rise in the dispersion of earnings.

Table 12.3   Institutional settings, low pay and labour market outcomes

Cross-country correlations	Incidence of low pay (early to mid 1990s):			
Correlated with:	Total	Men	Women	Youth
Earnings inequality[b] (early to mid-1990s): earnings decile ratio (D5/D1)				
All persons	0.94 **	0.89 **	0.66 **	0.65 **
Men	x	0.91 **	x	x
Women	x	x	0.54 *	x
Institutional features[c]:				
Collective bargaining cov., '94	-0.78 **	-0.64 **	-0.76 **	-0.52 *
Union density, '90-'94	-0.65 **	-0.58 *	-0.69 **	-0.72 **
Unempl. benefit replacement rate, gross, '95	-0.59 *	-0.42	-0.57 *	-0.11
Unempl. benefit replacement rate, net, '94/'95	-0.58 *	-0.67 **	-0.22	-0.14
Labour market outcomes: full-time employment-population ratios, '90-'94				
All persons	0.17	x	x	x
Men	0.22	0.00		
Women	0.08	x	-0.20	x
Women relative to men	-0.01	x	-0.33	x
Youths (under 25)	0.13	x	x	-0.09
Youths relat. to adults (25-64)	0.08	x	x	-0.03
Labour market outcomes: total employment-population ratios by skill,[e] '92				
Low-skilled	-0.17	x	x	x
Low relative to high skilled	-0.07	x	x	x
Labour market outcomes: unemployment rates, '90-'94				
All persons	0.03	x	x	x
Men	0.11	0.33	x	x
Women	-0.10	x	-0.41	x
Women relative to men	-0.29	x	-0.06	x
Youths (under 25)	-0.08	x	x	-0.13
Youths relat. to adults (25-64)	-0.12	x	x	-0.32
Labour market outcomes: unemployment rates by skill,[e] '92				
Low-skilled	0.28	x	x	x
Low relative to high skilled	-0.04	x	x	x

Notes:

a.   15 countries are included: Australia, Austria, Belgium, Canada, Finland, France, Germany, Italy, Japan, Netherlands, New Zealand, Portugal, Sweden, Switzerland, the UK and the USA.

b.   D1 and D5 refer to, respectively, the upper earnings limit of the bottom decile of workers and median earnings.

c.   Collective bargaining coverage refers to the percentage of all employees covered by a collective agreement concerning their wages and/or working conditions. Trade union density refers to the percentage of all employees belonging to a trade union. The gross (net) replacement rate refers to the before-tax (after-tax) level of unemployment benefit entitlements relative to gross (net) earnings and represents an average across different family situations, durations of unempl. and earnings levels (for more details, see OECD 1994, Ch. 8, and OECD,1996, Ch. 2).

d.   Excluding Austria.

e.   Persons with less than upper secondary education are classified as low skilled and those with higher (tertiary level) education as high skilled.

f.   x = not applicable. * = significant at 5 per cent level. ** = significant at 1 per cent level.

Source:

See Appendix for the incidence of low pay; OECD Database on Earnings Inequality for the D5/D1 ratios; OECD (1997, Chapter 3) for collective bargaining coverage and union density; OECD Database on Taxation and Benefit Entitlements for unemployment benefit replacement rates; and OECD (1996, Statistical Annex) and OECD, Education at a Glance for the indicators of labour market outcomes.

Across OECD countries with statutory or national minimum wages, there appears to be a negative association between the level of minimum wages relative to average wages and the incidence of low pay: countries with a relatively low (high) minimum wage tend to have a high (low) incidence of low pay (Figure 12.5). Clearly, other factors will also be important in determining how close is the match between the level of the minimum wage and the incidence of low pay. If there is high collective bargaining coverage and the minima set in these agreements are higher than the statutory minimum wage, then even a low level of the statutory minimum might be associated with a low incidence of low pay. Conversely, a relatively high minimum wage may be associated with a high incidence of low pay because of non-compliance.

Figure 12.5   Statutory minimum wages and low pay, mid-1990s (percentages)

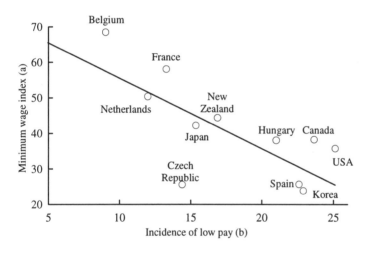

Notes:
a.   Statutory or national mimimum wage as a percentage of median full-time earnings.
b.   Percentage of full-time workers receiving less than two-thirds of median earnings.

Source: For the minimum-wage index, OECD Database on Minimum Wages; for the incidence of low pay, see Appendix.

It is also possible that unemployment and related benefits may create a wage floor below which workers will be reluctant to accept jobs. Table 12.3 shows that there is a significant and negative correlation between benefit replacement rates (both gross and net) and the incidence of low pay. The weaker result for youths compared with men and women probably reflects the fact that the replacement rate indicators have been averaged across different family situations, unemployment durations and earnings levels and so are less likely to be representative of the replacement rates typically faced by youths in each country. Of course, a high correlation between replacement rates and the incidence of low pay does not necessarily imply that there is a causal link. Differences across countries in social preferences more generally with respect to income inequality may imply both generous welfare benefits and a low incidence of low pay in some countries and the opposite in others.

Changes in some of these institutional settings also appear to be associated with changes in the incidence of low-paid work. As we have time series on the incidence of low pay for only a few countries we have used the dispersion of wages in the bottom half of the earnings distribution as a proxy measure for the incidence of low pay. As shown in Table 12.4, changes over the last 10 years in bargaining coverage and unionization appear to be correlated

Table 12.4   Changes in institutional settings, wage dispersion and labour market outcomes

Cross-country correlations[a]	Wage dispersion (D5/D1)		
Correlated with:	Total	Men	Women
Institutional features:			
Collective bargaining coverage	-0.19	-0.59 *	-0.23
Union density	-0.10	-0.47	-0.01
Unempl. benefit gross replacement rate	-0.07	0.06	-0.17
Labour market outcomes: full-time employment-population ratios			
All persons	0.07	x	x
Men	-0.02	0.02	x
Women	0.22	x	0.10
Youths (under 25)	-0.09	x	x
Labour market outcomes: unemployment rates			
All persons	-0.10	x	x
Men	-0.10	-0.28	x
Women	-0.10	x	0.02
Youths (under 25)	-0.01	x	x

Notes:
a. The change in each variable is calculated as the difference in its level around the mid-1990s and 10 years earlier. 14 countries are included: Australia, Belgium, Canada, Finland, France, Germany, Italy, Japan, Netherlands, New Zealand, Portugal, Sweden, United Kingdom and the United States. Wage dispersion is measured as the ratio of median earnings (D5) to the upper earnings limit of the bottom decile of workers (D1). See Table 12.3 for definitions of collective bargaining coverage, union density and unemployment benefit replacement rate.
b. x = not applicable. * = significant at the 5 per cent level.

Source: See Table 12.3.

with changes in the dispersion of earnings. The correlations are less significant than when levels are compared in Table 12.3 but, nevertheless, do suggest that changes in wage setting institutions can partly explain different trends across countries with respect to the relative wages of low-paid workers, particularly for men. These results are consistent with those of a number of US studies which have also found that declines in unionization contributed to rising earnings inequality (Freeman 1993, Mishel and Bernstein 1994, Dinardo et al. 1996).

There is little correlation, however, between changes in replacement rates and changes in the dispersion of earnings. This most likely reflects the fact that for most of the countries included in the correlations there has been very little variation in replacement rates over the last 10 years (see Chart 2.2 of OECD 1996, p. 29) compared with much greater variation in earnings inequality. In other words, while the generosity of welfare benefits does appear to be related to the incidence of low pay, changes in benefit generosity have generally been small compared to changes in other factors which influence the distribution of earnings.

Other institutional settings apart from those relating to wage determination and welfare benefits may influence indirectly the incidence of low pay. For instance, labour turnover (but not necessarily job turnover) is lower in most European countries compared with North America and, in part, this appears to be related to differences in the degree of 'strictness' of employment protection legislation (see OECD 1996, Chapter 5). Several US studies (e.g. Podgursky and Swaim 1987, Farber 1996) show that displaced workers face large and persistent declines in earnings upon re-employment compared with their previous level of earnings. Thus part of the higher incidence of low pay in the USA than in other countries may be explained by the relatively larger pool of displaced or laid-off workers at any point in time. Moreover, in Belgium, where there are relatively few low-paid workers, it would appear that displaced workers suffer only small earnings losses upon re-employment (Leonard and Van Audenrode 1995). The UK, on the other hand, follows the US pattern; earnings losses following a spell of unemployment tend to be substantial and the overall incidence of low pay is quite high (Gregory and Jukes 1996).

3.2 Low Pay and Labour Market Outcomes

If high minimum wages or generous welfare benefits limit low-paid employment by establishing artificially high wage floors which lock some workers out of a job, then we would expect this impact to be strongest for low-skilled workers or for workers with little job experience. However, as shown in Table 12.3, employment opportunities for these groups do not appear to be strongly correlated with the overall incidence of low pay. In several cases the correlation coefficients between the incidence of low pay and employment–population ratios for women, youths and unskilled workers are negative rather than positive and even when positive are never significant at conventional levels. On the other hand, there does appear to be a weak tendency for unemployment rates of women and youths to be somewhat higher in those countries where the incidence of low pay is lowest but again the correlations are not significant. For all persons with few qualifications there appears to be a weakly positive rather than negative correlation between low pay and unemployment or no correlation at all when unemployment rates of unskilled workers are measured relative to skilled workers.

Of course, based on these simple correlations across countries it is not possible to rule out the existence of a trade-off between earnings inequality and labour market outcomes in terms of employment and unemployment. Country differences in the proportion of women or youths that are in employment are driven by many factors other than just the degree of wage dispersion and it is possible that these factors dominate the impact of any wage floors that might exist in some countries. In the case of youths, factors such as overall labour market conditions, and institutional and social differences across countries in training and school retention rates, may be particularly important in explaining their labour-market outcomes (some of these factors are examined in OECD 1996, Chapter 4).

In addition, the number of observations in our cross-country comparisons is small and the absence of any significant correlations may be the result of one or two outliers. In fact, as can been seen in Figure 12.6, Finland and Sweden stand out for displaying both a high proportion of women in full-time employment and the lowest incidence of low-paid employment. If these two countries are excluded then the correlation coefficient between female full-time employment–population ratios and the incidence of low pay among female workers becomes positive (0.27), although it is still not significant, and the correlation with the incidence of low pay for all workers rises to 0.65, which is significant at the 5 per cent level. In the correlations of low pay with employment of low-skilled workers, Sweden appears as an outlier in the company of Japan, but, in this case, removing these countries does not result in any appreciably closer relationship between the two variables.

Sweden also shows up as an outlier in Figure 12.7 by virtue of its low unemployment rate for women in comparison with most other countries. Again, excluding Finland and Sweden results in a stronger (negative) correlation between low pay and unemployment for women. In this case, the correlation coefficient (−0.65) becomes significant at the 5 per cent level when the incidence of low pay is measured with respect to female workers but remains insignificant (−0.21) when measured with respect to all workers. Finally,

Figure 12.6   Incidence of low pay and employment–population ratios,
mid-1990s

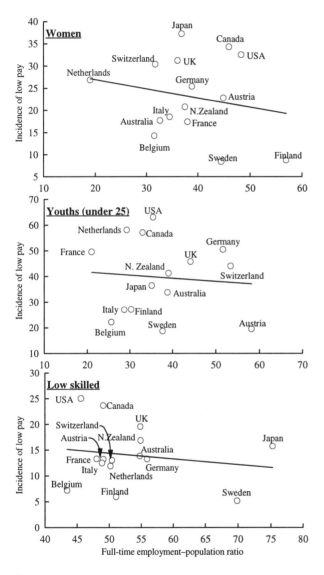

Notes:
The incidence of low pay refers to the percentage of full-time workers receiving less than two-thirds of median earnings.

Source: See Appendix and Table 12.3.

Figure 12.7   Incidence of low pay and unemployment rates,
            mid-1990s

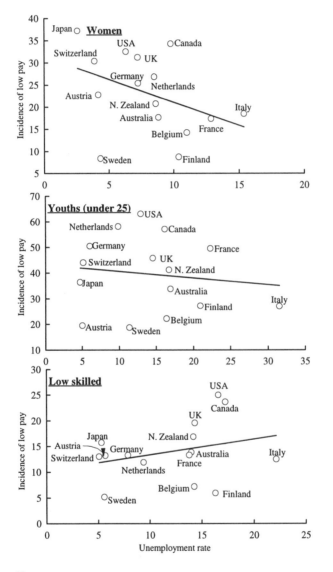

Notes:
The incidence of low pay refers to the percentage of full-time workers receiving less than two-thirds of median earnings.

Source: See Appendix and Table 12.3.

Austria appears to be somewhat of an outlier in both Figures 12.6 and 12.7 because relatively few Austrian youths appear to be in low-paid jobs, but this could be because apprentices have been excluded from the low-pay measure. If Austria is excluded the correlation between youth employment–population ratios and both the overall incidence of low pay and the youth incidence of low pay does become slightly stronger (0.18 and 0.15, respectively) but is still not significant.

An additional reason for the lack of any strong correlations between the incidence of low pay and employment outcomes could be that in some countries the public sector acts as an 'employer of last resort' and provides jobs for unskilled and inexperienced workers at wage rates in excess of the market value of their marginal productivity. In the Nordic countries, for instance, the high employment rates of women are sometimes attributed to the large public sector in these countries as well as to generous maternity leave and child care provisions. In order to check whether employment in the public sector has tended to offset an underlying positive relationship between earnings differentials and employment outcomes, a number of regressions have been carried out with the government share of total employment added as an explanatory variable to the incidence of low-paid employment for explaining cross-country differences in full-time employment–population ratios. The results of the regressions are summarized in Table 12.5. Not surprisingly given the few observations and the small number of independent variables the regressions have very low explanatory power. However, the regression results do suggest that government employment does account for part of the variation across countries in employment–population ratios for women but not for men or youths. After controlling for this factor, women's full-time employment rates become positively related, but not significantly, to both the incidence of low-paid employment among all workers and among female workers only.

Another approach to controlling for other factors which might influence the level of employment or unemployment rates is to examine correlations of changes over time in these variables with changes in the incidence of low pay. This will not control for all other factors but may control for those factors which change little over time but which nevertheless may explain a large part of the level difference across countries in employment and unemployment rates. In Table 12.4, changes in employment and unemployment rates over the last 10 years are correlated with changes in wage differentials between low paid and median paid workers. The results are generally not significant, although for women there is some tendency for an increase in wage dispersion to be associated with a rise in their employment rates and a fall in their unemployment rates.

Table 12.5   *Low pay, employment–population ratios and government*
            employment

Dependent variable: Full-time employment– population ratio for:	Explanatory variables:				Adjusted R^2
	Incidence of low pay			Gov't share	
	Constant	Total	Specific[b]	of tot. empl.	
Total	0.446	0.263	x	0.348	0.054
t-value	*7.2*	*1.1*		*1.5*	
Men	0.711	0.148	x	-0.136	-0.085
t-value	*10.4*	*0.6*		*0.5*	
Men	0.745	x	-0.044	-0.188	-0.112
t-value	*12.7*		*0.1*	*0.8*	
Women	0.176	0.400	x	0.832	0.169
t-value	*1.7*	*1.0*		*2.2*	
Women	0.208	x	0.118	0.815	0.110
t-value	*1.5*		*0.4*	*1.8*	
Youths (under 25)	0.357	0.215	x	-0.068	-0.146
t-value	*2.4*	*0.4*		*0.1*	
Youths (under 25)	0.452	x	-0.095	-0.217	-0.143
t-value	*2.9*		*0.4*	*0.4*	

Notes:
a. The regressions are carried out for a single point in time corresponding to the early to mid 1990s (the precise year depending on the variable and country). The 16 countries included are: Australia, Austria, Belgium, Canada, Finland, France, Germany, Italy, Japan, Netherlands, New Zealand, Portugal, Sweden, Switzerland, United Kingdom and the United States.
b. For men, women and youths, two regressions are carried out: the first against the total incidence of low pay and the second against the incidence specific to each group.
c. x = not applicable.

Source: The government share in total employment comes from the OECD Economic Outlook Database; for all other data see Table 12.3.

The lack of any significant correlation between changes in wage dispersion and changes in either employment and unemployment is also evident in Figure 12.8. Irrespective of the direction of changes in wage dispersion, full-time employment–population ratios have risen for women in most countries and have declined for youths in all countries, with France, Finland and Sweden recording particularly large falls. This, in and of itself, suggests that other factors apart from wage dispersion may play a more important role in explaining labour market developments for women and youths. The widespread increase in the proportion of women in full-time employment also indicates that the trend rise in women's labour force participation which has been observed in most OECD countries has not just been the result of more women taking up part-time jobs.

Figure 12.8   Changes in wage dispersion and labour market outcomes over 10 years to mid-1990s

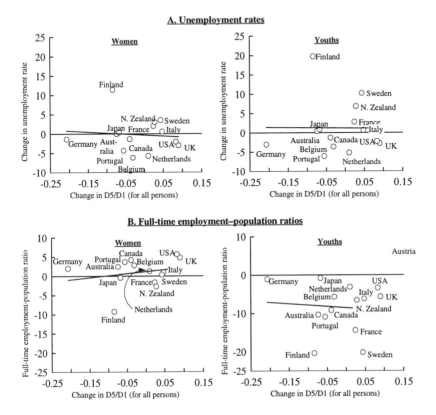

Note: The change in each variable is calculated as the difference between its level around the mid-1990s and 10 years earlier.

Source: See Appendix and Table 12.3.

The absence of any strong association for women and youths between changes in wage dispersion and changes in employment and unemployment is not being driven by a few extreme or aberrant observations. Finland does stand out as an obvious outlier in each of the graphs, reflecting the particularly severe recession it experienced during the early 1990s, but none of the correlations come even close to being significant if it is excluded. In fact, excluding Finland results in a positive, instead of a negative, coefficient for most of the correlations between changes in wage dispersion and changes in unemployment.

In sum, at this level of aggregation it appears difficult to detect any uniform evidence of a strong relationship across countries which would suggest that greater wage inequality is associated with better labour market outcomes in terms of higher employment and lower unemployment. The evidence from studies at the micro level is also somewhat mixed. Based on their analysis of comparable micro-data, Card et al. (1996) do not find that less wage flexibility over time in Canada and France than in the United States has generated substantially different patterns of relative employment growth by skill. On the other hand, Blau and Kahn (1996) find in their study of a larger number of countries than Card et al. that employment–population ratios for the low skilled tend to be lower in those countries where the earnings distribution is the most compressed. These contradictory findings suggest that further work is warranted into examining whether greater earnings inequality really is a necessary price to pay for better employment and unemployment outcomes.

4 EARNINGS MOBILITY OF LOW-PAID WORKERS

The extent to which low-paid employment results in poverty and social exclusion will partly depend on the extent to which it is a permanent or transitory phenomenon. Most workers start off their careers in relatively low-paid jobs but obtain earnings increases as they gain experience and settle into a career. Nevertheless, some workers may experience very little upward earnings mobility or may be stuck cycling between poorly-paid jobs and unemployment. In this section, we use longitudinal data for 1986–91 to analyse the earnings mobility of low-paid workers in seven OECD countries: Denmark, France, Germany, Italy, Sweden, the United Kingdom and the United States.[6]

Our analysis of earnings mobility addresses two issues. Firstly, we want to measure the degree of mobility both into and out of low-paid employment. If the overwhelming majority of low-paid workers quickly move on to better jobs then the implications for policy will be very different than if we observe that there is a significant core of low-paid workers that remain stuck at the bottom of the earnings ladder. The second issue we explore is the extent to which the mobility of low-paid workers differs across countries. As shown above, the incidence of low pay according to our relative measure is significantly higher in the United States than in Europe. We now ask whether the higher incidence of low pay in the less regulated US labour market is compensated for by higher upward mobility out of low-paid jobs.[7]

4.1 Data and Measurement Issues

Many of the issues concerning the definition and measure of low pay have already been discussed in section 2. In keeping with the cross-section analysis, the mobility analysis is mainly restricted to full-time workers. We also retain earnings of less than two-thirds of the median earnings level as our primary definition of low-paid employment.[8]

Setting the low-pay threshold at two-thirds of median earnings unambiguously identifies those earning significantly less than a typical worker. For this reason it is our preferred criterion. This threshold produces an important non-comparability, however, which has important implications for making international comparisons of low-pay mobility patterns: as shown in section 2, a far larger share of the workforce is classified as low paid in countries with widely dispersed earnings, such as the United States, than in countries with less cross-sectional wage inequality, such as Denmark and Italy. Thus, we also examine low-pay mobility when the low-paid threshold is defined as the upper limit of the first quintile of the earnings distribution (the 20th percentile). The first quintile definition is comparable across counties in the sense that attention is focused on the lowest fifth of all earners in each country. However, it is not comparable in another sense, because the extent to which these workers' earnings fall short of average earnings varies greatly across countries.

Both thresholds for low pay are calculated each year using the distribution of earnings across *all* workers in that year, regardless of whether they were employed during the rest of the 1986–91 period. This yields thresholds comparable to those used in our cross-sectional analysis. However, most of the mobility measures examined below require earnings data for multiple years and are calculated *only* for workers employed during all of those years. Since workers with more continuous employment tend to have higher earnings than more intermittent workers, the single-year low-pay incidence rates for the workers included in our mobility calculations are lower than they would be if intermittent workers were also included in the calculations. Thus, the low-pay incidence rates reported in this section can be meaningfully compared with each other, but are not easily compared with incidence measures calculated with cross-sectional data.

Our mobility analysis requires longitudinal or panel data which follow the same workers over multiple years. Table 12.6 provides an overview of the longitudinal data sets that we used. The limited availability of such data means that many of the countries included in the cross-sectional analysis could not be included in this analysis. As in our cross-section analysis it has not been possible to use exactly the same type of data for each country. The German and United States data are derived exclusively from household surveys, while the Danish, French and Italian data are derived exclusively from administrative sources. The Swedish data are primarily from household surveys, but administrative tax data were used to refine the earnings measures for some of the observations. The data source for the United Kingdom is also a hybrid. The sample of workers is drawn from administrative data, but most of the information – including workers' earnings – was gathered from a survey of employers. When comparing mobility measures, it should be borne in mind that the earnings data collected from administrative sources are likely to be more accurate than those collected from survey interviews (Westergård-Nielsen 1989).

Table 12.6   Overview of longitudinal data sets used in earnings mobility analysis

Source of data	Type of data	Wage & salary workers missed by sampling frame	Data on the nonempl.	Sample size: total working age population	Sample size: full-time wage & salary workers in both '86 & '91	Earnings concept
Denmark Data from the Danish Longitudinal Database (DLD), supplied by Niels Westergård-Nielsen and Paul Bingley, Centre for Labour Market and Social Research, Aarhus Business School.	Administr.		Yes	14 438	6 422	Gross weekly earnings
France Data from Déclarations Annuelles des Données Sociales (DADS), supplied by Yves Guillotin and Alain Bigard, Groupe d'Analyse et Analyse des Itinéraires et Niveaux Salariaux (GAINS), Université du Maine.	Administr.	General gov't	No	856 422	287 821	Net monthly earnings
Germany Data from the German Socio-Economic Panel (GSOEP), supplied by Viktor Steiner, Zentrum fur Europaeische Wirtschaftsforschung (ZEW), Mannheim.	Hhold Survey		Yes	8 775	2 168	Gross monthly earnings
Italy Data from the Instituto Nazionale de Previdenza Sociale Dataset (INPSD), supplied by Claudio Malpede, Lia Pacelli and Riccardo Revelli, R&P, Ricerche e Progetti, Torino.	Administr.	General gov't	No	143 851	52 877	Gross monthly earnings
Sweden Data from the HUS, supplied by Anders Klevmarken and Sten Hansen, University of Uppsala.	Hhold Survey (matched to administr. tax data)		Yes	1 362	615	Gross monthly earnings
UK Data from the New Earnings Survey Panel Dataset (NESPD), supplied by Peter Elias, Warwick University.	Establishment Survey (sampled from admin. data)	Very low earners	No	219 201	71 453	Gross monthly earnings
USA Data from the Panel Study of Income Dynamics (PSID), supplied by David Fasenfest, Purdue University.	Hhold survey		Yes	9 776	3 915	Gross weekly earnings

Several additional measurement issues affect our mobility analysis. One important concern is that panel data tend to exacerbate the problems of non-response and measurement error already present in cross-sectional data. Non-response tends to cumulate over time in panel data, because it is not always possible to track individuals or to induce them to continue to participate in the survey. The resulting sample attrition can be very high and, if it is not random, could lead to erroneous conclusions (Westergård-Nielsen 1989, Baudelot 1983).[9] The surveys for Germany and the United States provide sophisticated probability weights intended to correct for attrition bias and these weights have been used in the analysis. Analogous corrections could not be made for the other data sets.

Longitudinal analysis may also be particularly susceptible to measurement error in earnings or other variables. For example, it might not matter greatly for a cross-sectional analysis of earnings if individuals report their earnings somewhat imprecisely, say within a range of plus or minus five per cent of the true value. However, the same reporting error would tend to have a much larger effect on the results of an analysis of earnings mobility, because year-to-year changes in random reporting error would tend to be much more than five per cent of the true changes in earnings. Several validation studies of the Panel Study of Income Dynamics, our data source for the United States, are somewhat reassuring about these issues in that these problems were not found to be serious (Hill 1992, Bound et al. 1994). Nonetheless, relatively little is known about how accurately panel data sets reflect individual earnings histories. A related concern is that the statistical reliability of earnings mobility estimates calculated from the different data sets varies considerably owing to large differences in sample sizes. Sample sizes are particularly small for Sweden and some of the measures discussed below are not reported for this country because they could not be estimated with sufficient precision.

Our use of different types of longitudinal data sources to estimate mobility patterns introduces additional problems of comparability. Some of the data sets, typically those constructed from administrative data, do not cover the entire working-age population, or even the entire wage and salary workforce. For example, the French and Italian data are collected from tax and social security records that exclude much of the public sector and all persons not in work. It is not possible to analyse mobility between low-paid employment and non-employment for these countries, since non-employment is indistinguishable from certain forms of employment. Even when the analysis is limited to workers observed to be employed in all of the years being considered, these data sets may give rise to highly selective forms of sample attrition and renewal. For example, all persons switching from a private-sector job to a public-sector job effectively disappear from the employed sample, while all persons moving from the public to the private sector appear as new entrants to the sample.[10] It is not clear whether international comparisons of mobility are significantly affected by this problem.

4.2 Aggregate Mobility of Low-Paid Workers

Before turning to the mobility of low-paid workers, it may be useful to summarize our results concerning earnings mobility for all workers whether low
paid or not. We find that similar and substantial levels of *relative* mobility
prevail across the countries included in our study. Approximately half the
workers in all of the countries were in a different earnings quintile in 1991
than in 1986, and between 11 and 17 per cent were at least two quintiles
higher or lower than they had been, indicating large changes in relative
earnings. Despite this mobility, a large share of cross-sectional earnings inequality appears to be quite persistent.[11] The cross-country results differ
much more markedly for measures of *absolute* earnings mobility, such as the
percentage growth in real earnings during 1986–91. The growth in average
earnings of continuously employed workers was strongest in the United
Kingdom and was weakest in the United States. Individuals' real earnings
paths fan out widely around the average in all countries, but particularly so in
the United States. This variability across individuals, which is the source of
relative earnings mobility, includes falling real earnings for a significant
number of workers, despite the tendency for earnings to rise with experience.
The share of workers with real earnings reductions ranged from 6 per cent in
Germany to 29 per cent in the United States.[12]

Table 12.7 presents summary measures of earnings mobility over the period 1986–91 for low-paid workers according to two definitions of low pay:
workers in the bottom quintile and workers earning less than two-thirds of
median earnings. Five-year transition probabilities are shown both for exits
from low-paid employment for workers who were low paid in 1986 and by
source of entry into low pay for workers who were low paid in 1991. In both
cases we calculate exit and entry probabilities both for all low-paid workers
irrespective of their subsequent or previous work status and for 'persistently'
full-time workers only.

The transition probabilities in Table 12.7 (upper half) indicate that there is
considerable movement out of low-paid jobs in all countries, but also considerable variation about the prospects of these workers across countries.
Focusing first on the four countries for which all low-paid workers can be
tracked, regardless of their subsequent work status, we find that only 27 to 35
per cent of the 1986 bottom quintile workers were still in the bottom quintile
in 1991. Cross-country differences in the share of low earners in 1986 who
were still low earners five years later are quite large, however, when low pay
is instead defined as less than two-thirds of median earnings. This share
ranged from a low of 6 per cent in Denmark to around 40 per cent in the
USA. In countries with a more egalitarian earnings distribution, the relatively
fewer workers earning less than two-thirds of median earnings in any single

year also have a relatively lower risk of remaining below this threshold for an extended period of time.

Table 12.7   Five-year earnings mobility of low-paid workers

	Low paid defined as bottom quintile				Low paid defined as below 0.65 median earnings			
	Not empl. full-time	In bottom quintile	In second quintile	In quintiles 3-5	Not empl. full-time	Below 0.65 median	0.65 to 0.95 median	Above 0.95 median
1991 earnings status of 1986 low-paid workers: A. Including moves out of full-time employment								
Denmark	26.7	32.1	20.5	20.7	25.7	6.0	43.1	25.2
Germany	39.3	27.4	16.8	16.6	40.5	15.5	29.7	14.3
Sweden	27.6	35.5	18.4	18.4	31.6	10.5	34.2	23.7
USA	32.3	34.9	21.2	11.6	30.4	40.5	17.8	11.3
1991 earnings status of 1986 low-paid workers: B. Full-time in both years								
Denmark	x	43.8	27.9	28.3	x	8.1	58.1	33.9
France	x	46.1	30.7	23.2	x	31.6	48.2	20.2
Germany	x	45.1	27.6	27.3	x	26.0	50.0	24.0
Italy	x	47.8	27.4	24.8	x	21.8	58.3	19.9
Sweden	x	49.1	25.5	25.5	x	–	–	–
UK	x	41.1	31.9	27.1	x	39.0	39.9	21.1
USA	x	51.6	31.3	17.2	x	58.1	25.6	16.3
1986 earnings status of 1991 low-paid workers: A. Including moves into full-time employment								
Denmark	38.3	33.3	15.3	13.2	52.7	10.4	25.2	11.8
Germany	39.1	32.1	22.0	6.8	45.5	28.2	23.3	3.0
Sweden	43.4	32.5	13.3	10.8	62.8	11.4	20.0	5.7
USA	50.9	33.3	11.3	4.6	46.8	39.8	9.4	4.1
1986 earnings status of 1991 low-paid workers: B. Full-time in both years								
Denmark	x	54.0	24.7	21.3	x	22.0	53.2	24.8
France	x	56.5	25.4	18.0	x	38.4	43.4	18.2
Germany	x	52.8	36.1	11.2	x	51.7	42.9	5.4
Italy	x	52.5	26.8	20.7	x	43.4	41.4	15.1
Sweden	x	57.5	23.4	19.2	x	–	–	–
UK	x	64.0	21.3	14.7	x	61.2	27.2	11.6
USA	x	67.7	23.0	9.3	x	74.7	17.7	7.6

Notes: x = not applicable. – = not reported (less than 30 observations).

Source: OECD (1996, Chapter 3).

In all countries much of the movement out of a low-paid job is out of full-time paid employment altogether, rather than into higher earnings ranges. For example, just under 16 per cent of German workers below two-thirds of median earnings in 1986 were still in that earnings range in 1991, but nearly as many had dropped out of full-time employment (40 per cent) as had moved up the earnings distribution (44 per cent). From the perspective of policy, it would be desirable to know why such a substantial number left full-time employment. Two insights can be gleaned from our mobility analysis. First, in all countries for which we have information, a large majority of those leaving full-time employment left employment altogether, rather than moving into part-time jobs or self-employment. Second, the exit rate is substantially higher for workers with low earnings than for better-paid workers. Averaging over the countries in our sample, first-quintile earners were about twice as likely to leave full-time employment as were third-quintile workers. These patterns suggest that the border between low-paid employment and non-employment is highly permeable when a multi-year period is considered. Thus a full account of low-pay dynamics would have to treat intermittent (and part-time) workers more extensively than is done here. Doing so, however, would raise data and methodological issues that go well beyond the scope of this analysis. The remainder of our mobility analysis focuses on continuously full-time workers.

When attention is restricted to low-paid workers remaining full-time employed, seven countries can be compared. Among persistently full-time workers who were in the bottom quintile of the 1986 earnings distribution approximately half were still in the bottom quintile in 1991 while the rest had moved higher in the distribution. Of the workers moving higher in the earnings distribution, a third to a half experienced large enough gains to skip over the second quintile and enter the top three quintiles. Again, cross-country differences are far greater when low pay is defined as earning less than two-thirds of median earnings and the USA stands out for the much greater extent to which low-pay workers are at risk of remaining low paid.

The patterns of movements into low-paid jobs suggest that low-paid workers in any given year also have very diverse histories (see lower half of Table 12.7). Again a large part of all entries into low-paid jobs is accounted for by shifts from outside full-time employment. There is, for example, a large inflow of young people from part-time work or non-employment. For many of them, a low-paid job will be a relatively brief phase of the school-to-work transition. However, a considerable share of low-paid workers in 1991 was either also low-paid workers in 1986 or had experienced downward earnings mobility. The former group shows considerable persistence in low-paid employment and probably has relatively poor prospects for obtaining significantly better jobs. The prospects for workers experiencing downward mobility are more difficult to assess and are probably quite diverse. However, studies of displaced workers in the United States have found substantial persistence of wage losses (Podgursky and Swaim 1987, Ruhm 1991).

Figure 12.9 examines the relationship between overall earnings inequality and the upward mobility of low-paid workers. When our preferred low-pay threshold of two-thirds of median earnings is used, it appears that low-paid workers have greater difficulty moving up in national labour markets in which cross-sectional inequality is higher (right-hand scatter plot). Since we saw earlier that the incidence of low-paid employment climbs in virtual lock-step with earnings inequality, this association can be paraphrased as follows: a higher share of low-paid workers become trapped in countries where the pool of low-paid workers, in any single year, is larger. It should be empha-sized, however, that this association does not generalize to alternative defini-tions of low-paid employment, such as the bottom quintile. Another impor-tant caveat is that more detailed and longer career-history data are required in order to characterize more adequately the complex dynamics of low-paid jobs and how they are affected by the level of static wage inequality. As men-tioned earlier, spells of part-time work and non-employment also would need to be incorporated into a comprehensive account of low-pay dynamics. We leave further exploration of these issues to future research, turning instead to the question how the aggregate mobility flows, summarized in Table 12.7, translate into low-pay incidence and persistence for individual workers.

Figure 12.9   *Upward mobility of low-paid workers and overall earnings*
inequality

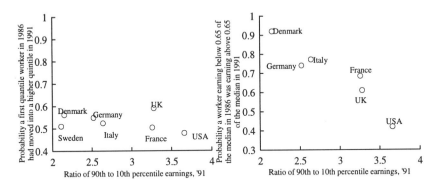

Note: The mobility of low-paid workers refers only to those workers employed full-time in 1986 and 1991.

Source: OECD (1996, Chapter 3).

4.3 A Closer Look at Low-Pay Incidence and Persistence [13]

Most often low-pay patterns are assessed using data for a single year. A longer-run view, incorporating worker mobility, increases the incidence of low pay and, hence, the share of the workforce potentially affected by its adverse effects, if emphasis is placed on all workers who are *ever* low paid. Owing to the considerable movements into low-paying jobs, the share of continuously employed workers who were low paid at any time during 1986–91 is one and one-half to two times as high as the share in a single year, such as 1986 (Figure 12.10).[14] Although many of these spells were short, this larger group may be relevant for assessing the share of the workforce at risk of low pay and the hardship that even temporarily low earnings may produce.

Figure 12.10 Alternative incidence measures for low-paid employment, 1986–91 (%)

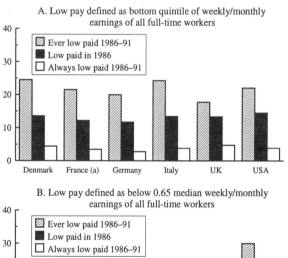

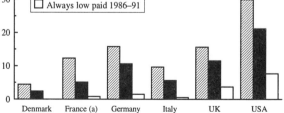

Note: a. Data for 1984–9.

Source: OECD (1997, Chapter 2).

When low-pay 'careers' – rather than low-pay jobs – are the focus of policy concern, the proportion of continuously employed workers *always* low paid over a multi-year period is a more natural incidence measure. The share of such workers over the period 1986–91 is much lower than their share in any single year. While the shares of continuously full-time employed workers who were ever in the bottom quintile ranged from 18 to 24 per cent, the shares of these who were always low paid over the period 1986–91 ranged from 3 to 5 per cent, suggesting that low-pay traps are much less common than low-pay stop-overs. It does not follow, however, that low-paid employment is confined to a single, short spell for most workers who are low paid at any given time (see below).

Cross-country differences in the incidence of low pay using the bottom quintile threshold are modest and not much affected by whether one compares the shares ever low paid, low paid in a single year or always low paid. Much larger differences emerge when low pay is defined as less than two-thirds of median earnings. All three incidence measures are significantly higher in the United States than elsewhere, due the greater dispersion of wages there, while Italy and, especially, Denmark have the lowest incidence rates.

As is clear from Figure 12.11 (Panel A), in all countries only a minority of low-paid workers in a given year remain so for an extended, consecutive period of time. Among bottom-quintile workers in 1986, between 60 and 75 per cent move above this low-pay threshold at some point over the next five years. International differences are more pronounced when low pay is defined as under two-thirds of median earnings: more than 80 per cent of French, German and Italian workers, and virtually all Danish workers who were low paid in 1986 escaped by 1991; the corresponding rate for the United Kingdom and the United States was a little over 60 per cent. Despite these differences, in all countries most workers who are low paid in any selected year move higher in the earnings distribution at some point during the next few years, provided they remain employed.

Focusing on these cumulative exit rates can exaggerate the extent of upward mobility and understate the amount of time workers spend in low-paid jobs. Despite the high exit rates, the average cumulated time in low pay grows quite steeply when workers are followed over time. By 1991, workers who were low paid in 1986 had cumulated an average of two to four years of low pay (Figure 12.11, Panel B). It should also be borne in mind that these figures understate total time low paid, since they do not account for low-pay years prior to 1986 or subsequent to 1991. Accounting for intermittent and part-time workers would also indicate greater persistence in low pay. Elsewhere (OECD 1997, Chapter 2), we reconcile these two, apparently paradoxical, faces of low pay: few of the 1986 low-paid workers were continuously low paid during 1986–91, yet, on average, these workers cumulated a significant number of low-paid years. Several factors are involved, including multiple spells of low-paid employment (i.e. many escapes are only temporary) and a strong negative association between time already low paid and the probability of upward earnings mobility.

Figure 12.11 Two views of the persistence of low pay 1986–91: continuously employed full-time workers

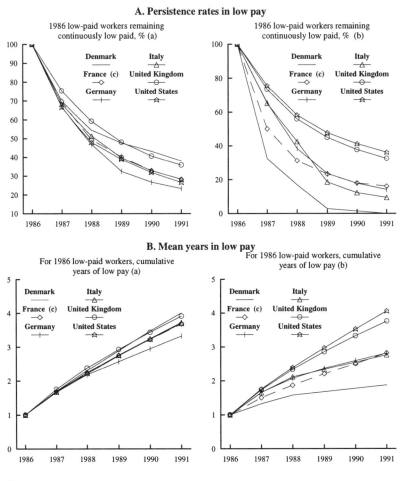

Notes:
a. Low pay defined as bottom quintile of weekly/monthly earnings of all full-time workers.
b. Low pay defined as below 0.65 median earnings of weekly/monthly earnings of all full-time workers.
c. Data for 1984–89.

Source: OECD (1997, Chapter 2).

In the now familiar pattern, international differences in cumulative low-paid years are small when low pay is defined as earnings in the bottom quintile. However, cumulative time in low-paid employment grows much more steeply in the United Kingdom and the United States than elsewhere, when low pay is defined as below two-thirds of median earnings. The labour market conditions or institutions that determine low pay persistence are not well understood, but this outcome may be related to the less regulated nature of the UK and US economies, including fewer barriers to low-paid employment. These two countries also experienced much greater increases in earnings inequality in recent years than other (non-transition) OECD countries (OECD 1996, Chapter 2), but have had considerable success at lowering unemployment.

Comparing estimates of average cumulated time in low pay shows that women, as well as older and less-educated workers, experience more time in low-paid employment than other workers (Table 12.8). Once in a low paid job, these groups have particular difficulty moving up the earnings distribution, at least in a sustained way. By contrast, youths in low-paid jobs have

Table 12.8   *Average cumulative years in low-paid employment during 1986–91 among low-paid workers in 1986: continuously employed full-time workers* [a]

		Denmark	France	Germany	Italy	UK	USA
Total		1.8	2.8	2.8	2.8	3.8	4.1
By sex:	Men	1.4	2.6	2.2	2.7	3.3	3.8
By sex:	Women	1.9	3.1	3.4	2.9	4.0	4.2
By age:	Under 25	1.6	2.6	2.4	2.5	3.1	4.0
By age:	25-34	1.6	2.8	3.0	2.7	4.1	3.9
By age:	35-49	2.2	3.0	3.5	3.5	4.6	4.2
By age:	50-64	2.0	3.3	5.1	3.8	5.1	4.2
By education:	Less than upper secondary	2.1	..	2.9	..	..	4.8
By education:	Upper secondary	1.6	..	2.9	..	..	4.0
By education:	Some tertiary[b]	1.0	..	1.2	..	..	3.8
By education:	University degree	1.0	..	x	..	..	2.7

Notes:
a.   Low pay defined as below 0.65 median earnings.
b.   Includes all tertiary (including university) education for Germany.
c.   x = Not applicable. .. = data not available.

Source: OECD (1997, Chapter 2).

An International Comparison

above-average prospects of moving up the earnings ladder. None the less, once in low-paid employment virtually all groups cumulate significantly additional low-paid years.

Of particular importance for targeting policy interventions designed to ameliorate problems resulting from low pay is that the demographic mix of low-paid employment varies depending on whether interest centres on the ever low paid, the single-year low paid or the always low paid (Figure 12.12).

Figure 12.12 Distribution of low-paid employment by age and sex, 1986–91: weekly/monthly earnings of continuously employed full-time workers [a]

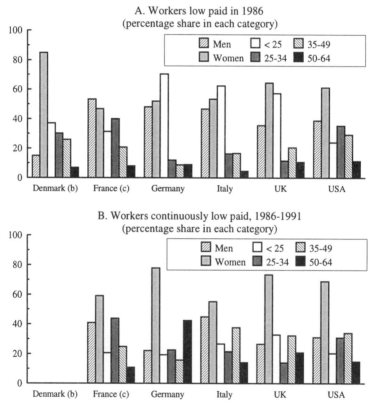

Notes:
a. Low pay is defined as below 0.65 median weekly/monthly earnings of all full-time workers.
b. Essentially no Danish workers were continuously low paid during 1986 to 1991.
c. Data refer to 1984–9.

Source: OECD (1997, Chapter 2).

Women, older and less-educated workers account for significantly larger shares of always low-paid workers than of the low paid in 1986, although the extent of these differences varies considerably across these six countries. These compositional differences are particularly striking for Germany: women accounted for 52 per cent of all low-paid workers in 1986, but almost 80 per cent of those who were continuously low-paid over the period 1986–91. The corresponding shares for workers aged 50–64 are 9 and 42 per cent, respectively (while the share for workers less than 25 years old falls from 70 to 19 per cent).

In sum, our analysis confirms the importance of earnings mobility for assessing the causes and consequences of low-paid employment, or designing policies to enhance the earnings potential of low-paid workers. A first lesson for policy is that the future earnings prospects and career histories of low-paid workers are very diverse. This heterogeneity means that any single policy intervention is unlikely to be appropriate for a large share of low-paid workers. Indeed, many of these workers appear to have strong upward mobility even in the absence of any assistance, although it is possible that their families have income-support needs during the period of low earnings. For another group, low-paid employment appears to be chronic, even if they periodically have a better year or cycle between low pay and no pay. The policy challenge for this group is to meet family-income needs while facilitating a durable escape from low pay.

5 CONCLUSIONS

There are a variety of different ways to measure low pay which reflect the fact that earnings represent both an important source of income for workers but are also an important component of overall labour costs. On the basis of a relative measure, the incidence of low-paid employment tends to be highest in those countries where earnings inequality is greatest; one-quarter of all full-time workers in the United States are low paid, compared with 6 per cent or less in Finland and Sweden. Even taking into account the high level of average earnings in the USA, it would still appear that the bottom 10 to 20 per cent of American workers in full-time jobs are low paid compared with equivalent workers in other advanced industrialized countries.

In all countries the incidence of low pay tends to be concentrated amongst low-skilled and inexperienced workers. Women and youths typically face a higher-than-average risk of being employed in low-paid jobs. Nevertheless, there are some country differences in this pattern. Relative to the average for all workers, the risk of being in a low-paid job is particularly high for women in Japan, Korea and Switzerland, for youths in Finland and for older workers in Japan and the United Kingdom.

Different institutional settings in terms of wage-setting practices and welfare provisions appear to have a significant impact on the incidence of low pay. Typically, countries with high rates of collective bargaining coverage and trade unionization tend to have a low incidence of low-paid employment. In countries where the legal minimum wage is high in relation to average earnings, the incidence of low pay also tends to be low. There is some evidence that generous welfare benefits may implicitly raise reservation wages. It is less clear, however, whether these wage floors, which limit the number of low-paid jobs, also adversely affect the overall chances of finding employment for lower-skilled and inexperienced workers. The employment or unemployment rates of youths, women and unskilled workers do not appear to be consistently or significantly correlated across countries with the incidence of low-paid employment. This suggests that factors other than relative wages, such as the overall level of aggregate demand or the amount of training received, may be more important for determining the labour market outcomes of these groups.

In many respects, earnings mobility is quite similar in the countries examined in detail. There is considerable turnover in low-paid jobs in all of the countries. Nevertheless, the share of low-paid workers in 1986 who were still low paid in 1991 ranged from below 10 per cent in Denmark to just over 40 per cent in the United States. For many youths, these jobs appear to provide an initial toe-hold in the labour market which initiates a period of significant wage growth. Older workers in low-paid jobs are much less likely than youths to experience upward mobility and sometimes cycle between low pay and non-employment. Countries with higher cross-sectional inequality of earnings appear to have lower upward mobility among low-paid workers, a pattern most evident in the United States. But in all countries low-paid workers have very diverse career histories and future employment prospects.

A number of issues concerning earnings inequality and mobility are touched upon in this study, but merit further attention. Whether countries face a trade-off between 'allowing' earnings inequality to rise or worsening the employment prospects of low-skilled workers is far from resolved. Earnings inequality has risen slightly or remained stable in a number of countries, but there is little evidence that the relatively low incidence of low-paid jobs in these countries is associated with lower employment rates for low-skilled and inexperienced workers. From a dynamic perspective, the situation is even more complex. Low-paid workers in any one year tend to have very diverse career and earnings prospects, with many moving up the earnings ladder, but also many remaining in low-pay jobs or leaving full-time employment altogether. The factors determining why some workers move into better jobs, but others do not, are not well understood. The relationship between trends in earnings inequality at any point in time and lifetime inequality of earnings needs to be developed further.

There are also several other directions where more useful internationally comparative work could be carried out in the area of low pay. More work is required on the labour cost aspect of earnings. For instance, it would be interesting to compare differences across countries in relative labour costs rather than just in terms of gross earnings. With respect to earnings as a source of income, more work is clearly required on the relationship between low pay and poverty. For instance, what is the proportion in different countries of low-paid workers that are also poor and how does this relate to a low-paid worker's family or household circumstances? In this area it may now be possible to do some comparative work using the results of the European Household Panel which are just now becoming available. As always, more work is also required on improving the international comparability of the data we are working with.

One final remark concerns the scope of our study which, in common with most other studies of low pay, is confined to the distribution of workers according to their wage rates rather than according to their earnings as such. At a broader level we could instead measure the number of labour-market participants with low earnings irrespective of how many hours they worked during the period considered. For example, we could examine the distribution of all individuals of working-age at work or seeking work according to their annual earnings. In this case, persons may have low earnings not simply because their wage rates are low but also because of a relative low number of hours worked during the year. However, widening the scope to look at low earnings more generally adds a whole new layer of complexity both in distinguishing the factors behind low earnings and for making cross-country comparisons, but, nevertheless, this warrants future work.

NOTES

1   The opinions expressed in this paper are those of the authors and do not necessarily represent those of the OECD or its member countries.

2   Of course, these comparisons of earnings levels need to be interpreted with some caution given both differences across countries in the data sources used and more general problems of currency conversion.

3   These comparisons suggest that Freeman (1993) may have somewhat overestimated the extent to which low-paid workers in the USA earn substantially less than equivalent workers in other advanced countries. For example, the bottom 10 per cent of full-time workers in the USA appear to earn roughly two-thirds of what comparable German workers earn and around almost 90 per cent compared with Italian workers and not 45 and 50 per cent, respectively, as estimated by Freeman based on average earnings of production workers.

4   According to the *New Earnings Survey* for April 1995, just under 20 per cent of all full-time workers on adult rates of pay were low paid based on their weekly earnings and just over 20 per cent of all workers (full-time and part-time on adult rates) were low paid in terms of hourly rates of pay.

5   Not all of the 19 countries shown in Table 12.2 could be included in these correlations because of missing data for some variables.

6   See OECD (1996, Chapter 3) and OECD (1997, Chapter 2) for a fuller presentation of this analysis.

7   While some forms of labour mobility tend to be higher in the USA than Europe, it is not clear *a priori* if this also translates into greater earnings mobility.

8   For the mobility analysis, we have actually specified low paid as earning less than or equal to 0.65 times median earnings. For expositional ease, we will refer to this as 'less than two-thirds median earnings'.

9   For example, if individuals whose economic fortunes change significantly are more difficult to follow because they are more likely to move or refuse to be interviewed, panel data would tend to underestimate the extent of earnings mobility unless an adjustment is made for the unrepresentative character of the remaining sample. This could be particularly important when the focus is on low-paid workers.

10 The UK data set presents a slight variant of this problem. While earnings are observed for workers in all sectors, there is some 'temporary' attrition and subsequent entry into the sample which can arise because of delays in tracing workers who have switched jobs.

11 Eighty per cent or more of the earnings inequality observed in a single year remains when earnings are averaged over the six-year period, 1986–91.

12 The similarity of relative mobility rates across countries reflects an approximate proportionality between cross-sectional earnings inequality (i.e. the width of the earnings quintiles) and the absolute volatility of earnings. Why such a proportionality should hold is not clear and is an interesting topic for future research.

13 Owing to small sample sizes, no results for Sweden are presented in this section.

14 As was explained above, the exclusion of intermittent workers from the sample explains why less than 20 per cent of the workers fall in the first quintile of the earnings distribution in 1986, in Figure 12.10.

REFERENCES

Baudelot, B. (1983), 'L'évolution individuelle des salaires (1970–1975)', Paris: INSEE, M102–103.

Blau, F.D. and L.M. Kahn (1995), 'The Gender Earnings Gap: Some International Evidence', in R. Freeman and L.M. Katz (eds), *Differences and Changes in Wage Structures*, Chicago: University of Chicago Press.

Blau, F.D. and L.M. Kahn (1996), 'International Differences in Male Wage Inequality: Institutions versus Market Forces', *Journal of Political Economy*, **104**, pp. 791–837.

Bound, J., C. Brown, G.J. Duncan and W.L. Rodgers (1994), 'Evidence on the Validity of Cross-Sectional and Longitudinal Labor Market Data', *Journal of Labor Economics*, **12**(3), pp. 345–68.

Card, D., F. Kramarz and T. Lemieux (1996*), Changes in the Relative Structure of Wages and Employment: A Comparison of the United States, Canada and France*, National Bureau of Economic Research, Working Paper No. 5487.

Dinardo, J., N. Fortin and T. Lemieux (1996), 'Labor Market Institutions and the Distribution of Wages, 1973–1992: A Semi-parametric Approach', *Econometrica*, **64**(5), pp. 1001–44.

Farber, H.S. (1996), *The Changing Face of Job Loss in the United States*, Princeton University: Industrial Relations Section, Working Paper, no. 360.

Freeman, R.B. (1993), 'How Much has De-Unionization Contributed to the Rise in Male Earnings Inequality?', in S. Danziger and P. Gottschalk (eds), *Uneven Tides: Rising Inequality in America*, New York: Russell Sage Foundation, pp. 99–164.

Gregory, M. and R. Jukes (1996), *The Effects of Unemployment on Future Earnings: A Panel Micro-Data Study of British Men, 1984–94*, paper prepared for the eighth EALE conference, Chania, Crete, 19–22 September.

Hill, M. (1992), *The Panel Study of Income Dynamics: A User's Guide*, Beverly Hills, CA: Sage Publications.

Leonard, J. and M. Van Audenrode (1995*)*, *The Duration of Unemployment and the Persistence of Wages*, CEPR Discussion Paper no. 1227.

Machin, S. and A. Manning (1994), 'Minimum Wages, Wage Dispersion and Employment: Evidence from the UK Wages Councils', *Industrial and Labour Relations Review*, no. 47, pp. 319–29.

Mishel, L. and J. Bernstein (1994), *The State of Working America, 1994–95*, New York: M.E. Sharpe, Inc.

OECD (1994), *The OECD Jobs Study: Evidence and Explanations*, Paris.

OECD (1996), *Employment Outlook*, Paris, July.

OECD (1997), *Employment Outlook*, Paris, July.

Podgursky, M. and P. Swaim (1987), 'Earnings Losses Following Displacement', *Industrial and Labor Relations Review*, October, pp. 17–29.

Ruhm, C.J. (1991), 'Are Workers Permanently Scarred by Job Displacements?', *American Economic Review*, March, pp. 319–24.

Rutkowski, J.J. (1996), *Changes in the Wage Structure during Economic Transition in Central and Eastern Europe*, World Bank Technical Paper no. 340.

Sloane, P.J. and I. Theodossiou (1996), 'Earnings Mobility, Family Income and Low Pay', *Economic Journal*, **106**, pp. 657–66.

Westergård-Nielsen, N. (1989), 'The Use of Register Data in Economic Analysis', *Zeitschrift für Volkswirtschaft und Statistik*, Heft 3/1989.

APPENDIX: SOURCES AND DEFINITIONS FOR CROSS-SECTIONAL DATA ON LOW PAY

Australia

Definition: Gross weekly earnings of full-time employees in their main job.

Sources: The Labour Force, Australia, ABS catalogue No. 6203.0, various issues, and unpublished tabulations provided by the Australian Bureau of Statistics (data for earlier years were published in *Weekly Earnings of Employees (Distribution), Australia*, ABS catalogue No. 6310.0). The data are obtained as an annual supplement (usually in August) to the monthly labour force survey and refer to the most recent pay period prior to the interview. The published data on the distribution of employees by earnings class have been interpolated to obtain the number of low-paid employees.

Austria
Definition: Net monthly earnings – standardized to a 40-hour working-week – for all employees.
Source: Results of the Austrian *Mikrozensus* of households for 1993. All data were supplied by the Austrian Central Statistical Office.

Belgium
Definition: Annual average of gross average daily earnings of full-time employees.
Source: Social security data provided by the Belgium Institut national d'assurance maladie-invalidité (INAMI). The incidence of low pay has been estimated based on grouped data on the distribution of employees by earnings class.

Canada
Definition: Gross annual earnings of full-time, year-round workers.
Source: Data supplied by the Analytical Studies Branch, Statistics Canada, based on the *Survey of Consumer Finances*.

Czech Republic
Definition: Gross annual earnings of full-time, year-round workers (i.e. workers who were paid for at least 1 700 hours of work during the year).
Source: Earnings Survey 1996, Czech Statistical Office. The published data on the distribution of employees by earnings class have been interpolated to obtain the number of low-paid employees.

Finland
Definition: Gross annual earnings of full-year, full-time employees.
Source: Data were supplied by Statistics Finland based on the preliminary 1994 results of the *Income Distribution Survey*.

France
Definition: Earnings of full-time employees (net of social security contributions) in month prior to the survey, adjusted to include annual bonuses.
Source: Data supplied by the Institut national de la statistique et des études économiques (INSEE) based on the March 1995 results of the labour force survey, *Enquête sur l'emploi.*

Germany (western Germany only)
Definition: Gross monthly earnings (not including annual bonuses) of full-time workers (including apprentices).

Source: Data provided by Victor Steiner, Zentrum für Europäische Wirtschaftsforschung, Mannheim, based on the *German Socio-Economic Panel*.
Additional data (as shown in Figures 12.2 and 12.3): The incidence of low pay has been estimated based on grouped social security data for full-time, full-year employees (excluding apprentices) by earnings class. The social security data come from the IAB-Beschäftigtenstichprobe (IABS). The IABS is a 1 per cent random sample of all dependent employees covered by the social security system. The data exclude civil servants, irregular workers and workers earning less than a certain minimum threshold (DM 590 in 1996).

Hungary
Definition: Gross monthly earnings (including 1/12th of non-regular payments from previous year) of full-time employees in May of each year.
Source: The data was provided by the Hungarian Ministry of Labour and the National Labour Centre based on their enterprise *Survey of Individual Wages and Earnings* which, since 1994, covers all enterprises with at least 10 employees.

Italy
Definition: Monthly net earnings (obtained by dividing annual earnings by the number of months worked) of wage and salary earners in their main job.
Source: Data provided by Andrea Brandolini and Paolo Sestito of the Bank of Italy based on the Bank of Italy's *Survey of Household Income and Wealth*.

Japan
Definition: Gross monthly scheduled earnings of regular employees (excluding part-time employees) aged 18 and over. The survey excludes establishments with less than five regular employees. Agriculture, forestry and fisheries, private household services, employees of foreign governments and the general government sector are also excluded from the scope of the survey.
Source: Basic Survey on Wage Structure 1994, Policy Planning and Research Department, Ministry of Labour, Japan. The published (establishment) data on the distribution of employees by earnings class have been interpolated to obtain the number of low-paid employees.

Korea
Definition: Gross monthly total cash earnings (including 1/12th of annual special payments) of regular full-time employees aged 18 and over. The data

excludes the general government sector, public enterprises, agriculture, forestry and fisheries, private household services, employees of foreign governments and all establishment with less than 10 regular employees.
Sources: Basic Survey of Wage Structures, Ministry of Labor, Korea, and data provided directly by the Korean Ministry of Labor. The published (establishment) data on the distribution of employees by earnings class have been interpolated to obtain the incidence and distribution of low-paid employment in Table 12.2.

Netherlands
Definition: Annual gross earnings, including occasional payments (overtime, holiday, etc.), of full-year equivalent, full-time employees.
Source: Survey of Earnings, Netherlands Central Bureau of Statistics, as reported in *Sociaal-Economische Maandstatistiek*, Netherlands Central Bureau of Statistics, December 1995. The published (establishment) data on the distribution of employees by earnings class have been interpolated to obtain the number of low-paid employees.

New Zealand
Definition: Gross annual earnings of full-time employees.
Source: Data provided by Statistics New Zealand based on the *Household Economic Survey*.

Poland
Definition: Gross monthly earnings of full-time employees (including monthly equivalent of periodic bonuses).
Source: Earnings Distribution in the National Economy as of September 1995, Polish Central Statistical Office. The data are from an establishment survey covering the whole national economy, except firms with less than 6 persons. The published data on the distribution of employees by earnings class have been interpolated to obtain the number of low-paid employees.

Sweden
Definition: Gross annual earnings of full-year, full-time employees aged 18 and over.
Source: Data supplied by Statistics Sweden based on the 1993 results of the *Income Distribution Survey*.

Switzerland
Definition: Gross annual earnings of full-time, full-year equivalent employees.
Source: Data provided by the Swiss Office fédéral de la statistique based on the results for the second quarter of 1995 of the annual Swiss labour force survey, *Enquête Suisse de la Population Active* (EPSA).

United Kingdom (Great Britain only)
Definition: Gross weekly earnings of full-time employees paid at adult rates, whose pay for the survey week was not affected by absence.
Source: UK Office for National Statistics, *New Earnings Survey* .

United States
Definition: Gross annual earnings of full-year, full-time employees.
Source: Data provided by US Bureau of the Census based on the March supplement to the *Current Population Survey*.
Additional data (as used in Figures 12.2 and 12.3): The incidence of low pay has been estimated based on data from unpublished tabulations by the Bureau of Labor Statistics of full-time employees by class of usual weekly earnings. The original source of the data is the *Current Population Survey*.

Index